C

MIKHAILOVSKY AND
RUSSIAN POPULISM

MIKHAILOVSKY AND RUSSIAN POPULISM

BY

JAMES H. BILLINGTON

OXFORD
AT THE CLARENDON PRESS
1958

Oxford University Press, Amen House, London E.C.4

GLASGOW NEW YORK TORONTO MELBOURNE WELLINGTON
BOMBAY CALCUTTA MADRAS KARACHI KUALA LUMPUR
CAPE TOWN IBADAN NAIROBI ACCRA

———

PRINTED IN GREAT BRITAIN

PREFACE

'I CAN understand the French bourgeois bringing about the Revolution to get rights, but how am I to comprehend the Russian nobleman making a revolution to lose them?'[1] This question—first asked by the military governor of Moscow about the ill-fated Decembrist uprising of 1825—remains the most challenging one for any student of nineteenth-century Russian radicalism. To attempt an answer one must be willing to move into fields unfamiliar to the contemporary Western mind, to project oneself into an age and a society in which ideas were as real and compelling as economic or political forces. In seeking an answer one may gain a deeper understanding both of the Russian past and of the hopes and trials of contemporary radicals in other undeveloped and semi-westernized countries.

Of all the periods of nineteenth-century Russian thought, the most intense and turbulent was that which followed the reform period of the early 1860's and lasted until the early 1880's. During this period books were read and ideas discussed with a voracious enthusiasm that knows perhaps no modern Western parallel. During these years thousands of Russia's privileged classes went voluntarily among the destitute masses, and more attempts were made on the life of the Tsar than in any comparable period of modern Russian history. This was the Indian Summer of Imperial Russia—an age of passionate intensity which gave birth to the great creative works of Dostoevsky, Tolstoy, Turgenev, Musorgsky, and Repin. Yet the populist movement, which was so central to it, has been largely ignored or distorted into caricature by historians.

This is an attempt to reconstruct in the context of its own time and place the story—not of the decline of the old Russia or the rise of the new—but of the radicalism of this age, and of Nicholas Mikhailovsky, who best expressed its ideas and most fully lived through its hopes and disappointments.

Mikhailovsky, like the age he lived in, has been long neglected by Soviet historians; and Western writers have, on the whole, collaborated in constructing a hagiography of early

[1] Leo Tikhomirov, *Russia Political and Social*, London, 1888, ii. 15.

revolutionaries which includes only Herzen, Belinsky, Cherny-shevsky, Dobrolyubov, and Pisarev. Since all of these figures were either dead or in prison by the late sixties, the impression has been created of a historical vacuum during the three decades leading up to the coming of Marxism in the late nineties. Western scholars have tended to further confuse the picture by approaching the populist age through the lives and thought of romantic *émigré* figures such as Lavrov, Bakunin, Kravchinsky (Stepnyak), and Kropotkin. None of these figures spent more than a few months within Russia after 1870, or exercised more than a peripheral influence on internal Russian developments. Thus, the widely accepted description of Russian radicalism in this period as the work of 'Bakuninists' and 'Lavrovists' is, at best, artificial and incomplete.

Alone of all the leaders of the populist movement, Mikhailov-sky remained alive and active within Russia from the early sixties until the eve of the Revolution of 1905. As the editor successively of the two most influential radical journals of the period, the *Annals of the Fatherland* and the *Wealth of Russia*, he brings us closer than any other figure to the inner springs of the populist movement. He played a decisive part in introducing into Russia the ideas of Mill, Spencer, Marx, and above all Proudhon—thinkers who would deeply influence the radical thought of the period. He played an intimate personal role in all the most important radical organizations of the age: the Chaikovsky circle, the organization of 'The People's Will', and the party of 'The People's Right'.

Endowed with a sympathetic manner, a contagious love of books, and unbridled confidence in the future, Mikhailovsky was almost the only radical of the period who was able to remain above petty faction and 'satisfy in some way all the warring groups'.[1] Even more important, however, for a move-ment that was more one of ideas than of personalities was the leading role Mikhailovsky played in shaping the ideas of popu-lism. He provided a formula of progress and a theory of history which helped fill the void of despair and check the drift toward extremism which followed the rampant iconoclasm of the early sixties. He helped develop the two great myths which lay behind the populist faith: the 'idea of the people' and the vision of a

[1] N. S. Rusanov, 'The Politics of N. K. Mikhailovsky', *Byloe*, 1907, no. 7, p. 128.

'new Christianity'. He was a major factor in linking the populist movement indissolubly with the moralistic and subjective socialism of Proudhon and the French radicals rather than the doctrinaire socialism of Marx and the German Social Democrats. Thus, we will be concerned with Mikhailovsky primarily as the mirror and spokesman of a long-neglected age in Russian history. Relatively little can be said of his purely personal life. Living in fear of the police and the censorship, Mikhailovsky destroyed his private papers before his death and wrote few personal letters.[1] Little should be said of much of his discursive writing on literary themes, or of his grey style of prose, which the more fluent Herzen was fully justified in calling 'atrocious'.[2] Moreover, many of the pseudo-scientific controversies in which he was involved have lost whatever interest they might have possessed, and his Victorian moralism and optimism are difficult to appreciate in an age that has seen the horrors of total war and totalitarian peace.

Nevertheless, Mikhailovsky deserves attention not only as the moving spirit of a forgotten age, but as a radical humanist in his own right. The transcendental idealists of the early twentieth century could with some justice call him 'a philosopher among publicists and a publicist among philosophers',[3] for he offered his contemporaries no clear dogma or final synthesis. His column was labelled that of a 'layman', and his writings were invariably called 'sketches' or 'notes'. Yet his very refusal to develop a system in these writings reflected a deep moral idealism, which transcends his pedantic style and naïvely optimistic tone.

Mikhailovsky was one of the first socialists in Russia, and one of the first sociologists in Europe, to insist that all social theory must begin with the individual personality. He was an uncompromising foe of any force—intellectual or political—which would, in the name of some abstract goal, impose cruelty on real people, who alone 'think, feel, and suffer', or restrict their universal 'struggle for individuality'. At the same time, despite

---

[1] X. xxxix; and Rusanov, 'The Archives of N. K. Mikhailovsky', *R.B.*, 1914, no. 1, pp. 129–32.

[2] A. I. Herzen, *Polnoe Sobranie Sochinenii* (ed. Lemke), Petrograd, 1923, xxi. 329.

[3] Nicholas Berdyaev, *Subektivizm i Individualizm v Obshchestvennoy Filosofii*, St. Petersburg, 1901, p. 216.

his passionate hatred of systems, Mikhailovsky was one of the first Russian radical intellectuals to recognize the need for a political channel for reform. Precisely at that moment in 1879 when the strong anarchistic strain of Russian populism appeared dominant, Mikhailovsky courageously sought to steer the radical camp into recognizing the need for democratic political forms. Finally, Mikhailovsky made an interesting and determined attempt to recapture in a hostile intellectual atmosphere another of the beliefs that underlay the growth of the democratic idea in the West—belief in an objective moral law. However insistent he was in calling his outlook subjective, he came increasingly to realize that belief in a transcendent truth was a necessary corollary to his belief in human dignity. He was one of the few survivors of the iconoclastic revolution of the sixties to acknowledge without renouncing radicalism the need for a belief in *pravda*—a truth which for him included both factual, objective truth (*pravda-istina*) and moral truth (*pravda-spravedlivost*).

Thus, despite his verbosity and seeming eclecticism, there was in Mikhailovsky—as in the best radical humanists of all ages— an inner core of value and belief. He was, indeed, but one of those European thinkers in the late nineteenth century who, while seeing great progress in the advance of science, felt that social reform should not be based on any body of 'scientific' dogma. In his doctrine of the two-sided truth one finds the first clear separation by a Russian radical theorist of 'the science of the spirit' from natural sciences, of *Geisteswissenschaften* from *Naturwissenschaften*.

Mikhailovsky was perhaps the greatest of Russia's nineteenth-century radical humanists. Unlike Belinsky, whom he most admired, he did not reach a faith in human personality only shortly before his death and after violent philosophical gyrations. Unlike Herzen, whom he most resembled, he was able to remain in Russia all of his life and exert a sustained and direct influence. Like these two great predecessors, Mikhailovsky retained throughout his life an uncompromising opposition to apathy and bourgeois mediocrity. Yet for him the alternative to apathy was not utopian fanaticism; the alternative to mediocrity was not extremism. He was in essence an evolutionist who believed in values which defined the means as well as the ends of his activity. He sought to maintain the communal type of old

Russian society while moving to a higher level of economic development, and to preserve as well the sense of honour and moral obligation of the old aristocracy while building the new society. He avoided extremes and remained true to Proudhon, his original teacher in social affairs, by rejecting all orthodoxies and all 'books of fate however learned'. Like all great humanists Mikhailovsky chose life rather than logic, the unresolved paradoxes of humanity rather than the monolithic leviathans of the totalitarian.

In charting a path across this unfamiliar terrain, we will seek to avoid both the speculative peaks of private theories about the Russian soul and the discursive quagmires of unrelated minutiae. Speculative peaks may be found in the works of *émigré* writers like Berdyaev and Ivanov-Razumnik; quagmires may be explored in the innumerable memoirs, articles, and collections on the period published between the repeal of the censorship in 1905 and the late twenties. The former offer frequent insights; the latter provide the indispensable raw material for any historical study—all the more valuable for not having been subjected to rigid interpretation. The present work attempts to provide what neither Soviet nor Western historians have yet supplied: an interpretation of the populist movement in its own terms and a study of its most important figure.

It may be that the recent Soviet call for a revision of pre-Bolshevik Russian revolutionary history will bring to an end the lamentable and now self-confessed Soviet practice of dismissing populism 'with the stroke of a pen'.[1] However, since every comment of Lenin on the subject will almost certainly still be regarded as holy writ, we can probably expect little more than refinements of Lenin's prejudices and caricatures. Mikhailovsky will probably remain for many years to come a 'petty bourgeois' 'amateur philistine', who 'pharasaically lifts up his eyes to the hills', voicing 'with the nonchalance of a society fop' argument which are 'insipid trash' 'stereotyped to the point of nausea'.[1]

Past ideas which did not create and do not reinforce the prejudices of the present may thus continue to be treated by

[1] 'The Twentieth Congress of the CP/USSR and Problems in the Study of the History of the Party', *Voprosy Istorii*, 1956, no. 3, pp. 5–6.

Soviet historians with the condescension and contempt with
which the closed and self-centred mind always regards the rest
of human kind. It is true, of course, that the populists did not
succeed in gaining power in Russia, and indeed, that their
movement was not dependent on Mikhailovsky in the same
sense that Bolshevism was dependent on Lenin. But populism
was not focused primarily on attaining power, and thus never
required a clear power centre. It would be unfortunate for the
writing of history if historians in the West were to look only for
those developments in past ages which had either immediate
power significance or bizarre amusement value. I shall not
attempt to obscure the utopianism of the populists or their lack
of material achievement. But their story will not be told as the
superfluous romanticism of a crumbling nobility or the product of various glandular disorders. I shall try to retell their
story, in so far as I am able, with determination not to 'play
tricks upon the dead', and in confidence that no chapter in the
history of human thought and aspiration deserves to remain
unwritten.

Among the many to whom I am indebted, I wish particularly to thank: Mr. J. S. G. Simmons of Oxford and Mr. Alexis
Struve of Paris for invaluable bibliographical assistance; the
staffs of the Library of Congress, the New York Public Library,
the libraries of Princeton and Columbia Universities, the British
Museum, the Bodleian, the Bibliothèque de Documentation
Internationale Contemporaine, and the Bibliothèque de l'In-
stitut d'Études Slaves for their help and co-operation; Messrs.
Max Hayward and E. E. Orchard for lending me a number of
rare Soviet publications; and the late Warden of All Souls,
Mr. B. H. Sumner, and Professor Hugh Seton-Watson of
London, for their advice and encouragement as supervisors of
my original doctoral thesis on this subject at Oxford. I owe
special thanks to the principal supervisor of that work, Mr.
Isaiah Berlin, for the stimulus of his ranging mind, for his contagious enthusiasm about the movement of ideas in history, and
for many valuable suggestions in the early stages of my research.
I am grateful to the Rhodes Trust for the support of my research,

    [1] Phrases used by Lenin to describe Mikhailovsky in 'What the "Friends of the
People" are and how they fight the Social Democrats', *Selected Works*, London,
1939, vol. xi.

and to numerous friends who have made valuable suggestions during the preparation of the present text. Finally, I must speak of the profound personal debt which I owe to my parents, to whom I dedicate whatever may be of value in this work.

J. H. B.

Narberth, Penna., U.S.A.
17 December 1956

CONTENTS

CONTENTS

ABBREVIATIONS

Mikhailovsky's works:

I–VI   *Sochineniya N. K. Mikhailovskago*, St. Petersburg, 1896–7, six volumes.

X   *Polnoe Sobranie Sochinenii N. K. Mikhailovskago*, St. Petersburg, 1913, volume ten.

(Roman numerals used by themselves will refer to these standard editions.)

Lit. V., I, II   *Literaturnyya Vospominaniya i Sovremennaya Smuta*, St. Petersburg, 1910, volumes one and two.

Ot., I, II   *Otkliki*, St. Petersburg, 1904, volumes one and two.

Q.Q.P.   *Qu'est-ce que le progrès?* (tr. Paul Louis), Paris, 1897.

Rev. St.   *Revolyutsionnyya Stati*, Berlin, 1906.

(Throughout the text capitalized Roman numerals will be used only to refer to Mikhailovsky's works. All other volume numbers will be indicated by small Roman numerals.)

Journals:

G.M.	*Golos Minuvshago*
Ist. V.	*Istorichesky Vestnik*
K.A.	*Krasny Arkhiv*
K.i S.	*Katorga i Ssylka*
M.G.	*Minuvshie Gody*
O.Z.	*Otechestvennye Zapiski*
R.B.	*Russkoe Bogatstvo*
R.S.	*Russkoe Slovo*
Sov.	*Sovremennik*

NOTE

THE attempt has been made to render most terms and titles into English in the text, providing the original Russian the first time each is mentioned. Titles in footnotes will, however, be left in Russian throughout to facilitate reference for the reader. In almost all cases the correct name will be used for authors, and revolutionary *noms de plume* will be given in parenthesis only where they have become as well or better known than the actual name. For the sake of simplicity a few minor changes have been made in the usual method of transliterating Russian, such as not indicating soft signs and rendering all nominative singular adjectival endings as 'y'. All dates pertaining only to Russia are given in the old style, but both dates are given where the event also involves the West or where confusion might arise.

The Golden Age is the most unlikely of all the dreams that ever have been; but for it men have given up their life and all their strength, for the sake of it prophets have died and been slain, without it the peoples will not live and cannot die . . .

From the dream of Versilov in Dostoevsky's *Raw Youth*

I

ELEMENTS OF THE DRAMA

The Youth

NICHOLAS KONSTANTINOVICH MIKHAILOVSKY was
born on 15 November 1842, near the provincial town
of Meshchovsk, 130 miles to the south-west of Moscow.
He was born in the heart of Russia, the centre of the vast, semi-
wooded plain of Muscovy from which the Tsarist Empire of all
the Russias had been slowly expanding for nearly five hundred
years. The physical milieu into which he was born is one that
Western man with his urbanized tastes and command over dis-
tances can only with great difficulty sympathetically re-create.
One Western visitor, the Marquis de Custine, who had come to
Russia only a few years before, has left a vivid description of the
region outside Moscow in which Mikhailovsky was born.

The silence is profound in these unvarying scenes: and sometimes
it becomes sublime as on a desert plain, of which the only boundaries
are our power of vision. The distant forest, it is true, presents no
variety; it is not beautiful: but who can fathom it? . . .
The landscape remains the same. The villages still present the
same double line of small wooden houses. . . . The country still
continues the same monotonous though undulating plain, sometimes
marshy, sometimes sandy; a few fields, wide pasture-ranges bounded
by forests of fir, now at a distance, now close upon the road, sometimes well grown, more frequently scattered and stunted: such is the
aspect of all these vast regions. Here and there is to be seen a country
house, or large and mansion-like farm, to which an avenue of birch
trees forms the approach. These are the manor houses or residences
of the proprietors of the land: and the traveller welcomes them on
the road as he would an oasis in the desert.[1]

It was in one of these manor-house 'oases' that Mikhailovsky
was born and spent his early childhood; for his father was a land-
owner, and both of his parents were members of the favoured
dvoryanstvo or gentry class. These early years of Mikhailovsky's

---

[1] Marquis de Custine, *Russia*, London, 1854, p. 378.

B

life coincided with the high tide of Tsarist autocratic rule. Nicholas I, who had come to power after crushing the abortive Decembrist rising of 1825, had gradually extended the scope of Imperial and bureaucratic authority to an unprecedented degree. He had endeavoured to consolidate his political achievement by the maintenance of the traditional social class structure of Russia. At the top of this class stratification were members of the landed gentry, like Mikhailovsky's father, who exercised varying degrees of control over a large section of the vast peasant population of Russia. Constantine Mikhailovsky had served as an army officer and police official in Kaluga province before retiring to his estate in the late thirties. It was upon such loyal landowners that the Tsar depended for support, considering them the 'unsleeping watchdogs guarding the state'.

Young Nicholas, however, was not harmoniously brought into the world of the rural aristocracy. Although he was the only son, his elderly father took little interest in him, and his mother died when he was too young to remember her. The deep moral sense which was to be his most distinctive characteristic was evidenced in his early reactions to incidents on the estate. A story that his father told jocularly about a Jew who had cursed him and his family during his days as a police official deeply distressed young Nicholas, as did the attempted suicide of one of his father's servants. He was pleased on another occasion when a young serf, who had been beaten for a prank which the two youths had committed together, agreed to remain his friend and to apply a token beating to young Nicholas. Indeed, Mikhailovsky's happiest recollections of his childhood at Meshchovsk were not of his family and their 'nest of gentlefolk', but of the young children of his father's serfs.[1] As with so many members of the nineteenth-century nobility in Russia, the psychological basis was established early for the contrast which would be drawn between the repressive life of the privileged class and the idealized spontaneity of the peasantry.

Mikhailovsky was also exposed at an early age to some of the economic tensions which were to help undermine the impres-

---

[1] See autobiographical passages in Mikhailovsky's 'In the Interim' (*V Peremezhku*), IV. 222–6, 239; and B. I. Goldman (Gorev), *N. K. Mikhailovsky*, Moscow, 1925, pp. 8–9. Mikhailovsky acknowledges that he had a sister (IV. 208 note) but there is no subsequent reference to her in his writings.

sive political edifice of Nicholaevan Russia. Throughout the forties, the financial position of the Mikhailovsky estate was steadily deteriorating. The possession of serfs became more an economic burden for Mikhailovsky's father than a source of income, and at the end of the forties he sold his land and serfs and moved into the town of Kostroma. His relatives lived in this city on the upper reaches of the Volga some 200 miles north-east of Moscow. It was there that Nicholas's young sister could be cared for and Nicholas himself entered in a *gymnasiya*.

During Nicholas's fourth year at the Kostroma school his father died. His relatives appear to have taken little more personal interest in him than his father had, and they made immediate arrangements to send him away for an advanced course of study. Since he had shown considerable interest in the natural sciences, he was enrolled in the second class of the St. Petersburg Mining Institute. In 1856, at the age of thirteen, Mikhailovsky left for St. Petersburg, carrying with him only his acceptance certificates to the Institute and the money that he had been given as his inheritance from his father's sale of the Meshchovsk property. Mikhailovsky left behind a childhood to which he would seldom refer in his subsequent writings. The idealized memory of provincial life lived on in the back of his mind and deeply influenced the social philosophy which he would preach. But in a very real sense life began for Mikhailovsky with his arrival in St. Petersburg, for he brought with him no deep parental or provincial ties. In order to place him into the context of his age, it is necessary to consider the setting of Russia and St. Petersburg in this post-Crimean period, and the unique traditions that had developed within the Russian intelligentsia.

The Setting

In the Europe of the mid-nineteenth century, the Russian Empire presented a unique and curious picture. It encompassed an area greater than that of the entire North American continent, with a population twice as great as that of any other European power. Yet this vast land island had been almost completely untouched by the industrial revolution. Throughout the great age of bourgeois, industrial expansion in the West,

Russia had remained proudly aloof—sealed off by rigid tariffs, by a large army, and by the uncompromising autocratic philosophy of Nicholas I. During the period of urbanization and constitutional liberalism Russia had remained the land of the peasant and the Tsar. In 1856 Russia had only 650 miles of railroads and only three cities with populations of more than 100,000. Fifty million of the sixty million citizens of European Russia were serfs: peasants who were still in various degrees of bondage, with no right to own property. Only a few more than a quarter of a million were, like Mikhailovsky, members of the landed and literate aristocracy.

After forty years of uninterrupted peace, Russia suddenly found herself at war with Turkey, England, and France in the spring of 1854. By the time the war limped to a halt in March 1856, it had become clear that the Crimean conflict—like every other major war in the nineteenth and early twentieth centuries —was to have an effect on Russian society of no less importance than its effect on international politics as a whole. Unsupported by any major European power, Russia had fought and lost on her own soil. The incompetence and backwardness of Nicholas's régime had been vividly demonstrated. Russia could no longer afford the luxury of neglecting domestic problems and looking with scorn on developments in the industrial West.

The force of events had shaken opinion loose from the pall of fatalism and inertia which had long lain over the sedentary, agrarian life of the Empire. 'The discouragement of the masses after a moment of exaltation'[1] produced a desire for change among people of all classes; while the deteriorating financial position of the Empire produced a pressing necessity for change which even the most authoritarian members of the Tsar's entourage could not neglect. With the death of Nicholas in 1855, and the conclusion of peace early in 1856, the stage seemed set for far-reaching social and economic changes.

As this sense of expectation grew, the defeat and the very issues of the war became soon forgotten. Russians of all classes became caught up in the accelerated tenor of activity that set in almost immediately after the end of the war. A serious programme of railroad building was launched, and the volume

---

[1] Description of Russia in a letter of 15 May 1855 by an anonymous German diplomat in Vicomte de Guichen, *La Guerre de Crimée*, Paris, 1936, p. 265.

of trade, which had been only slowly increasing throughout the nineteenth century, suddenly mushroomed, so that in the five-year period after Crimea the total volume was more than 50 per cent. higher than that of the highest previous five-year period.[1]

The principal class through which demands for change could become effective was still the privileged *dvoryanstvo*. But the dislocations of war had swollen the ranks of another social grouping that was to play an increasingly important role in Russian social and political developments—the *raznochintsy* or people belonging to no class or rank. This group, which was composed primarily of minor officials, merchants, writers, and descendants of priests or minority groups, had no place in the hierarchical class structure of Nicholaevan society and eagerly joined elements of the aristocracy who looked to the West for guidance in solving Russia's problems. No longer, however, did literate Russians look to the West of the Hohenzollerns and the Hapsburgs, but to the West of England and France. These countries had proven their superiority by defeating Russia in her own territory, and Russians of all shades of opinion felt impelled to turn to them in the years after Crimea as much for ideas about man and society as for financial and technical aid.

The centre both of this accelerated economic activity and of this turn to the West was St. Petersburg, the city which had been the capital of Russia and her symbolic 'window into Europe' ever since its creation by Peter the Great. With a population of nearly a half million in 1856, St. Petersburg was the largest city, the leading port, and the commercial capital of Russia. It was to be the centre of the major industrial and intellectual development of the next two decades and the leading port of entry into Russia from the West. The physical transformations which Russia as a whole would not undergo until the twentieth century were already taking place in St. Petersburg in 1856. Two new railway stations were under construction for railroad lines that were to connect St. Petersburg with the West and the interior of Russia respectively.[2] At the same time large block housing, springing up to accommodate

---

[1] M. W. Kovalevsky, *La Russie à la fin du XIXᵉ siècle*, Paris, 1900, p. 688.

[2] The word still used in Russian for station, *vokzal* (from Vauxhall), bears witness to the way in which this was viewed as an English innovation.

the steady influx of population, was beginning to change the physical appearance of much of the city.

St. Petersburg was the city in which construction and activism had most taken hold, the channel through which the material and ideological forces of the West were flowing into Russia. It was to this city that Mikhailovsky came in this first year after Crimea. He lived there almost permanently for a half century, and for most of that period Russian radicalism also unfolded against the background of the busy metropolis.

The Tradition

Social radicalism in nineteenth-century Russia was almost exclusively the product of an intelligentsia. Since Mikhailovsky rapidly took up ideas as his main stock in trade and joined this small but powerful group, some understanding of its origins and traditions is clearly required for any understanding of Mikhailovsky and Russian radicalism.

Historically, the intelligentsia was a product of the revolution in Russian society which reached its climax under Peter the Great. Before Peter, most institutions and forms of life in Russia had developed apart from the influence of critical secular thought. Even in the Church there had been almost no scholastic intellectual tradition to balance the contemplative tradition of Orthodoxy and the compassionate traditions of popular Russian spirituality. By supporting the modifications in Russian forms of worship instituted by the Greek-educated Patriarch Nikon, Peter asserted the supremacy of the critical intellect over spiritual tradition and widened the gulf which the schism in the Church under Tsar Alexis had first opened. Moreover, Peter established, with the counsel of Leibniz, the Academy of Sciences and other secondary secular institutions of learning which provided the opportunity for pursuing the quest for truth outside the Church. Peter, more than any other of his predecessors, introduced the techniques and thought of Western Europe to Russia, posing to her most sensitive minds the problem of Russia's backwardness. By building St. Petersburg he provided Russia with the city which was to become in many respects the spiritual home of the Russian intelligentsia.

Not until the influx of *philosophes* at the time of Catherine the

Great in the late eighteenth century, however, did the modern intelligentsia begin to take coherent form. Under her and her two successors, Paul and Alexander I, an *élite* court intelligentsia began to appear, which drew its beliefs from the French encyclopedists and the esoteric cults of the early romantics. This aristocratic intelligentsia turned to social radicalism in the ill-fated Decembrist rising of 1825. With the harsh repression of the Decembrist constitutionalists and the accession of Nicholas I, the period of exclusive dominance by a court intelligentsia came to an end, and the distinctive traditions of the nineteenth-century intelligentsia began to form.

The institutions on which the intelligentsia began to centre in the thirties were the universities and the periodic journals within Russia rather than the courts and the international *salons* of an earlier age. In the universities, above all in Moscow, young students began to form new circles (*kruzhki*). Even more than the earlier circles these budding student groups were animated by a thirst for totality: a desire to find not only ideal truth, but social justice and individual fulfilment as well. These student groups of the thirties were for the most part under the spell of German metaphysical idealism, which provided them with an all-embracing world picture. The philosophy of Schelling or Hegel lay behind most of the new journals that began to appear in the thirties, as well as the most important student group, the Stankevich circle. When Nicholas began to draw his bureaucratic reins tighter by shutting down several of the new journals and putting sharp restrictions on the universities in the mid thirties, the Stankevich group began to focus its attention on social questions—which had long been the particular concern of the smaller rival circle of Alexander Herzen.

In the late thirties and the forties, the intelligentsia coalesced into two fairly distinct groups; the 'Slavophils' and 'westernizers'. Many of the Stankevich group, such as Constantine Aksakov and Yury Samarin, were pioneers in the former group, which saw in the organic communal traditions of early Russian society the regenerative hope for the future. But some of the same Stankevich group, such as Vissarion Belinsky and Michael Bakunin, joined Herzen in the ranks of those who looked to the West for the key to social emancipation. For all their differences, however, these two groups were united in opposition to the

harsh reign of Nicholas, which as one Slavophil said, had as its
ideal 'not the Russia of tomorrow but the Austria of yesterday'.[1]
They were united as well in a common concern for the Russian
peasantry and in a common realization of the gap between
their lofty ideals and the sordid realities of contemporary Russia.

The united opposition of the intelligentsia to both serfdom
and autocracy increased greatly during the final seven years of
Nicholas's long reign. For, after the revolutionary uprisings of
1848 in the West, Nicholas drew in his own reins of authority
even tighter. He brought to a halt the activities of the peasant
commissions, which had been investigating possible reforms in
the institution of serfdom, and called for greater regulation of
the press through the preliminary censorship. Finally, Nicholas
harshly repressed the Petrashevsky circle, where early utopian
socialist ideas had been discussed in the late forties by a growing
number of intellectuals. With the exile to Siberia in 1849 of the
Petrashevsky leaders, including Dostoevsky, the closest Russian
facsimile to the European revolutionary movement of 1848 was
crushed. The fact that Russia had not participated in the unrest
of 1848 added to the repressive measures of the final seven years
of Nicholas's reign to produce a deep sense of frustration. The
passionate intensity with which the intelligentsia returned to
activity in the universities and new journals in the more tolerant
atmosphere of post-Crimean Russia thus represents in many
ways the bursting forth of artificially contained energies. Whatever the ultimate causes of radical unrest, the immediate conditioning factors were the frustrations and fascinations of a still
privileged intelligentsia rather than the sufferings of an oppressed peasantry.

By the fifties the intelligentsia had coalesced as a distinct and
self-conscious group. Although most were members of the
gentry and economically self-sufficient, their sense of unity was
based not on social or economic bonds, but on common beliefs.
Two of these binding assumptions may be isolated as the central
articles of faith for any *intelligent* in the latter years of Nicholas's
reign: a thirst for philosophic totality and an opposition to the
social institution of serfdom.

The fundamental importance of philosophy—in the broadest

[1] Yury Samarin, in N. V. Riasanovsky, *Russia and the West in the Teaching of the
Slavophiles*, Harvard, 1952, p. 153.

sense of the posing of great questions and seeking of total answers—can hardly be overestimated in discussing the formation of the intelligentsia under Nicholas. Peter Chaadaev, in the first of his famed 'Philosophical Letters' in 1829, had insisted that 'ideas have always preceded interests, that only in searching for truth does one find freedom and well-being'.[1] Throughout the following two decades this passion for endless questioning and speculation became such a central tradition among the intelligentsia that in 1850 Nicholas I finally declared philosophy illegal as an academic subject. Despite Nicholas's move, however, and despite the rejection by subsequent generations of the philosophic systems of Hegel and Schelling, German metaphysical idealism left a permanent legacy of dissatisfaction with partial answers and tentative positions.

It was this passion for philosophic totality, a sense of unity in the common search for truth, which makes it essential to distinguish from the beginning the Russian term *intelligent* from 'intellectual', in the specialized, somewhat pedantic sense in which the term is often understood in the West. Belinsky confessed in the forties that 'for me, to think, feel, understand and suffer are one and the same thing'.[2] For the Russian *intelligent*, thought was inextricable from the totality of human experience. The problems with which 'thinkers' should deal could not be anything less than the total problems of meaning and purpose. Many of the distinctive characteristics of the intelligentsia— hatred of Tsarist bureaucracy, repudiation of *meshchanstvo* (bourgeois philistinism), hostility to pure form in art, and opposition to the *posredstvennost* (mediocrity) that enshrouds lives unmoved by great questions—are merely corollaries to this belief that their quest was for ultimates.

The intelligentsia was animated not only by a thirst for truth, but by a passion for social justice; and the all-consuming social issue of the intelligentsia in the late forties and fifties was the liberation of the serfs. More than anything else, a common opposition to the institution of serfdom united Slavophils and westernizers in the final, repressive years under Nicholas. Sympathy for the plight of the peasant was, as Herzen recalled, 'the one strong, unaccountable, physiological, passionate idea,

---

[1] P. Ya. Chaadaev, *Sochineniya i Pisma*, Moscow (ed. Gershenzon), 1913, i. 89.
[2] V. G. Belinsky, *Izbrannye Filosofskie Sochineniya*, Moscow, 1941, p. 163.

which they found in recollection and we, in prophecy. . . . Like Janus or like a two-headed eagle we looked in different directions while the same heart was throbbing within us.'[1] A thirst for absolute answers and a concern for the immediate issue of peasant emancipation were the most distinctive characteristics of the intelligentsia as it stepped forth on the turbulent stage of post-Crimean Russia.

[1] A. I. Herzen, *Polnoe Sobranie Sochinenii*, xi. 11.

II

THE ICONOCLASTIC REVOLUTION
(1856–66)

I N the St. Petersburg to which Mikhailovsky came in 1856,
the accelerated pace of life was already beginning to con-
verge with the established intensity of the Russian intelligentsia to produce what would soon be known as 'Bazarovism',
the thoroughgoing iconoclasm of the 'new men' of the sixties.
The decade after the Crimean War, from 1856 to 1866, known
as 'the sixties' in Russian social history, was a period of great
disruption and change in the social and intellectual life of
Russia. During these years Mikhailovsky served his apprentice-
ship as an *intelligent* in St. Petersburg. Although essentially a
minor character on the stage of the sixties, Mikhailovsky became indelibly stamped with the sense of passion and outrage
which underlay all the literary controversies, the utopian experiments, and student unrest of the decade.

There were logical as well as psychological reasons for the
great wave of optimism that swept through the intelligentsia
after the war. The need for reforms had been vaguely acknowledged by the new Tsar in his peace manifesto of 1856; there
had been an immediate liberalization in the preliminary censorship, in the regulations governing foreign travel, and in university curricular restrictions.

These early moves lent credence to a widespread belief in
the late fifties that the Tsar would initiate a programme of
'reform from above'. Herzen voiced such optimistic expectations
in the early issues of the *Bell* (*Kolokol*)—the first illegal *émigré*
journal in modern Russian history, which began to appear in
London in the summer of 1857. Liberation of the serfs stood first
on the list of social demands presented in the *Bell*, and the
matter was a constant subject of discussion among the intelligentsia of the late fifties, as news of impending reform leaked
out from the investigating and editing committees appointed
by Alexander II.

On 19 February 1861 the Tsar announced the emancipation

of the serfs, thus gratifying this long-standing goal of the intelligentsia. Yet a whole series of events—beginning with nation-wide disorders in this same month and climaxing in a mysterious fire and a series of revolutionary publications in St. Petersburg early in June—revealed far more continued unrest than gratified contentment. This wave of discontent was produced in good measure by a set of essentially intellectual problems—by the unsatisfied thirst for philosophic totality which had again risen to the fore once the question of emancipation had been resolved. Indeed, just as important for the course of Russian history as the practical economic problems lying behind the peasant *Jacqueries* of the early sixties were the ideas raging in the minds of the young intelligentsia. However insufficient the emancipation act might have been to satisfy the material wants of the peasantry, it is improbable that a more liberal edict would have satisfied the intelligentsia. For the hearts of the intelligentsia throbbed not only for their 'younger brother the peasant', but for their own hopes of finding answers to the ultimate questions of meaning and purpose. The 'new men' of the sixties were to turn their backs on their intellectual as well as their religious heritage; but, in truth, they were only extending the search for a total truth and faith which the earlier intelligentsia —and the Church before it—had long pursued.

'Bazarovism'

The distinctive new characteristic of the post-Crimean radical intelligentsia was its thoroughgoing rejection of past tradition. This attitude of denial and rejection among the young generation of students and writers was in part conditioned by such factors as dislocation from a rural background, unsettling experiences in the Crimean War, the impoverishment of the landed aristocracy, and the sudden profusion of uprooted *raznochintsy* elements within the intelligentsia. Basically, however, this negative attitude was the result of widespread disillusionment in the metaphysical and idealistic framework in which the earlier intelligentsia had cast its thought. The growing desire to follow Belinsky's injunction to go 'from the blue heavens into the kitchen' created a great wave of interest in the materialist and utilitarian thinkers of the West.

The most influential spokesman for the young generation in the first five years after Crimea was Nicholas Chernyshevsky. As a student in the late forties he had followed Belinsky in rejecting Hegel for the materialism of Feuerbach. As a writer for Nekrasov's influential journal, the *Contemporary* (*Sovremennik*) in the early years after Crimea, he led the intelligentsia in turning to the dispassionate studies of human relationships that had been made by the English utilitarians. In the pages of the *Contemporary*, he translated and annotated John Stuart Mill's *Utilitarianism* and *Political Economy*, and suggested a new ethical outlook, based not on ideal considerations, but on 'rational egoism'. 'Good' was to be determined not by metaphysical criteria for Chernyshevsky, but by the concrete criteria of pleasure and the rational principle of the greatest amount. Chernyshevsky's famous protégé on the *Contemporary*, Dobrolyubov, championed the rational socialism of Robert Owen over the more visionary, emotion-based socialisms of Lamennais and Fourier, which had appealed to the pre-Crimean radicals. Chernyshevsky and Dobrolyubov together began to attack the prevailing political, religious, and above all aesthetic world-picture of nineteenth-century Russia. They insisted that art must serve a beneficial social purpose, separating' Pushkinians', for whom satisfaction lay in the creation of beauty, from 'Gogolians', for whom the demands of humanity superseded those of artistic form.

The older generation viewed with misgivings the tendency of the new intelligentsia to negate all that was not coldly rational or deducible from empirical evidence. In 1861 Turgenev gave graphic expression to this clash in his novel, *Fathers and Sons*, where Bazarov, a young medical student scoffs at all established codes of honour, religious superstition, and aesthetic values. His *credo* is that 'two and two is four and everything else is rubbish'; and the word that he uses to describe Bazarov's philosophy is the term that subsequent history has come to associate with the unrest of the post-Crimean period—nihilism.[1] Dobrolyubov rejected Bazarov as a caricature of the entire

---

[1] The term 'nihilism' was first used in modern times by Jacobi, in the late eighteenth century, and in Russia by Nadezhdin, in 1829. It was generally used as synonymous with Feuerbachian materialism throughout the forties in both Germany and Russia. Benoît-P. Hepner, *Bakounine et le panslavisme révolutionnaire*, Paris, 1950, pp. 192–6. Only after Turgenev's novel did the term come into general use as a synonym for a believer in the universal validity of scientific methodology. It

radical movement. But another rising young radical publicist, Dmitry Pisarev, accepted Bazarov as an exemplary prototype for the new men of the sixties. With Dobrolyubov's death in 1861 and Chernyshevsky's arrest in the following year, Pisarev rapidly emerged as the dominant spokesman for the new generation during the second half of the decade after Crimea. The nihilistic materialism which had represented only one facet of Chernyshevsky's fertile thought now became for Pisarev and his followers an inflexible dogma.

In the pages of the *Russian Word* (*Russkoe Slovo*), Pisarev insisted that there was no reality apart from the material world and the mechanical principles governing its operations. For Pisarev, the task of the young generation was to create a new intellectual *élite* consecrated to a belief in materialism and natural science and to the immediate task of negative criticism: the destruction of all the aesthetic and emotional shibboleths of past centuries. Not only religion but all speculative philosophy represents idle day-dreaming; all artistic creation becomes 'as pretty as Brussels lace and almost as useless';[1] and human friendship must be based solely on rational self-interest and common labour. With Pisarev the philosophical negativism of the new *déclassé* intelligentsia reached its full height, and the rakish dress and unconventional behaviour of student circles in the sixties gave testimony to the popularity of social iconoclasm. The real importance of this negative outlook lay not so much in its outward manifestations, however, as in its permeating influence on Russian thinkers of all complexions. Whether espoused or cursed, this philosophy of denial represented a startling new world-picture which no one could ignore.

Politically, 'Bazarovism' had the important effect of breaking down the intelligentsia's common front *vis-à-vis* the government. Indeed the young iconoclasts opened up a gulf that would never be successfully bridged between themselves and their older rivals, the Slavophils and moderate liberals. It is not

now appears that Turgenev took the term from Katkov, who used it as a rather imprecise label of abuse for all radicals—a use which has been common in historical writing ever since. B. P. Kozmin, 'Two Words on the Word "Nihilist" ', *Izvestiya Akademiya Nauk SSSR* (*otd. lit. i yaz.*), 1951, no. 4, pp. 381-4.

[1] D. I. Pisarev, 'Pisemsky, Turgenev, and Goncharov', *R.S.*, 1861, no. 12 in Armand Coquart, *Dmitri Pisarev, 1840-1868, et l'idéologie du nihilisme russe*, Paris, 1946, p. 119.

surprising that the idealistic world-picture which had given cohesion to the Moscow Slavophils was rejected and seriously discredited by the young realists in St. Petersburg. However, Slavophilism as a movement had largely died of its own accord by the early sixties.[1] The split which opened up between the young realists and the cosmopolitan liberals, the 'westernizers' of the forties, was of far greater importance.

The rejection of moderate liberalism was caused basically by the deep suspicion the intelligentsia had developed for all traces of mediocrity and philistinism. The progressive estrangement of moderates from the new radicalism began when two of the original westernizers, Granovsky and Chicherin, successively cautioned Herzen of the need for gradualness and the dangers of fomenting irresponsible criticism by illegally publishing the *Bell*. When Herzen himself was attacked from the left in 1858, he found himself for the first time in the position of counselling moderation to his Russian readers.

If Herzen expressed alarm at the negativism of the young generation, it is hardly surprising that enlightened liberals less radical than he should begin to dissociate themselves altogether from the 'new men' of the sixties. The older generation of writers on the *Contemporary*—literary critics like Druzhinin and Botkin and novelists like Turgenev and Goncharov, who had all been active in the general clamour for emancipation in the forties—fought unsuccessfully with their younger colleagues. Turgenev broke with the *Contemporary* in 1860, and two years later, after immortalizing the conflict in *Fathers and Sons*, he left Russia altogether.

This estrangement of the enlightened moderates from the enthusiastic realists helped to leave the legacy of mutual mistrust between liberal and extremist that was to be so characteristic of Russian social thought. Both liberals and radicals would recruit their followers from the intelligentsia; but it was the latter who were the true heirs to the old intelligentsia's passion for knowledge not just of truths, but of Truth, and for changing not just institutions, but lives. The rising realists rejected all formalism and 'neutralism' in art as in life. For them, the artist like the citizen must be an active propagandist of the truth. They rejected the world-view of the Slavophils more decisively than

[1] See *Note A*, p. 188.

that of the more eclectic westernizers; but they were in greater
basic agreement with the former in believing that what Russia
needed was not a cosmopolitan tolerance of ideas, but a passionate rock-bed of belief on which to act. However one may judge
this new outlook, one must agree with Pisarev's contention that,
for the sixties, 'if Bazarovism is a malady, it is the malady of
our time'.[1]

The Young Iconoclast

The story of Mikhailovsky's early years in St. Petersburg is
that of the typical man of the sixties: enthusiastic, fearless, and
deeply involved in the student circles, new journals, and communal experiments of the period. When he arrived in St.
Petersburg to begin his studies, Mikhailovsky was the uprooted
intellectual *par excellence*. Like so many of his generation, he was
to develop his only real attachment to the rising tide of social
and intellectual unrest in St. Petersburg.

Mikhailovsky was an industrious student, excelling in both
the humanistic and the scientific courses offered at the institute.
But he soon transferred his interests from his school curriculum
to the wider horizons offered by the new social and political
journals of the post-Crimean period. These 'thick journals', as
they were popularly called, appeared monthly or bi-weekly
and were read by the young students with an eagerness and
intensity that can hardly be exaggerated. Particular attention
was usually paid to the 'bibliographical section', which
contained reprints and reviews of the latest works of Western
philosophers and social theorists. Totally unlike the dry compen-
dium which the word 'bibliography' suggests in English, the
bibliographical section (together with the traditional 'internal
review') provided the principal medium for veiled propaganda
on social issues.

As a student, Mikhailovsky had been influenced by Herzen's
Bell, Nekrasov's *Contemporary*, and Eliseev's 'Chronicle of Progress' in the satirical journal, the *Spark* (*Iskra*). At the early age
of eighteen he established his first personal contact with this
world of radical journalism, when an admiring friend at the
institute introduced him to the editor of a newly-founded
journal, *Daybreak* (*Rassvet*). This journal was dedicated to one

[1] D. I. Pisarev, *Izbrannye Sochineniya*, Moscow, 1934, i. 228.

of the young generation's fondest beliefs: the equality of the sexes. Its editor, Valerian Krempin, had retired from service as an artillery colonel to devote himself to his 'journal for mature young women'. He typified a somewhat older element active in the sixties: the disillusioned professional man newly enamoured of a 'cause'.

Mikhailovsky was instinctively attracted to this cause. 'Woman wants to and can become a person', he later recalled. 'To understand and fathom this required no special knowledge or experience . . . [but] simple common sense and good will that could be found alike in an artillery officer and in an exalted, half-grown mining cadet.'[1] Accordingly, in April 1860, he made his début as a journalist in *Daybreak* with an article criticizing the recently-published story by Goncharov, *Episodes from the Life of Raisky*. Following the established radical practice of using literary criticism as a medium for social propaganda, Mikhailovsky attacked Goncharov for both the shallowness of the characters in his story and its lack of a social message.[2]

Mikhailovsky had always enjoyed writing and had even tried his hand at poetry while at the gymnasium, so it is not surprising that he felt proud of his youthful composition and of the thirteen roubles he received as payment. The article betrays the boyish enthusiasm of its author by the repeated use of rhetorical questions such as 'Is he a man?' or 'Can he be living?' It betrays as well the early influence on Mikhailovsky of John Stuart Mill, the first of a long line of Western thinkers to whom he turned. It was on the basis of Mill's utilitarian philosophy that Mikhailovsky questioned Goncharov, for the servile status of women in society seemed to Mikhailovsky a clear challenge to a rational ethic of human relationships. Throughout the sixties Mikhailovsky continued to view the emancipation of women as his special journalistic 'cause', publishing a series of articles on the subject, culminating in a laudatory preface to the Russian translation of Mill's *Rights of Women* in 1869.[3]

---

[1] *Lit. V.* I. 8. See 1–41 for most biographical details of this section.

[2] X. 369–82, esp. 374. The *Episodes* were the beginning of Goncharov's novel, *The Precipice (Obryv)*.

[3] His most important articles on this subject ('The Masculine Question or the Feminine', *Rus*, 1864, no. 18; 'On the Feminine Question', *Yakor*, 1864, nos. 46, 47; and 'On the Means of Combating Prostitution', *O.Z.*, 1869, no. 7) are reprinted X. 381–424. His introduction to Mill's *Rights of Women* is republished in X. 293–310.

Mikhailovsky rapidly became caught up not only in the journalistic life of the sixties, but in the second main channel of radical ardour: student agitation. Student life in post-Crimean St. Petersburg was unusually turbulent and intense, even by Russian standards. Uprooted youth like Mikhailovsky came to St. Petersburg in these years with great expectations for study and stimulation. In their view a university was 'the dream of our provincial youth . . . an indescribable sanctuary . . . a place where the young man can solve all problems'.[1] If disillusionment usually followed from the rigidity of the curriculum and the pedantry of their professors, faith in the educational process itself was only intensified by their frustration and close association with students sharing the same feelings.

The main centre of student discontent was the University of St. Petersburg, where student opposition to both government and university administration was most highly developed. In early 1861 student excitement ran particularly high. A sense of outrage was caused not only by the limited nature of the emancipation edict, but also by the arbitrary cancellation of an address to be given by the popular historian Kostomarov just a few days before, and by an officially-sponsored massacre of Polish peasants just a few weeks after the edict. Mikhailovsky, who was in the last year of his studies, immediately assumed leadership of the protest movement within the Mining Institute. At an unauthorized student meeting he delivered an address of protest in which he particularly denounced the repression in Poland.

Throughout the spring of 1861 student requiems were celebrated for Polish revolutionaries who had been hanged in Warsaw and for numerous peasants who had been shot for demonstrating against the régime. As student unrest mounted, Mikhailovsky presented a petition to the institute authorities on behalf of his fellow students demanding the right of the student body to organize and help administer their own affairs. For this action he was expelled from the institute, and thus was prevented from receiving the diploma for which he had completed all his formal work.

[1] Leo Tikhomirov, *Russia Social and Political*, ii. 64. For the best pictures of student activities of the period see the accounts of two radicals who, like Mikhailovsky, began their journalistic careers on *Daybreak*: A. M. Skabichevsky (*Literaturnye Vospominaniya*, Moscow-Leningrad, 1928, pp. 73-107, 117-73) and D. I. Pisarev (*Sochineniya*, St. Petersburg, 1901, iii. 1-110).

He retired to the country with the intention of returning in the autumn and using his remaining money to enter the Jurisprudence Faculty of the University. But the St. Petersburg to which he returned was in even greater turmoil than that which he had left. On 14 September a young radical poet, M. L. Mikhailov, had been imprisoned and held *incommunicado*—the first writer to be so treated under Alexander II—for allegedly writing the anti-governmental pamphlet, *To the Young Generation*.[1] Student protest meetings were so widespread that when Mikhailovsky returned, he was denied admission under new emergency regulations. Administrative perplexity in the face of student agitation was finally resolved by closing St. Petersburg University on 20 December.

Even moderate elements were shocked by this arbitrary act. Five distinguished professors resigned from their posts in protest, including Spasovich and Utin, who had championed the adoption of the English legal system in Russia. Mikhailovsky had been impressed while still at the institute with the critiques of the Russian criminal code written by these professors. Encouraged by their voluntary identification with the student demands, Mikhailovsky began to propagate their view that justice is served better by a flexible, constantly-evolving body of law than by a rigid corpus such as that of Imperial Russia.[2]

The writings of these men helped raise the ground-swell of protest at the Russian legal system, which in turn led to the juridical reforms of 1864 and the adoption of trial by jury. This reform gave Mikhailovsky the idea of becoming an active barrister. 'Upon the issuance of the court reform of 20 November 1864', a close friend later recalled, 'Mikhailovsky thought of an advocate's career, dreaming not only of the noble profession of a defender of "widows and orphans", but about the social role of an advocate in political affairs working for the good of his fatherland.'[3]

Mikhailovsky might well have become a lawyer had he not become involved during 1863-4 in the third of the great radical institutions of the period; the communal experiment or artel.

[1] Actually written for the most part by Nicholas Shelgunov, *infra*, p. 47.

[2] *Lit. V.* I. 10–15. The best statement of Mikhailovsky's views on liberalization of the legal code are contained in 'Crime and Punishment', a review (reprinted II. 1–96) of A. Lyubavsky's *Russkie Ugolovnye Protsessy*, St. Petersburg, 1866-7.

[3] N. V. Reinhardt, 'Memoirs', *Bayan*, 1908, no. 1, p. 23; in X. lxii.

His interest in these radical egalitarian experiments was in part inspired by Chernyshevsky's widely discussed *What is to be done?*

In this celebrated valedictory to the young generation, written from prison in 1863, Chernyshevsky had urged the formation of communal enterprises not for sentimental or even moral considerations, but simply in order to apply the utilitarian calculus for maximizing material happiness. Chernyshevsky's argument was that

> The theory is cold, but it teaches man to create warmth. A match is cold, the side of the box on which one strikes it is cold, the firewood is cold. But from them comes fire which prepares food for man and warms his body.

He does not deny that 'the theory is pitiless'; but insists that

> following it, people will be no more the wretched objects of idle commiseration. The scalpel should not flinch out of sympathy for the patient, who will be no better off for our compassion.[1]

Mikhailovsky was, however, more directly influenced by the purely moral arguments advanced by Chernyshevsky's lesser-known colleague on the *Contemporary*, Gregory Eliseev. Eliseev accepted the idea that economic enterprises should be run on functional lines and a profit-sharing basis—the essence of the old Russian artel system. In setting up the first two journals to be founded on artel lines—the weekly *Century* (*Vek*) in 1862, and the daily *Sketches* (*Ocherki*) in 1863[2]—Eliseev established the precedent for a co-operative enterprise run on a family-like basis. This type of co-operative would not become commonplace until the seventies, when the influence of Chernyshevsky's ideas receded sharply. Yet Eliseev's influence was dominant on Mikhailovsky almost from the moment they began their lifelong friendship in 1862, and was probably responsible for Mikhailovsky's early decision to invest most of his inheritance in a small book-binding establishment, to be operated as an artel.[3]

The choice of a book-binding business was significant; during the early sixties Mikhailovsky had become such an avid biblio-

---

[1] N. G. Chernyshevsky, *Chto Delat*, Moscow-Leningrad, 1933, p. 95.

[2] Neither lasted a year. For Eliseev's role in them see S. Breytburg, 'Toward a History of the Gazette *Ocherki*', and B. P. Kozmin, 'The Artel Journal *Vek*', in *Russkaya Zhurnalistika: I. Shestidesyatye Gody* (ed. Polyansky), Moscow, 1930.

[3] Reinhardt, 'Memoirs', in X. lviii.

phil that he was attracted to anything which would keep him in contact with books. Reading both French and German, he shared the general enthusiasm for the latest works from Western Europe and was able to support himself during these years by tutoring wealthy young foreigners in St. Petersburg. Because of his passion for books, he soon became well known in St. Petersburg publishing circles. And it was through a book-seller, Nicholas Kurochkin, that Mikhailovsky was finally hired permanently in 1865, on the type of journal for which he was ideally suited: a bibliographical review, the *Book Herald* (*Knizhny Vestnik*).

This 'bibliographical work' into which Mikhailovsky was plunged continued to be a major medium for developing radical social ideas under the eyes of the censor. The old preliminary, or preventive, censorship had been replaced by the less restrictive punitive censorship early in 1865. But the problem of veiling anti-governmental propaganda remained; and the tradition of expounding radical ideas in bibliographical critiques was to grow even stronger in the years after 1865.

The two years Mikhailovsky spent on the *Book Herald* were among the happiest of his life. He was stimulated by a whole new range of personalities that he met through Kurochkin; and in his critiques of new books he began to formulate a radical philosophy of his own. He had spent most of his money on his short-lived artel experiment and was living in a small attic flat near the Voznesensky bridge on 12 roubles a month for lodging and 9 for food. However, the thrill of his new job as a reviewer free to write as he pleased more than compensated for his financial predicament. 'Like an impoverished Spanish *hidalgo*, proudly draped in my moth-eaten cape, full of my own editorial importance, every day I strolled in worn-out shoes along the Nevsky Prospect to the bookstore.'[1]

Thus, Mikhailovsky shared in the student unrest, the radical publication, and the communal experiments of the decade. But, as he settled down to regular work on a journal in 1865, his attention began to turn to some of the intellectual problems posed by the ferment of the age. He began to look to the West for some means of reconciling the philosophical paradox which had underlain the *Sturm und Drang* of the sixties: between the

[1] *Lit. V.* I. 19.

violent rejection of all unscientific belief and the passionate affirmation of an eminently visionary belief in progress and perfectibility. In 1865 and early 1866 Mikhailovsky turned for inspiration to the strange compound of rejection and affirmation offered by the French anarcho-socialist and lover of paradox, Pierre Joseph Proudhon.

By the mid sixties Proudhon had already become probably the most important single ideological influence on the radical intelligentsia.[1] His influence was decisive on Mikhailovsky and his closest friends. They were attracted both by Proudhon's opposition—to the 'fantastic reveries' of the early utopians, the 'philistinism' of bourgeois politics, and the inhumanity of all system makers—and by his affirmation of man's perfectibility when freed from coercive authority. A reading of Proudhon's *Système des Contradictions* in the early sixties was directly responsible for turning Mikhailovsky away from his early resolve to become a lawyer.[2] The book, with its picture of irreconcilable social tensions and unbridgeable paradoxes, convinced him that the injustices of the legal system were but a by-product of more fundamental conflicts in society. He thus put aside his early intention to work for social reform by becoming a 'defender of widows and orphans' in the newly reformed courts. 'The social role of an advocate in political affairs' seemed, after reading Proudhon, a much too prosaic way of 'working for the good of the fatherland'. The idea of justice as something to be furthered through institutional media was abandoned for the exultant Proudhonist idea that justice lay in defending human personality by shattering all institutional bonds.

Mikhailovsky's principal collaborator on the *Book Herald* was Bartholomew Zaitsev, an outspoken Proudhonist who had taken over from the incarcerated Pisarev the role of leading iconoclast for the *Russian Word*. Through Zaitsev, Mikhailovsky became a close friend of the economic editor of the *Russian Word*, Nicholas Sokolov, who in turn had become a personal friend and follower of Proudhon when in Brussels in 1860. During this period, Sokolov was putting the finishing touches on his famous book, *The Heretics*, a restatement of Proudhon's apologia for perennial dissent in which Proudhon was characterized as the last, the greatest, and indeed 'the model heretic'.[3]

---

[1] See *Note B*, p. 188.   [2] *Lit. V.* I. 13.   [3] *Infra*, p. 132.

The editor of the *Book Herald*, Nicholas Kurochkin, and his brother Vasily were avid Francophils with a large library of French works. It was probably from them that Mikhailovsky first borrowed and began reading intensively the works of this exciting new French thinker late in 1865.

In April 1866 he published his first article on Proudhon, urging a clearer understanding of Proudhon who was 'decidedly not a negative figure, but on the contrary a positive one by preference'.[1] In the same year he began a translation of Proudhon's posthumously published *De la capacité politique des classes ouvrières*, which was published in 1867, as *Frantsuzkaya Demokratiya* (French Democracy). Almost every major article by Mikhailovsky for the next fifteen years contained some citation or reference to Proudhon. This rough-hewn French provincial played a major role for Mikhailovsky and his generation in transforming a philosophic nihilism based on materialism and empiricism into a social nihilism—a denial of all authority over the individual, whether political, philosophical, or religious. Largely through Proudhon, Mikhailovsky gave to his own iconoclasm a positive and social orientation. By 1865 he had been directed towards his own deepest article of faith: the search for social justice in Proudhon's sense of 'the defence of human dignity wherever it is compromised'.[2]

But there was still too much radical activity and expectation to allow time for extended philosophizing. In the winter of 1865 a new radical circle had formed around the young Proudhonists of the *Book Herald*. The *enfant terrible* of this circle was a young scientist recently returned from Western Europe, Nicholas Nozhin, whom Kurochkin had recruited to write for the *Book Herald*. To the unsympathetic outsider, this new figure was just another man of the sixties 'with a leporine profile and bulging gray eyes . . . dressed in ridiculously extreme nihilistic fashion'.[3] But for Mikhailovsky, Nozhin 'flashed before me like a meteor . . . having nothing in common with the ordinary phenomena of nature'.[4] Mikhailovsky moved in to share a flat

---

[1] 'Proudhon and Our Publicists', *Knizhny Vestnik*, 1866, no. 8, in X. 506. Vasily Kurochkin was editor of *Iskra*.

[2] P. J. Proudhon, *De la justice dans la révolution et dans l'église*, Paris, 1858, i. 182.

[3] L. I. Mechnikov, 'M. A. Bakunin in Italy in 1864', *Ist V.*, 1897, no. 3, p. 818.

[4] IV. 265–6. Spoken about the character of Bukhartsev, whom Mikhailovsky later admitted to be a portrayal of Nozhin.

with Nozhin in the latter part of 1865, and they began to attend 'evenings' together to discuss 'advanced ideas' with Eliseev, Zaitsev, several naval officers from Kronstadt, and transient students from Moscow and the provinces.

The atmosphere in these circles was charged with anticipation, but a rapid series of events in April brought to a sudden end their great expectations. On 3 April Nozhin suddenly died; and on the following day a member of another St. Petersburg circle, Dmitry Karakozov, attempted to assassinate the Tsar. In the wake of this unprecedented act, the *Contemporary* and the *Russian Word* were shut down for ever, and Mikhailovsky and the entire *Book Herald* circle arrested. The young iconoclasts were forced into regrouping their forces and formulating at last a positive philosophy and programme of action. More than any other single man, Mikhailovsky created during this forced 'withdrawal and return' of the late sixties the positive ideology that would suddenly blossom forth amidst the ruins left by a decade of iconoclasm.

III

A THEORY OF HISTORY

THE attempted assassination of 1866 ended the hope of further reform from above. The high tide had in fact been reached in 1865; and by any Western yardstick the water-line was still abysmally low. Important as Alexander's reforms were and far-reaching as their implications may have been, they had not in any major respect aided the position of the social reformer in Russia. The cumbersome preliminary censorship had been abolished, but the punitive powers of the censor remained. More important, there was still no political channel through which opposition or even discussion could find legal expression.

In rapid succession the last of the moderate ministers, Golovnin and Valuev, were dismissed from their posts after the Karakozov affair; mass and indiscriminate arrests were made; and Count Muravev, the suppressor of the Polish rebellion of 1863, was appointed to head a committee of inquiry with virtually dictatorial powers. Nekrasov of the *Contemporary* added to the demoralization of the radical camp by consenting to read an ode to Muravev at the fashionable English Club. There seemed to the radicals to be symbolic significance in the fact that Glinka's opera, *A Life for the Tsar*, was enjoying record popularity during this period.[1] Emphatically, as one of Mikhailovsky's friends later recalled: '1866 finished off what is known as the sixties, if we define it not in its strict chronological sense, but in its basic meaning of a period of hope, of reform and social renovation. . . .'[2] For Mikhailovsky, as for his colleagues, the early summer of 1866 was a period of discouragement verging on despair.

Mikhailovsky was released from prison earlier than his collaborators on the *Book Herald*, Zaitsev and Kurochkin; and during the summer of 1866 he was its sole editor. He could not make it a going concern, however, and the eventual release of

[1] I. A. Khudyakov, 'Memoirs', *Ist V.*, 1906, no. 11, p. 90.
[2] N. F. Annensky, in *Na Slavnom Postu*, St. Petersburg, 1906, p. 433.

Zaitsev and Kurochkin came too late to save the magazine from dissolution in the autumn. In a bitter article, 'The Fourth of April and Russian Journalism', Mikhailovsky accused the government of stifling freedom of thought and censured the motives as well as the policies of the administration.[1] The only radical journal still in operation to which he could turn for employment in the winter of 1866 was the *Cause* (*Delo*), which had been taken over in 1865 by Blagosvetlov, the former editor of the *Russian Word*. Mikhailovsky wrote anonymous literary reviews for the *Cause*, but stayed on the journal only long enough to form a dislike of Blagosvetlov.[2] The negativism of the *Russian Word* was no longer enough for Mikhailovsky. With no regular source of income and his own resources severely depleted, Mikhailovsky left St. Petersburg in the early spring of 1867 for the provincial home of the Kurochkin brothers at Chernaya Rechka in the Crimea.

The atmosphere on the country estate was even more depressing than that of St. Petersburg. Nicholas Kurochkin's *Book Herald* had just failed, and his brother's satirical journal, the *Spark*, was at its lowest ebb. Many of the principal contributors to the *Spark* had left St. Petersburg to spend their summer with the Kurochkins. Denied normal outlet for their talents, they began to suffer from 'that well-known Russian weakness', which, Mikhailovsky explained, was 'the pseudonym for drunkenness'. The alcoholism and general moral laxity of his contemporaries shocked and saddened Mikhailovsky. Yet he was repelled even more by the derisive portrayal of the young generation as irresponsible libertines in the novels of former radicals like Leskov and Pisemsky. His friends turned to drink, Mikhailovsky later insisted, because of their 'sorrowful circumstances which strengthened, if they did not actually produce, this pernicious habit'.[3]

The rest of 1867 and all of 1868 were years of sporadic contributions to the few sympathetic 'thick journals' that remained. On the invitation of P. A. Gaideburov, one of the visitors to the Kurochkins, Mikhailovsky accepted in the summer of 1867 the position of literary editor on a new journal,

---

[1] The article was never published, but is discussed in *Lit. V.* I. 18.
[2] Ibid. 20–22.
[3] Ibid. 32.

the *Public Court* (*Glasny Sud*), but left after only two issues.[1] He
then thought of turning for employment to a new journal for
'progressive women', the *Woman's Herald* (*Zhensky Vestnik*); but
this journal, like the *Cause*, was too closely linked with the purely
negative traditions of the *Russian Word*.[2] Not until 1 January
1868 did another radical journal appear in St. Petersburg—
the *Contemporary Review* (*Sovremennoe Obozrenie*)—which could
legitimately claim to be the heir to the *Contemporary*. This new
journal, which was edited by former collaborators on the *Contemporary*, appealed to the young Mikhailovsky; and he agreed to
begin publishing a series of 'Letters on the Russian Intelligentsia' in the July issue.[3] When this journal failed in June, Mikhailovsky turned to Nicholas Kurochkin, who gave him a position
writing a regular 'Journalistic Review' for the bibliographical
section of the *Week*. But, when a minor figure whom Mikhailovsky disliked was appointed editor over Kurochkin, Mikhailovsky
joined the latter in resigning from that journal as well, in
March 1869.

The periodical on which they both found permanent employment was the newly-reformed *Annals of the Fatherland* (*Otechestvennye Zapiski*), the second and most important heir of the
Contemporary, and one which was to become the most influential
of all the 'thick journals' in post-Crimean radicalism. It was on
the pages of the *Annals* that Mikhailovsky set forth the thoughts
that he had drawn together during his period of withdrawal.

The 'Subjective Method'

Throughout this period Mikhailovsky had been preoccupied
with drawing together a positive message for the radical camp.
He had tried his hand at a novel, *The Struggle* (*Borba*), which he

[1] Gaideburov was a student of early Russian history, whose name was alleged
to have been taken from that of the *gaidemaks*—Ukrainian insurrectionists of the
eighteenth century. Mikhailovsky and Gaideburov (whom Mikhailovsky had
probably met in 1863, when Gaideburov was working with Eliseev on *St. Peter-
burgskiya Vedomosti*) became major protagonists within the populist movement after
Gaideburov assumed permanent editorship of the *Week* (*Nedelya*) in 1875. *Infra*,
pp. 95–96, 105 note 1, 145.

[2] The editor was A. K. Sheller-Mikhailov, the last editor of the *Russian Word*,
and the publisher was a pompous and uncritical admirer of the West. 'I wish the
infant well', Mikhailovsky wrote, 'but would change its mother and father.'
(Quoted from an unspecified article in the *Week* of 1868 by M. Klevensky, in
Russkaya Zhurnalistika, Moscow, 1930, p. 119.)

[3] See *Note C*, p. 188.

hoped would tell the story of the men of the sixties. But soon he turned to philosophy, writing a lengthy essay, 'What is Progress?' Published in instalments throughout 1869 and 1870, this work was perhaps the most influential of many attempts by radicals to synthesize the ideas of the sixties. This was the closest Mikhailovsky ever came to a *profession de foi*. For many of his contemporaries it helped to reconcile a belief in scientific method with an eminently non-scientific belief in human perfectibility.

The uncritical optimists of the early sixties had not been bothered by this basic inconsistency in their outlook. But as radical disillusionment grew in the late sixties they began to feel the need for a doctrine that would harmonize science and progress, a causal and a teleological understanding of the world. In order to fill this need, Mikhailovsky turned to the newly-discovered evolutionary thought of the West. The subtitle of Mikhailovsky's 'What is Progress?' was 'an examination of the ideas of Herbert Spencer'. Since this, and most of his articles in the next few years, were concerned with Spencer, Darwin, and other evolutionary thinkers, it is important to trace how their ideas entered into Russian radical thought in the late sixties.

Evolutionary thought was introduced into Russia in 1864 with a translation of Darwin's *Origin of the Species* and a series of popular articles on Darwin by Pisarev, then at the height of his prestige.[1] Pisarev accepted as scientific truth Darwin's theory of natural selection and used it as a means for reconciling his belief in scientific truth with his certainty of human progress. For Pisarev, and for most of the men of the sixties, progress simply became a scientific law—since all would admit the ape to represent progress over the amoeba, and man progress over the ape.

Darwinism was used to justify struggles of all sorts by the iconoclasts. Pisarev's reading of Darwin led him to conclude 'that each species acts in a constant way exclusively for its own good and that the most absolute egoism constitutes the basic law of life of the entire organic world'.[2] Zaitsev concluded that

[1] D. I. Pisarev, *Sochineniya*, St. Petersburg, 1912, iii. 311–498. 'Progress in the Animal and Plant World', *R.S.*, 1864, nos. 4, 5, 6, 7, 9. See also an anonymous series on 'The Book of Darwin: Its Critics and Commentators', *O.Z.*, 1864, nos. 8, 10, 12.

[2] Pisarev, *Sochineniya*, iii. 362.

the present superiority of the white races must be the result of natural selection, and that other races which were failing in the 'struggle for survival' would soon become extinct.[1]

Equating the struggle for survival with progress shocked the moral idealism of the intelligentsia, and Nozhin, Mikhailovsky's closest friend in the mid sixties, pointed out the lines along which the radical camp would reject social Darwinism. In an attack on Zaitsev in 1865, Nozhin conceded that the struggle for existence was a valid description of the relationship of one species to another.[2] But he insisted that such a struggle was not at all necessary among members of the same species, particularly among human beings. Nozhin insisted that co-operation was more natural than competition among members of a common species, and indeed, that only by co-operation was survival possible at all.[3] In the pontifical, pseudo-scientific language of the day, Nozhin concluded that 'the union of physiological interests is possible between like entities'.[4]

Mikhailovsky expanded the argument in a series of articles in the late sixties, accepting the thesis that Darwin's theory of evolution is correct in describing man's relationship to nature, but not in describing his relationship to his fellow-men. In the course of his many articles on Darwinism,[5] Mikhailovsky helped to give the term 'Darwinism' the synonymity with 'predatory self-seeking' which it would acquire among radicals of the seventies and eighties.[6]

Mikhailovsky followed Nozhin in rejecting Darwin's theory of evolution, because in human society concepts like chance

[1] V. A. Zaitsev, 'A Reply to My Critics on My Way of Looking on the Coloured Races', *R.S.*, 1864, no. 12.

[2] N. D. Nozhin, 'On the Appearance of the Articles of *Russkoe Slovo* on Slavery', *Iskra*, 1865, no. 8.

[3] The prevalence of co-operation in the natural world was a theme being sounded by many members of geographic and zoological expeditions which were then exploring the vast eastern regions of Russia. Nozhin based his scientific argumentation for this point on the works of the leading Russian zoologist, Karl Kessler.

[4] From an unspecified issue of *Knizhny Vestnik* of 1866 in *Na Slavnom Postu*, p. 213.

[5] I. 1–422.

[6] For one of the best radical critiques of social Darwinism see Chernyshevsky, 'The Origin of the Theory Favourable to the Fight for Survival', *Russkaya Mysl*, 1888, no. 9. Only the philosophical reactionaries accepted a doctrine of social Darwinism. Danilevsky's *Russia and Europe*, St. Petersburg, 1869, for example, was based on strict analogies of society with the laws of struggle in the biological world.

variation and natural selection implied purposeless struggle. 'I was still under the spell of Nozhin', he later wrote of this period of withdrawal. 'I interested myself in the question of the boundaries of biology and sociology and the possibilities of bringing them closer together.'[1] In his search for a theory of social development that would justify a belief in both science and progress (biology and sociology) Mikhailovsky turned to the pre-Darwinian doctrine of purposive evolution preached by Herbert Spencer.

Spencer's works were introduced into Russia in 1866, when the first of a projected seven-volume translation of Spencer's works was published in St. Petersburg. Mikhailovsky systematically studied this latest prophet from the West in the early months of his forced withdrawal from St. Petersburg; two articles on Spencer, which appeared in July 1867, mark the beginning of this new interest.[2]

There was much in both the thought and personality of Herbert Spencer to commend him to the radical intelligentsia. A nonconformist and an iconoclast, Spencer expressed a view which Mikhailovsky heartily endorsed that:

To the true reformer no institution is sacred, no belief above criticism. Everything shall conform to equity and reason. Nothing shall be saved by its prestige.[3]

Spencer's faith in the individual personality as an end in itself and more than a mere economic entity appealed to Mikhailovsky's Proudhonist sentiments. Mikhailovsky also saw in Spencer a man who sensed danger in the growing power of all authorities, especially that of the state. Most important, Spencer's concept of progress as a continual process of dissociation from accepted norms, in a progression 'from the homogeneous to the heterogeneous', offered a convenient 'scientific' formula for a position already held by Mikhailovsky's associates.[4]

At the beginning of 'What is Progress?', Mikhailovsky follows Spencer in accepting as a criterion for measuring human progress the biological 'law' that an organism is further developed as it becomes more complex and as the division of labour among

[1] *Lit. V.* I. 44.
[2] 'Literary Review', in *Glasny Sud*, 11 and 20 July 1867, in X. 425–42.
[3] See *Note D*, p. 189.
[4] Spencer, 'Progress, its Law and Cause', the *Westminster Review*, April 1857.

members of the organism becomes more complete. Having accepted Spencer's law, however, Mikhailovsky reaches an impasse over the question: What, in society, is this organism? If the 'organism' means society as a whole, then the increase in productivity resulting from specialization is in itself progress. If, on the other hand, the 'organism' in the formula is the individual personality, progress would have to be measured primarily by the variety of tasks and functions assigned to each individual. As society becomes heterogeneous, the individual 'organism' becomes specialized; conversely, as the individual becomes many-sided, the social 'organism' tends to become homogeneous, with everyone doing a bit of everything. 'Which one of these two types of development, which are mutually exclusive, can one consider truly progressive?' asks Mikhailovsky. 'The objective point of view does not help solve this problem. It only shows that progress consists in a change from the homogeneous to the heterogeneous.'[1]

Since 'the objective point of view' offered no solution, Mikhailovsky introduced into his arguments what he would call the 'subjective method'—and what his later admirer, the historian Kareev, would more accurately call the 'subjective point of view'. Mikhailovsky's point of view was clearly conditioned by 'the spell of Nozhin', for Nozhin, in his argument against the 'objective' laws of social Darwinism, had ultimately fallen back on his deep belief in the natural goodness of man and in 'full health, freedom and anarchy for the self-sufficient individual'. In Nozhin's view the unnatural fight for existence arose among men not just because of the advent of the machine, but 'because of conflicting interests, or what is exactly the same —the division of labour'.[2]

Mikhailovsky insists that the individual is the only 'organism' in terms of which one may speak of progress. He claims that utilitarian philosophers, by speaking of values in terms of social utility, share with apologists for the organic state the sin of defining worth in terms of impersonal abstractions. Mikhailovsky insists that any true reformer must 'take the point of view that society as an abstract personality does not live or die or suffer or rejoice'. It is therefore essential in Mikhailovsky's view

[1] Q.Q.P., p. 81.
[2] Na Slavnom Postu, pp. 212-13.

to 'make the personality, which thinks, feels and desires, the centre of our examination'.[1]

Thus the personality, which 'thinks, feels and desires', is the organism in terms of which alone progress can be measured. Following Nozhin, Mikhailovsky sees the division of labour as the major dehumanizing force of modern times, recalling in particular his own visits to the arms factory at Tula, where intense specialization was already dehumanizing a second generation of workers.[2] Mikhailovsky turns for discussion of the awesome problems raised by specialization not to the economists, but to the socialists of the West such as Proudhon and to other Western writers such as Schiller and de Tocqueville.[3] Reinforced by the arguments of such diverse thinkers, Mikhailovsky insists, in his final definition of progress, on the centrality of the individual personality:

Progress is the gradual drawing to completion of the indivisible personality: the most complete and varied division of labour possible between man's organs, and the smallest possible division of labour between men ... all which diminishes the heterogeneity of society and in so doing strengthens the heterogeneity of its members is moral, just, reasonable, and useful.[4]

In arriving at this oft-repeated 'formula of progress', Mikhailovsky had turned from the post-Crimean flood of English utilitarian thought to the more long-standing influence of French radicalism, and above all to the positivist philosophy of Auguste Comte. By the late sixties Comte's grandiose ideas on human history and society were attracting even greater attention in Russia than had the ideas of his predecessor and teacher, St.-Simon.[5] Comte's optimistic theory of history with its rich picture of progress unfolding in all areas of life captured Mikhailovsky's imagination. Yet, just as Mikhailovsky detected a germ of possible absolutism in St.-Simon's concept of rule by

[1] *Q.Q.P.*, p. 81. Mikhailovsky's attack on utilitarian social philosophy for its neglect of the individual was taken by his own acknowledgement from the work of the American scientist and social historian, John William Draper, particularly *The History of Intellectual Development in Europe*, N.Y., 1862, and *The History of Civil Development in America*, N.Y., 1865. See *Q.Q.P.*, pp. 71–74.

[2] Ibid., p. 48.

[3] Ibid., pp. 48–50.

[4] Ibid., p. 200.

[5] See *Note E*, p. 189

an *élite* of dedicated experts,[1] so he developed strong reservations about Comte's system.

In Comte's *Cours de philosophie positive*, sociology and ethics were classed as sciences subject to discernible laws, different from the physical sciences only in that they would be the last to arrive at the positive stage. For Mikhailovsky this explanation erred seriously by destroying a vital distinction in the name of an abstract system.

This principle in terms of which all phenomena are subject to laws is pure and irreproachable like a virgin. But it may also remain sterile like a virgin, for it does not possess in itself an element of fertility.[2]

This 'element of fertility' can only be provided by a frank recognition of the 'subjective element' which makes the sciences of humanity profoundly different from the natural sciences.

In the domain of social life, observation is so inevitably linked to moral appreciation that only at the risk of misunderstanding the significance of political developments has one the right to exclude admiration and reprobation.[3]

Although Comte claimed that positive philosophy will realize 'all the legitimate desires of the political revolutionaries',[4] his philosophy can never, in Mikhailovsky's view, determine what these legitimate desires are. Thus, the wide variety of 'causes' which the followers of St.-Simon and Comte were championing did not surprise Mikhailovsky; for the positivist 'can veer off to either right or left; he might become, like Dumas, Nélaton, and other scientific notables of contemporary France, a zealous servant of the Second Empire; but he might equally well choose a completely different programme'.[5] To be a servant of a new Napoleon in the centre of bourgeois capitalism was as unthinkable a career as a Russian radical could imagine. By pointing out that the doctrine of St.-Simon and Comte did not clearly

---

[1] In his 'Parallels and Contrasts' (published in a collection gathered by Vasily Kurochkin, *Nevsky Sbornik*, St. Petersburg, 1867) Mikhailovsky challenges St.-Simon with Mill's maxim that logic does not cover human beings, and with citations from Proudhon. Cf. the latter's similar objections to St.-Simon in his *Confessions d'un révolutionnaire*, Paris, 1850, p. 324.

[2] *Q.Q.P.*, p. 96.   [3] Ibid., p. 97.

[4] Ibid., p. 102, quoted from Comte, *Cours de philosophie positive*, Paris, 1864, iv. 148.   [5] *Q.Q.P.*, p. 103.

rule out such activity, Mikhailovsky effectively indicated to his Russian radical audience the insufficiency of positivism as a social outlook.

No system of objective truth, including that of Comte with which he is most in sympathy, can be acceptable to Mikhailovsky if 'it is deaf to the sufferings of humanity'.[1] The dependence of positivism on scientific method is both its greatness and its limitation, for 'one still has desires. Every positivist has them, but positivism itself poses no ideal, for an ideal is the result of a subjective state.'[2] There had to be clear recognition of a subjective or moral truth as well as an objective or scientific truth. As he later wrote:

> I could never believe, and do not now believe that it is forbidden to find a point of view in which truth-as-verity (*pravda-istina*) and truth-as-justice (*pravda-spravedlivost*) could not go hand-in-hand, one enriching the other.[3]

Neither type of truth should, however, obscure the other. Indeed, in Mikhailovsky's view the task of life should be

> fearlessly to look in the eye of reality and its reflections—truth-as-verity, objective truth—and at same time to defend truth-as-justice—subjective truth.[4]

It is significant that, during the period when he was writing 'What is Progress?', Mikhailovsky bought a bust of Belinsky, which he was to keep over his bookshelf for the rest of his life. Belinsky had been the first of the great Russian radicals to establish by his own example the idea among the intelligentsia that truth itself was not enough without justice. Like Belinsky, who had rejected Hegelian idealism because of its indifference to the fate of the individual, Mikhailovsky rejected those parts of Comte which might lead to determinism. He sought a social philosophy which would satisfy his moral passions for justice as well as his intellectual belief that a new age was dawning.

The only social philosophy compatible with this new age was, for Mikhailovsky, a practical or subjective socialism. He accepts a distinction drawn by Littré, the principal disciple of Comte and a friend of many Russian radicals, between the 'two

---

[1] *Q.Q.P.*, p. 100.   [2] Ibid., pp. 102-3.
[3] From an article written in 1889, chosen by Mikhailovsky for the introduction to the 1896 edition of his collected works, I. v.   [4] I. v.

socialisms . . . the one metaphysical, the other practical, experimental and, in its limits, positive'.[1] Mikhailovsky rejects the
'metaphysical revolutionaries', whose historical utility ended
when they had fulfilled their negative function of overthrowing
Catholicism and feudalism. Attributing a metaphysical significance to such abstract terms as 'the people' or 'the general will'
was, for Mikhailovsky as for Comte, 'a sort of transfer to the
people of the divine right that had been so resented in kings'.[2]
All of these metaphysical concepts belong to the second, metaphysical period of history, but not to the third, positive epoch
on which man has now embarked.

For Mikhailovsky, the socialism of the positive age would
have to be completely free of abstract dogma and mystical
concepts. It would have to be 'practical and experimental',
accepting the idea that subjective man just as he is is a superior
value to any objective idea of truth that men could ever evolve.

Pure beauty, absolute justice, pure truth . . . —all these points of
view are too narrow for a phenomenon as complex as man in society.
. . . There is nothing more beautiful for man than man himself; and
the worst of men is far above the best photographic apparatus. . . .[3]

Man as man thus came to represent for Mikhailovsky the
supreme value in this new and unique third age. It was only in
the past, 'in the eccentric period, that man with his flesh and
blood, his thoughts and feelings, his loves and hates could be
forgotten for an abstract category'.[4] Like Comte, Mikhailovsky
looks forward to the development of altruism as the hope of the
new positive age. But, for Mikhailovsky, altruism itself should
not become an abstract idea, since it involves the constant
sympathetic penetration into the experience of others—the
'subjective method' rather than passive observation of social
phenomena. This Proudhonist emphasis on moral feeling rather
than dispassionate appraisal lies at the root of all the hatred of
pedants, bureaucrats, and statisticians which was to become so
characteristic of Mikhailovsky and the radicalism of the seventies.

[1] Ibid., p. 104. Quoted from *La Philosophie Positive*, 1867, no. 1, p. 140.
[2] *Q.Q.P.*, p. 92. Quoted from *Cours*, iv. 56. Cf. Proudhon's criticism of the old
tyranny which Rousseau 'made respectable by making it proceed from the people'.
P. J. Proudhon, *De la justice*, Paris, 1858, i. 182.
[3] *Q.Q.P.*, p. 182.   [4] Ibid., p. 183.

Mikhailovsky had begun 'What is Progress?' in an attempt to reconcile the two things in which the sixties believed: natural science and human progress. But by the end he was calling forth the new belief which was to dominate the seventies: faith in the intrinsic worth of the human personality and in his moral ideals. He had begun with an examination of the system of Herbert Spencer and Auguste Comte—and would continue to use the terminology of these great system builders. But the mainsprings in his social philosophy were provided by the anti-systematic moral humanism of Proudhon and Belinsky. They were the true authors of the 'subjective method', and Mikhailovsky, in the longest of his famous 'layman's notes' in the mid-seventies, suggested as his ideal a combination of the best qualities of these two men.[1]

The Struggle for Individuality

It is a tribute to the depth of Hegel's influence on Russian thought that even those who rejected his philosophy still sought to base their activities on a philosophy of history. By the late sixties the young iconoclasts had already begun to turn from Chernyshevsky's question 'What is to be done?' to the long-standing Hegelian question 'Where are we going?' As one man of the sixties recalled: 'from 1864 on I began to think about the interplay and interdependence of the forces and laws of physical and human nature—about their unfolding in history, about their meaning in the future social order and the development of the people.'[2] In the second half of the decade, Mikhailovsky and his contemporaries began to look on history itself as a source of hope.

The most influential of the new optimistic philosophies of history was that of Peter Lavrov—an older figure whose intellectual development had begun under the influence of Hegel. Like Mikhailovsky, Lavrov recognized the need for 'standing in the position of the suffering and desiring ranks of society and not in the position of a detached on-looker . . .'.[3] Lavrov also shared Mikhailovsky's recognition of the difference between

---

[1] 'Proudhon and Belinsky', O.Z., 1875, no. 11, in III. 923–85.

[2] A. P. Shchapov in N. A. Rubakin, Sredi Knig, Moscow, 1913, ii. 219.

[3] P. L. Lavrov, Formula Progressa N. K. Mikhailovskago, St. Petersburg, 1906, p. 36.

natural science and human history. In his famous *Historical Letters* of 1868–70, Lavrov insisted that scientific laws had little relevance to history, which is moved by 'those mental and moral aims which in every epoch are recognized by the most developed personalities as the highest aim, as truth and the moral ideal'.[1] As the ideal for his own generation, Lavrov held out an almost mystical concept of progress. But his appeal—like that of all revolutionary Hegelians—was to the select few capable of becoming possessed by the new ideal. The challenge at the end of the *Letters* was a throwback to the revolutionary Hegelianism of Bakunin:

> Wilt thou be one of those who are ready for all sacrifices and sufferings if only he can succeed in being a conscious, knowing agent of progress? Or wilt thou stand aside as a passive spectator on the terrible mass of evil committed around thee, conscious of your own betrayal?[2]

Mikhailovsky shared with Lavrov a faith in progress—as well as many common experiences in the circles of the late sixties. But he was not sympathetic with Lavrov's attempt to intoxicate men with an ideal, and lose their identity in serving it. For Mikhailovsky, it was necessary to define progress in terms of ethical benefits to individuals; for Lavrov 'what is necessary is only the evaluation of historical movements from the point of view of progress as the final goal'.[3] Personal controversy between the two men began when Mikhailovsky, as an editor of the *Week*, pronounced Lavrov's first 'Letter' too dense and Germanic for publication. The Letter was eventually published; but knowledge of Mikhailovsky's action may have helped prompt Lavrov to write a critique of Mikhailovsky,[4] in which the latter's concept of progress was called too mechanical, and his formula too narrowly focused on contemporary problems. Lavrov's arguments were as ponderous as those of his original Letters, and perhaps their greatest importance lay in stimulating Mikhailovsky to spell out his own philosophy of history in greater detail for the radical camp. Although contained in no single work as celebrated as the *Historical Letters*, Mikhailovsky's

---

[1] P. L. Lavrov, *Istoricheskie Pisma*, St. Petersburg, 1906, p. 34.
[2] Ibid., p. 358.   [3] Ibid., p. 296.
[4] P. L. Lavrov, 'The Formula of Progress of N. K. Mikhailovsky', *O.Z.*, 1870, no. 2.

views, as set forth in many articles in the *Annals*, exerted a greater cumulative influence than those of Lavrov, Bakunin, or any other radical figure of the time.

The constant factor in Mikhailovsky's quest for a broadened 'formula of progress' was his repeated use of the familiar concept of three ages. He discussed a whole series of triadic formulas and formulated an original one of his own in a celebrated essay, 'The Struggle for Individuality'.

Mikhailovsky had borrowed heavily from Comte in 'What is Progress?'; and in February 1871 he adopted the Comtean scheme of three historical ages: (1) the age of absolutism, theology, war, and feudal land-holding; (2) the age of constitutional monarchy, metaphysics, and capital accumulation; and (3) the age of science, objective laws, and the right to work.[1] Mikhailovsky would often subsequently use this formula, but it was too impersonal and devoid of social message for him to accept it fully. In August and September of the same year he turned with greater enthusiasm to the theories of Louis Blanc.

In 1871 the Russian translation was published of the first half of the French socialist's twelve-volume *Histoire de la Révolution française*. Mikhailovsky's lengthy review, 'The Philosophy of History of Louis Blanc', revealed the extent of Mikhailovsky's interest in philosophies of history during this period. In his view Blanc was like the Russians of the late sixties and seventies in that he 'had to create a philosophy of history . . . Plato, Moore, and Campanella could and had to be satisfied with only a logical and ethical sanction for their ideals. They were utopians, noble dreamers, naïve builders on the sand. . . . Louis Blanc could and had to add to the sanction of logic and ethics, the historical sanction. This is one of the signs of the times.'[2]

Mikhailovsky finds in Blanc's work a new and more satisfying trio of historical epochs—the ages of authority, individualism, and brotherhood. Blanc's first two ages correspond closely to those of Comte; but the concept of the third age as an age of brotherhood appeals more to his moral idealism than had Comte's impersonal age of 'science and universal order'.

Mikhailovsky suggests, however, several revealing alterations in Blanc's picture of the development of European history. For

[1] VI. 105. Mikhailovsky acknowledges his debt to Comte more explicitly in an article of April 1870 (IV. 100).   [2] III. 13.

instance, Blanc's assertion that the age of authority gave way
to the age of individualism with Luther is rejected. 'Luther was
still a pope; he still stood firm on the ground of authority . . .
Cartesianism, with which begins the latest metaphysic, was the
real revolution, the real rebellion of human personality in the
realm of thought against the legends of Catholicism.'[1] But even
Descartes only began the process leading to 'the latest metaphysic' (i.e. exclusive belief in the methods of natural science)
and is thus linked only with the second age. For science in
Mikhailovsky's view cannot by itself bring about the age of
brotherhood.

In November of 1872 Mikhailovsky brought forth another
tripartite theory, that of the early Neapolitan, Giambattista
Vico. In reading Michelet's translation of Vico, Mikhailovsky
found corroboration of his own belief that human studies
differ completely from those of the natural sciences. Vico foreshadowed German romanticism in contending that history
must be written subjectively, in insisting that a *scienza nuova* was
needed to deal with human affairs; and it is this idea which
Mikhailovsky discusses in his 'Vico and His "New Science"'.

Mikhailovsky pays tribute to Vico as the first to see that 'the
new science is the philosophy of history';[2] and he finds new
insight in Vico's trio of historical epochs: (1) the divine age of
theocracy and fetishism, (2) the heroic age of aristocracy and
polytheism, and (3) the human age of democracy. Mikhailovsky
accepts the theory, but rejects Vico's doctrine of necessary
cyclic repetition. History for Mikhailovsky is essentially linear,
a process of moving forward into a new age which would combine Comte's positive age, Blanc's age of brotherhood, and
Vico's human age.

Mikhailovsky's own historical triad had something in common with each of the others that he studied. The first stage in
Mikhailovsky's theory of history is the *objective anthropocentric*
stage, in which man instinctively recognizes himself to be the
centre of nature. In this completely self-centred period, man is
ruled by his own predatory instincts; his highest achievement is
the creation of anthropomorphic religion. The second age is the
eccentric stage, in which man loses his sense of wholeness and
becomes perplexed with the separation between body and soul,

[1] III. 48.   [2] III. 89.

his material and his speculative concerns. During this age metaphysical systems arise as an attempt to restore the wholeness of man's world-picture. But these systems only confuse man further; and the fragmentation of personality is accelerated by the tendency towards specialization, which develops rapidly during this period.

The third and golden age is for Mikhailovsky the *subjective anthropocentric* stage, in which man regains the idea that he is the measure of all things, but adds to it a mastery over nature. He recaptures the simple, unifying idea of the first age, but is no longer subject to the competitive laws of nature, having gained the knowledge to harness her powers during the eccentric age. The first age gives birth to a higher *type* of society than the second; but the second is at a higher *level* of development. Russia with her survival of the primitive village commune is thus a higher type of society than England with its depersonalized competitiveness; but England because of her greater ability to harness the forces of nature is a higher level of society. The third age would combine the high type of the 'noble savage' with the high level of technical power developed by the man of civilization.[1]

This triad represents Mikhailovsky's revised 'formula of progress', the more universally applicable formula which Lavrov had demanded. Yet each of these successive steps are but part of one central, progressive development in the history of humanity: 'the fight for individuality.'

Any philosophy of history must claim to disentangle from the fabric of human events some guiding thread of paramount significance. For Hegel it was the many-coloured strand of the world-spirit; for Marx, the knotty cord of class struggle. For Mikhailovsky the thread of meaning was the universal struggle for the fullness of human personality. There was no higher end in history than the individual's struggle to be himself. 'I am not the goal of nature; nature has no goal', declared Mikhailovsky. 'But I have a goal and I shall attain it.'[2] In the world of men, as distinct from that of animals, the goal of one is not the destruction of another, but the full realization of each. And the struggle of man's highest moral instincts to create an ideal human society is the path through which the new age will

[1] I. 199–215.   [2] I. 215.

come into being. The future is not 'written down in an immutable book of fate, that is unfolded by fatalists—even the most learned'.[1] For Mikhailovsky, all deterministic philosophies of history were the products of the eccentric age. They all crushed rather than fulfilled individuality. The picture Mikhailovsky held of all such systems was that of a raven looking at the guillotined body of the last human being and croaking: *fiat justitia pereat mundus.*[2]

Mikhailovsky's philosophy of history was derived from his scheme of values which began and ended with the human personality. But by providing, together with Lavrov, a theory of history and a formula of progress, Mikhailovsky helped to give the subjective idealists of the seventies the feeling that their struggle was integrally related to that of the entire historical process.

[1] III. 206.   [2] *Q.Q.P.*, pp. 182–3.

IV

A SOCIAL PHILOSOPHY

IN social as well as general philosophy, the ferment of the sixties completely altered the established patterns of Russian thought. The old foundations of authority and belief were swept away, and by the late sixties political thought had become polarized into revolutionary and reactionary positions. One is faced with the ironic fact that although the decade after Crimea saw more liberal reforms than any comparable period since the time of Peter the Great, the net effect among the intelligentsia was the emergence of two highly illiberal ideologies. To appreciate the full significance of the populist middle way which Mikhailovsky was evolving, it is essential to trace briefly this polarization of Russian political thought in the sixties.

Growing Extremism

The philosophic reactionaries were for the most part not old-style conservatives, but converted iconoclasts who had literally reacted to the unrest they had helped create. The most influential reactionaries were not detached elderly poets like Tyutchev and Fet, but young writers like Constantine Leontev, who had been caught up in the fervour of the iconoclastic revolution, and then had rebelled at its social implications. Leontev concluded that the doctrines of 'the young generation' would lead to destruction of the beauty and variety of Russian life, and rejected 'the horrible prose' of those who would fill the world with 'little houses as alike as two peas or six-storied barracks like those on the Nevsky Prospect'.[1]

This attachment to a way of life that offers variety and beauty even at the expense of suffering, is at the base of the emotional reaction which reached its climax in the creative work of another former radical, Fedor Dostoevsky. In his journals of the early sixties, *Time* (*Vremya*) and the *Epoch* (*Epokha*), and in his

[1] Quoted in Nicholas Berdyaev, *Leontiev*, London, 1940, pp. 27–28.

Notes from the Underground (1864), he had already begun his campaign of opposition to the new materialistic world-order.

There were elements of mystical nationalism in Dostoevsky and in the new reaction generally. Particularly after the Polish uprising of 1863 a wave of Great-Russian chauvinism arose that would drown out forever the mellow Slavophilism of an earlier day. Another former radical, Michael Katkov, led an attack on the radicals for their links with the Poles. His journal, *Moscow News* (*Moskovskiya Vedomosti*), justly called itself 'the organ of a party which may be called Russian, ultra-Russian, exclusively Russian',[1] and soon attained the highest circulation yet reached by a Russian journal.[2] He turned the military leaders of the Polish repression into national heroes, and during the reaction of 1866 discredited liberal ministers by accusing them of Polish sympathies. With Katkov thus conditioning opinion, the Tsar increasingly put his trust in those whose reputations had been inflated by the chauvinist press—men like Trepov, the new military governor of St. Petersburg, and Muravev, head of the special governmental committee of inquiry. In 1869–70 the new chauvinism received its fullest expression in *Russia and Europe*, the work of a former colleague of Dostoevsky in the Petrashevsky circle, Nicholas Danilevsky. A biologist as well as a former radical, Danilevsky foresaw a struggle for survival among the nations in which autocratic Russia would triumph over the Romano-German world of Western Europe. Danilevsky's work came close to becoming 'the "Household Companion" of every Russian'.[3] It provided the arguments with which many radicals crossed over into the camp of reaction and prepared the way for the reactionary Panslavism of the seventies.

The drift towards the right in the late sixties was paralleled by an equally unmistakable drift towards the extreme left. Just as liberal ministers were gradually being replaced by militarists

---

[1] M. K. Lemke, *Ocherki po Istorii Russkoy Tsenzury i Zhurnalistiki XIX stoletiya*, St. Petersburg, 1904, p. 279. This narrow chauvinism characterizes not only his many journals of the next two decades, but the two other most popular new journals of the late nineteenth century, Kraevsky's *The Voice* (*Golos*) and Suvorin's *New Time* (*Novoe Vremya*).

[2] The circulation was 12,000, 4,000 more than its nearest competitor and 3,000 higher than the highest circulation attained during the Crimean War. Ibid., pp. 279, 358.

[3] As predicted in Dostoevsky's letter of 18/30 March 1869, in *Letters of F. M. Dostoevsky*, London, 1914, p. 174.

in governmental circles, so Jacobin revolutionaries were bidding fair to dominate the radical camp.

The drift towards revolution began in several smaller circles within *Zemlya i Volya*, particularly that which published in May 1862 the proclamation, *Young Russia*. Probably written by the most important survivor of the circle, Peter Tkachev, the pamphlet was signed by a mysterious 'Central Revolutionary Committee', and rebuked Herzen and other reformers for 'their lack of faith in revolution'.[1] Secretive organizational mystique was also noticeable in the 'Petersburg Commune', a small group which came to dominate *Zemlya i Volya* late in 1862.[2]

The wave of chauvinism following the Polish uprising swept *Zemlya i Volya* out of existence altogether in 1863. But new laws restricting student activity only encouraged the tendency towards secretive and disciplined organization. Moreover, regular contact was established in 1863 with the revolutionary exiles gathered about Bakunin in Switzerland. Tkachev reappeared from imprisonment in 1865 to quote for the first time in the Russian press Marx's *Critique of Political Economy*, in brushing aside legal and moral objections to his own revolutionary outlook.[3] A new journal, the *Popular Chronicle* (*Narodnaya Letopis*), which began to appear in the same year, exemplified the growing organizational mystique and political extremism. The writing as well as the organization was communal, and reflected an extreme anti-monarchic outlook. Crown Prince Nicholas's death on 12 April 1865 was not even announced on its pages, while the death of Abraham Lincoln two days later was announced on the front page with a black border of mourning.

This unprecedented insult expressed the growing exasperation of many radicals who by the mid sixties had lost faith in the power of reason and moral persuasion. Such disillusionment was common both to the hard corps of revolutionaries gathered about Bakunin in Geneva and to a growing number of intellectuals within Russia. In the latter half of the decade there were two major attempts to unite these two groups in a common

---

[1] V. Ya. Yakovlev, *Materialy*, p. 28.

[2] L. Panteleev, *Iz Vospominanii Proshlogo*, Moscow, 1934, pp. 252-320.

[3] *R.S.*, 1865, no. 12, p. 30. Tkachev was reviewing an earlier article expounding the primacy of the economic factor, by Yury Zhukovsky, editor of the *Popular Chronicle*.

revolutionary programme. These two movements, known as the Karakozov and Nechaev affairs, carried the mysticism of revolution to new heights and helped to polarize further the intelligentsia into the extremes of right and left.

Just as Moscow had become the seat of the most powerful ideologists of the new reaction through Katkov and Leontev, so it was in Moscow that two new and extreme revolutionary circles appeared in 1865; that of N. A. Ishutin, from which Karakozov would emerge, and that of N. P. Nefedov, from which Nechaev came. Leader of the Ishutin group was I. A. Khudyakov, another of the many former seminarians from Kazan and students of early Russian culture to turn radical. After making contact with Bakuninist forces in Geneva in 1865 Khudyakov returned to Russia to organize a group of radical circles, within which there arose a secret, ascetic cadre of terrorists known as *Ad* (Hell). To join, one was required to give up all family ties, accept a new name, and even sacrifice one's life if the group so required. The sole aim of the society was 'endless love and devotion to the fatherland'.[1] What such 'devotion' required of them became dramatically clear when a young student from Kazan and member of 'Hell', Dmitry Karakozov, arrived in St. Petersburg unannounced early in 1866 and made his famous attempt to kill the Tsar on 4 April.

This crude measure of the extreme left helped precipitate the reaction and 'white terror' of 1866–7. It also served as a precedent and inspiration for the last and greatest of the revolutionary mystics, Serge Nechaev, for whom Karakozov's attempt was 'the beginning of our holy business'.[2]

Nechaev succeeded far more than Khudyakov in gaining the active support of Bakunin and the *émigré* extremists in Geneva. As with 'Hell', the circles which Nechaev organized on his return from Geneva in the summer 1869 were revolutionary in their attitude towards moderate liberals as well as toward the government. They were secret, strictly disciplined, and limited to five members each—whence their name, 'revolutionary fives'.

[1] 'The Karakozov Attempt', *K.A.*, 1926, no. 4, pp. 119–20. Karakozov was in touch with Khudyakov, who wrote for him a militantly egalitarian pamphlet, 'To Worker-Friends'. While Khudyakov later professed to be shocked at Karakozov's extremism, he must bear some of the responsibility for the attempted assassination. See E. E. Kolosov, 'The Disputed Questions of the Karakozov Affair', *K. i S.*, 1924, no. 3.   [2] B. P. Kozmin, *Tkachev*, Moscow, 1922, p. 156.

Most important of all, the disciplined hierarchy—the demands of which were to take precedence over all personal concerns—was set up *before* the ends in view had been clearly established. As in the early days of Ignatius Loyola's sixteenth-century student circle in Paris, which became the nucleus of the Jesuit order, dedication to a common cause was established before any clear concept of what the cause would be.

As a guide for the consecrated revolutionary, Nechaev drew up the famed 'revolutionary catechism' in collaboration with Bakunin. Independently, however, Nechaev developed a new revolutionary technique—that of gaining obedience through blackmailing fellow revolutionaries and deliberately involving them in common crimes. This technique was carried to its extreme on 21 November 1869 when Nechaev, together with the other members of a Moscow 'five', murdered a young student and fellow conspirator, I. I. Ivanov. When the body was discovered four days later and details of the group became known, 'the Nechaev affair' became a *cause célèbre* and provided dramatic evidence for those seeking to discredit *en bloc* all young radicals.

Thus one is faced with the ironic fact that the decade of so many liberalizing reforms saw the intelligentsia gradually drift toward the illiberal poles of reaction and revolution. A decade that began with Katkov and Khudyakov both as radical writers in St. Petersburg ended with the one a complete apologist for autocracy and the other an advocate of revolution and Tsaricide. Only against this background of growing extremism can the full significance be appreciated of the less negative middle position that was emerging in the late sixties: the social philosophy of *narodnichestvo* (populism) and of Mikhailovsky, its leading spokesman.

Between Scylla and Charybdis

The origins of the populist 'middle way' have been generally traced to the writings of Herzen in the months after the failure of the revolution of 1848. But Herzen's influence from abroad on movements in Russia was rapidly waning by 1863, the year in which populist ideas began to take root there. The man who did perhaps the most to father populism within Russia during these years was Mikhailovsky's earliest journalistic hero and his closest lifelong friend: Gregory Eliseev. Eliseev began the search which Mikhailovsky would lead for a special Russian path between the extremes of reaction and revolution.

Eliseev's efforts to create a moral social order in Russia began when he left a professorship at the Kazan Theological Academy to join the young radical group on the *Contemporary* in 1856 and set up a number of co-operative journals and socialistic experiments.[1] He gathered around him on the *Contemporary* a group of close and devoted followers who shared the socialist ideals, but not the materialistic world-view of the famous literary editors of the journal: Chernyshevsky and Dobrolyubov. There was Shchapov, who had studied early Russian Christianity under Eliseev at Kazan; Englehardt, an authority on agricultural chemistry; and Shelgunov, an expert on forestry and a student of socialist thought. All three had played active roles in *Zemlya i Volya* in 1862–3, and all three shared Eliseev's affiliation with the *Contemporary*. One of them, Shelgunov, gave in his famous 'Proclamation to the Young Generation' in 1861 the clearest early statement of the populists' passionate desire for a special path for Russia:

We have already been apes of the French and the Germans, are we now to give ourselves over as apes of the English? No, we do not want English economic maturity. . . . Why cannot Russia arrive at some new order unknown even to America? We not only can, we must. . . .[2]

The social institution through which Eliseev and his followers sought to implement their ideals was the village commune or *obshchina*. The commune had long been idealized by the intelligentsia, but for Eliseev the value of the institution lay only in its moral qualities.

The Slavophils correctly notice that in our present society there is a brotherhood which is not seen in Western society *despite the equality there of equal rights*. But they are mistaken when they think that this brotherhood is a peculiarity of our people developed in its religion. It necessarily accompanies all that is whole and complete,

---

[1] *Supra*, p. 20.

[2] V. Ya. Yakovlev, *Materialy*, p. 4. Yakovlev, writing before the opening of the police files in 1905, attributed the authorship of the proclamation to the poet M. L. Mikhailov, who played only a secondary role in its composition.

and composes itself not *mechanically*, but from the *natural* profusion
of types and the preserved family character of the village commune
—a commune not corrupted by bureaucratic transformations and
enforced changes. It existed in other countries as well until bureaucracy interfered in the internal life of the commune and violated the
moral element in it.[1]

Thus, impersonal mechanism and bureaucracy were the universal corrupters; and the still unsullied 'moral element' in the
commune made it the best hope for social regeneration. The
commune's worth lay neither in its hallowed Slavic or Orthodox
character nor in its potential for conversion into rationally-
ordered socialist communities (as with many 'westernizers').

The influence of the moral idealist wing of the *Contemporary*
was decisive in leading Mikhailovsky and his associates on the
Book Herald away from the revolutionary extremism of Khudyakov and 'Hell'. Eliseev's 'Chronicle of Progress', which began
appearing in the *Spark* in 1859, was the first radical column
which Mikhailovsky had read as a student. In 1862 a personal
friendship began between the two which deepened while they
were both working on communal-type journals and frequenting
the same circles in St. Petersburg in the mid sixties. When, in
the spring of 1865, the Moscow extremists linked with Ishutin
sought to establish contact with the St. Petersburg radicals,
Eliseev became a key point of contact. Eliseev journeyed to
Moscow but was from the beginning ill impressed with the crude
extremism of the Muscovite radicals who 'concerned themselves
not with hiding their most radical thoughts, but rather with
showing them off in order not to seem less progressive than their
comrades'.[2] Nozhin—who had been equally repelled by Bakhu-
nin's extremism on meeting him in Florence the year before—
must have joined Eliseev in influencing Mikhailovsky to avoid
all contact with the conspiratorial revolutionaries.[3] Indeed,
Nozhin's mysterious death on 3 April, the night before the
Karakozov attempt, was almost certainly the work of the 'Hell'
organization which feared he might intervene to prevent the
assassination.[4]

---

[1] *Ocherki*, 1 January 1863, in Breytburg, 'On the History of the Gazette *Ocherki*',
loc. cit., p. 65.
[2] From Eliseev's unpublished papers in *Lit. V.* I. 479.
[3] See *Note F*, p. 189.   [4] See *Note G*, p. 189.

Mikhailovsky thus inherited from Eliseev and Nozhin an antipathy to both reaction and revolution. The importance of Eliseev's group increased in 1868 when the poet Nekrasov chose them to provide the nucleus of the staff for his new journal, the reformed *Annals of the Fatherland*. As editor of the all-important 'publicistic section', Eliseev sought to steer the new journal along a 'middle way' in its critical early years. One of his first and most important steps was to rescue Mikhailovsky from his journalistic wanderings. In December 1868 Mikhailovsky published his first article in Eliseev's section of the *Annals*, thus beginning a collaboration which was to continue uninterrupted until 1884, when the journal was forcibly shut by Imperial authority.

The influence of Eliseev's opposition to the extremes can be seen in the subject of Mikhailovsky's polemic début in the *Annals*. Just as Eliseev had in 1861 been one of the first to attack Katkov for turning from radicalism to reaction, so Mikhailovsky in 1868 led the attack on one of the most celebrated of all radicals-turned-reactionary, Vasily Kelsiev.

Known to his fellow radicals by the Cossack title of 'Hetman', Kelsiev had led one of the most colourful clandestine lives of his generation.[1] When he announced in May 1867 that he had been converted to absolutism and published his memoirs in Katkov's *Russian Herald* early in 1868,[2] he became famous throughout Russia. Kelsiev styled his conversion to autocratic Pan-Slavism as the harbinger of a new age in Russian history; but Mikhailovsky entitled his refutation of Kelsiev, 'The Victim of Old Russian History', calling him a typical product of the old Russia of mysticism and *mechtaniya* (day-dreams). In Mikhailovsky's view, Kelsiev's conversion was merely a final caprice of the second, 'eccentric' age of history. Whether idolizing the West or glorifying the East, Kelsiev consistently lacked faith in 'the mental and moral development of society'. The truth-seeker must lend a receptive ear to all ideas, and 'if his ears had been equally open to all factors and sides Kelsiev would not perhaps have become either an *émigré* or a Pan-Slav'.[3]

The influence of Eliseev's anti-extremism was evident in Mikhailovsky's attitude towards the left as well as the right. In

[1] *Infra*, p. 123.
[2] V. I. Kelsiev, *Perezhitoe i Peredumannoe*, St. Petersburg, 1868.   [3] IV. 27.

1869–70 the most widely discussed of all revolutionary *émigrés* was Nechaev, who was generally thought to have set up inside Russia a wide circle of followers in communion with the awesome and semi-legendary figure of Bakunin. When the trial of Nechaev's alleged fellow conspirators took place in the summer of 1871, Mikhailovsky covered it for the *Annals*. He dissociated himself firmly from the extreme left by expressing general satisfaction with the conviction of twenty-seven of the defendants. Far from expressing outrage, Mikhailovsky praised the high quality of the defence counsel and the way in which trial by jury and laws of evidence had been put into practice in Russia.[1]

Even more important than the actual *Nechaevtsy* in focusing attention on the extremism of the left was Dostoevsky's characterization of them in *The Possessed*.[2] The principal theme of the novel is the dissolution of the main character, Stavrogin, a brilliant but enigmatic figure who, lacking any central ideal or sense of purpose, ends in suicide. Stavrogin may represent in part a picture of Bakunin, whom Dostoevsky had heard speak at Geneva in the autumn of 1868. But the figure of Peter Verkhovensky, one of Stavrogin's conspiratorial followers, is unquestionably Dostoevsky's representation of Nechaev. The fumbling murder of Shatov in the novel at Verkhovensky's behest is a detailed and almost entirely exact description of the murder of Ivanov by Nechaev.[3]

The appearance of *The Possessed* in book form in January 1873 was the signal for an outburst of indignation in radical circles. Tkachev, the only important radical still actively preaching the Nechaevan doctrine of immediate revolution, directed the most vitriolic attack at Dostoevsky.[4] But Mikhailov-

---

[1] X. 11–32. Among the eminent lawyers assigned to defend the *Nechaevtsy* were Spasovich and Urusov, both of whom Mikhailovsky had read as a youth. For details of the trial see B. P. Kozmin, *Nechaev i Nechaevtsy*, Moscow-Leningrad, 1931, pp. 9–142, 158–88.

[2] Published throughout 1871–2 in Katkov's *Russky Vestnik*.

[3] On the Stavrogin-Bakunin parallel see V. Polonsky and L. P. Grossman, *Spor o Bakunine i Dostoevskom*, Leningrad, 1926. Ivan Pryzhov (the oldest of the *Nechaevtsy* and a student of old Russian popular history) is represented in *The Possessed* by Tolkachenko. Like Dostoevsky, Mikhailovsky was particularly interested in this elderly figure—probably because Pryzhov, like Mikhailovsky in the Karakozov affair, was only unwittingly implicated. See M. Altman, *Ivan Gavrilovich Pryzhov*, Moscow 1932, pp. 129–45.

[4] In two anonymous articles, 'Sick People', *Delo*, 1873, nos. 3, 4, in P. N. Tkachev, *Izbrannye Sochineniya*, Moscow, 1933, iii. 5–48.

sky's critique of February 1873 was very different from the crude condemnation of Tkachev and offers a good example of Mikhailovsky's 'middle way'. Mikhailovsky did not agree with Tkachev that Dostoevsky had misrepresented the *Nechaevtsy*, but rather that Dostoevsky had 'seized on a sad, mistaken and criminal exception—the Nechaev affair' and tried to represent it as a picture of radical youth as a whole.

If Dostoevsky had taken into consideration the great mass of the Russian young people . . . then he would without question be convinced that the theories voiced by Shatov, Kirilov, and Stavrogin can occupy here only a microscopically small place. Moreover, he would be convinced that the Nechaev affair is such a monstrosity in every respect that it cannot serve as the theme for a novel with a more or less wide scope. . . . If Dostoevsky were deliberately to search for a milieu in which mystical theories would be completely out of place, he would find it in contemporary Russian youth.[1]

Whereas Mikhailovsky had read and admired Dostoevsky's *Crime and Punishment*,[2] he finds *The Possessed* a highly unsatisfactory novel. 'In place of types of people, given over to their ideas, in *The Possessed* there appear only *types, given over to ideas arbitrarily invented for them by the author*.'[3] Dostoevsky is thus accused of misrepresenting not only the radical camp, but the practical direction of thought which Mikhailovsky believed was characteristic of the new age. Dostoevsky and his 'psychiatric talent'[4] should not be applied to contemporary man, who was practical in outlook and integrated with both himself and society. 'Why', asks Mikhailovsky, 'doesn't Dostoevsky write a novel about European life of the fourteenth to sixteenth centuries?'[5]

Thus Mikhailovsky criticized those among the intelligentsia who rejected his own belief in the perfectibility of human nature—whether they did so in defence of revolution à la Nechaev and Tkachev or of mysticism and reaction in the manner of Dostoevsky's *Possessed* and *Diary of a Writer*. Mikhailovsky repeatedly characterized the reactionary and revolutionary

---

[1] I. 851–2.
[2] He may have taken the title of his own 1869 article on Russian law from Dostoevsky's novel.   [3] I. 849.
[4] Mikhailovsky would later call it a 'cruel talent'—the title of his 1882 essay on Dostoevsky: V. 1.   [5] I. 842.

trends as 'the Scylla and Charybdis' of Russian thought. He sought to avoid alike the frozen Russia of Leontev and the flaming Russia of Nechaev. Under the influence of Eliseev and the moral idealists on the *Annals* Mikhailovsky developed a more temperate and optimistic ideology, which was to dominate Russian radicalism in the early seventies.

V

THE FLOWERING OF POPULISM

A FAITH in human progress, an intense moral idealism, and
an opposition to the extremes of reaction and revolution
—these beliefs of Mikhailovsky became the banners of the
populist movement.

Unorganized and often confused, this movement was none
the less distinct and coherent in its broad outlines. It was based
not in the Moscow of the extremists, but in the St. Petersburg
to which the men of the sixties had looked so hopefully. It was
organized neither by the 'revolutionary fives' of Nechaev nor
by the chauvinistic societies of Katkov, but through the hallowed social institutions of the radical intelligentsia: the student
circle, the radical journal, and the communal experiment. It
was born in the late sixties, and would remain the dominant
form of radicalism in Russia until the emergence of formal
political parties in the early twentieth century. Mikhailovsky
alone of all the great radicals of the age remained alive and
active within Russia throughout this entire period. In his
career are mirrored most of the visions, successes, failures, and
uncertainties of this strange and uniquely Russian movement.
His most active and productive years, like those of the movement itself, were the first five years of the 1870's.

The Simple Life

By the end of the decade the social background of Russia
seemed propitious once more for optimism and renewed expectation. The shock of both the Karakozov affair and the
ensuing 'white terror' had worn off; and the intelligentsia were,
like Mikhailovsky, returning to activity in St. Petersburg, finding new interests, and feeling free to express themselves again.

A long period of peace and economic expansion was settling
on Russia—to be interrupted only briefly in the mid seventies by
a minor depression and a war with Turkey. In 1868 the Minister of Finance, Count Reutern, opened the gates for a new

influx of ideas and capital from the West by passing the last in a series of decrees guaranteeing economic *laissez-faire*. His programme for the rapid expansion of the railroad system, which more than tripled its total mileage in the period 1868–73,[1] was changing the face of Russia more than almost any economic development of the century.

At the centre of this new profusion of economic activity was St. Petersburg, increasing in population at the rate of 30,000 a year. It was not surprising that the new movement should originate in this great home of the intelligentsia, nor that its leaders should seek above all to build a bridge between the new world it represented and the old world of Russia's still primitive peasant empire.

As Mikhailovsky returned to full-time journalism in St. Petersburg late in 1868, he turned his attention to social questions, and above all to the question of the place of the peasantry in a changing social order. Mikhailovsky's stay on the Kurochkins' provincial estate in 1867 had exposed him for the first time since his childhood to the life and problems of the peasantry. While there, he met many of the 'provincial correspondents' who were a special feature of the Kurochkins' journal, the *Spark*, and shared a flat with a young writer, M. A. Demert, who had actually been a serf, emancipated under the edict of 1861. Since Demert was acting as a justice of the peace for arbitration of land claims, Mikhailovsky may well have learned much from him about the tribulations of the emancipated but still impoverished peasantry. A simple figure of high integrity, Demert must have seemed to be a prototype of the 'noble savage'. At any rate, Mikhailovsky insisted on bringing Demert with him to St. Petersburg when he returned briefly in 1867; and Demert remained a trusted friend and collaborator until his death in 1875.

Another figure who directed Mikhailovsky's attention to the problems of the peasantry was Gleb Uspensky, a gifted and sensitive young writer who specialized in realistic vignettes of peasant life. Mikhailovsky met him at the Kurochkins' in 1868, and struck up an intimate friendship that was to last throughout their lives.[2]

[1] M. W. Kovalevsky, *La Russie*, p. 854.
[2] *Gleb Uspensky v Zhizni*, Moscow, 1935, pp. 72–75.

Uspensky first suggested to Mikhailovsky that he apply for a permanent post on the *Annals* after he left the *Week* in March 1869. Mikhailovsky had already published his attack on Kelsiev in Eliseev's section of the journal in December 1868, but hesitated to become a full-time collaborator largely because of misgivings about the political beliefs of the editor-in-chief, Nekrasov.[1] Through the urgings of Uspensky, Eliseev, and Kurochkin, Mikhailovsky finally accepted a permanent position in July 1869.

Uspensky also introduced Mikhailovsky to the social life of St. Petersburg. Among those with whom Mikhailovsky came into frequent contact was a good friend of Uspensky's wife, an attractive, somewhat Bohemian member of an aristocratic St. Petersburg family, Mariya Evgrafovna Pavlovskaya. Mariya had been studying music for years at the St. Petersburg conservatory, and was considered by at least one of her contemporaries to have been the favourite pupil of the great Anton Rubinstein.[2] She had, however, also become caught up in the excitement of student circles in the sixties and had become engaged to an old school friend of Mikhailovsky's, P. V. Zasodimsky.

There is little doubt that Mariya was an attractive and vivacious woman. One contemporary described her as 'reminding me of some sort of gypsy . . . she had coarse sensitive lips; little bells seemed to jingle periodically in her low, chesty voice; a kind of wild merriment sparkled in her beautiful grey eyes'.[3] Mikhailovsky was strongly attracted to her although she was several years his senior; and, when Zasodimsky resigned his claim on her in the best spirit of the times,[4] Mikhailovsky married her some time in 1870 or 1871.[5]

During the early seventies the dacha which the Mikhailovskies

---

[1] Like most of his generation, Mikhailovsky had not forgiven Nekrasov for writing an ode to the reactionary Muravev at the height of the 'white terror' of 1866. Mikhailovsky also feared that the position of the formal editor, Kraevsky, might prove in practice more than that of a mere nominal editor. On balance, however, Mikhailovsky felt that the radical camp needed a journal and that Nekrasov could still serve as a symbolic rallying point. *Lit. V.* I. 80–85.

[2] V. V. Timofeeva, in *Uspensky v Zhizni*, p. 114.

[3] Ibid., p. 144.

[4] Ibid., p. 112.

[5] Mikhailovsky was already married and settled by the spring of 1872 when Uspensky's wife and Timofeeva visited him (ibid., pp. 111–18), but was still single when first visited by Skabichevsky 'in 1871 or 1870'. A. M. Skabichevsky, *Vospominaniya*, p. 274.

set up just south of St. Petersburg became the centre of
Mikhailovsky's activities and an important gathering place for
young radicals. The small town of Gatchina in which the dacha
was located was most famous as the site of the Tsar's country
palace and the point of departure for his lavish hunts. But
Mikhailovsky's cottage, which was located in one of Gatchina's
innumerable parks, offered few such luxuries. Indeed, it represented to those who visited it a living example of that return
to the people and simple living which was to become a distinctive feature of Russian populism.

One young visitor, who came with Uspensky's wife early in
1872, described the dacha and the effect it produced on those
who stayed there:

I remember with what tenderness I was welcomed into this poor
crowded dacha of barge planks with round spike holes through which
the summer wind freely blew and the sunbeams splashed their golden
rays. The entire setting—the simple unpainted tables, the benches
and stools, even the beds covered with plaids called forth sympathy
and delight within me.

After describing the 'primitive simplicity' of Mikhailovsky's
study and his wife's room, the visitor recalled that

. . . to Aleksandra Vasilevna they gave up the very best room, and
in the dining room they reserved for their guests a special sofa
brought out from the city. All that was told to me and showed to me
seemed so captivating and wonderful that I finally became moved,
went out into the garden, and gave myself over to the most delightful
reflections on 'the new life' and 'the new men'. Indeed, there was
something new here in this ravishing simplicity! A man approached
another directly and simply as man to man, entered into a circle of
close friends, became a member of one and the same family. . . .[1]

Discussions with visitors often continued—in the best traditions of the radical intelligentsia—till daybreak; and, although
the best rooms and the 'sofa for guests' were willingly ceded to
visitors, the only ones usually able to get any rest were those
who slept completely outside the dacha on the hay-covered
balcony.[2]

The ebullient and high-strung Mariya was, however, a rather

---

[1] Timofeeva, in *Uspensky v Zhizni*, p. 114. The Uspenskies also had a dacha in
Gatchina.   [2] Ibid., p. 115.

disturbing influence for her more seriously inclined husband. When Uspensky's wife read to her a letter from Uspensky telling of his visit to a dance in Paris, Mariya flew into a rage, hammered on the crude barge-plank partition of Mikhailovsky's study, swearing that she would never permit her husband to do such a thing. At one moment she shrieked: 'You'll never leave me. I warn you. I'll hang around your neck—either with me or not at all.' Yet in the next breath her mind wandered off: 'What a picture, (giggle) Gleb Ivanovich, the can-can—and some Suzon-Louison twitting him on the nose with "Qu'est-ce qu'il veut de moi, ce drôle-là?" (boisterous laughter).'[1]

Only in the hours when Nicholas Konstantinovich was working did she walk on tiptoes, hold her fingers to her lips, or go out of the house altogether 'in order not to disturb', taking with her the retinue —the incessantly arriving and forever departing guests.

But even then she apparently couldn't contain herself, and organized races in the park, or boisterous games of hopscotch over benches. She particularly enjoyed sending out cries to attract the police,

and was as happy as a child when a policeman would run up out of breath and look around him at the 'good clean public' sitting on the benches, not knowing what it was all about.[2]

The lives of Mikhailovsky and his wife gradually drew apart. When he left Russia early in 1873 to cover the Vienna exhibition for the *Annals*, his wife proved unfaithful to him; and shortly after his return she left him altogether after only a few years of childless marriage.[3] Early in 1875 he entered into a civil marriage with a second wife, Ludmilla Nikolaevna, who bore him two sons, in 1875 and 1877, but in a very real sense Mikhailovsky's heart lay elsewhere throughout the seventies. He was absorbed in the radical journals and circles of his day. He could be faithful only to the injunction which Kurochkin had given to the staff of the *Book Herald*, the first journal on which he had worked:

The man of journalism should separate himself from all personal

[1] Ibid., p. 116. [2] Ibid., p. 117.
[3] Ibid., p. 146; E. K. Pimenova, *Dni Minuvshie, Vospominaniya*, Leningrad, 1929, p. 140.

tastes and wishes . . . the knowledge that he is a useful and true servant of society is the only moral satisfaction of the man of journalism.[1]

The Circle and the Journal

Populism at the turn of the decade grew directly out of the favourite institutions of the radical intelligentsia: the student circle and the thick journal. Mikhailovsky played an important role in the leading example of each, the Chaikovsky circle and the *Annals of the Fatherland*.

The new circles formed in St. Petersburg early in 1869 under Nicholas Chaikovsky and Mark Natanson were set up in a deliberate attempt to counter the Nechaev pattern of cynical and conspiratorial organization. The two circles united late in 1869 consolidating opposition to the conspiratorial followers of Nechaev, whom, as one contemporary later recalled, 'the mass of the youth considered to have been a spy and agent-provocateur'.[2] The name *Chaikovtsy* came into widespread use in 1870, when their attempt to 'organize students sensibly and rationally' spread out from St. Petersburg to Kiev, Odessa, and other provincial student centres. By late 1870 numerous circles existed in both St. Petersburg and the provinces, organized along artel lines with each member often pledged to extend whatever financial aid or personal counsel another member might need. All members were engaged in self-improvement by reading in the illegal libraries that were the most characteristic feature of the *Chaikovtsy*. In contrast to the hierarchical structure and secretiveness of the *Nechaevtsy*, these circles sought to create a family-like atmosphere of mutual confidence and aid.

The aim is *self-development*. School studies do not give answers to a mass of disturbing and tormenting questions, to the searching mind and sensitive heart of youth. . . . Personality has to be developed in a wide and many-sided way. Without this, the moral purity of personality is inconceivable, and even *personal* happiness and *social* utility become inconceivable. *The ideal of personal self-perfection is thus the best means toward the end of social betterment.*[3]

[1] Quoted by Vladimir Rozenberg, 'N. K. Mikhailovsky on *Russkie Vedomosti*', *Rus. Ved.*, 1914, no. 22, p. 3.

[2] Leo Tikhomirov, *Vospominaniya*, Moscow-Leningrad, 1927, p. 46.

[3] An anonymous member of the circles known as *Zemlyavolets*, in P. L. Lavrov, *Narodniki-Propagandisty 1873–8 Godov*, St. Petersburg, 1907, p. 35.

Thus, self-perfection was intimately associated with the accumulation of knowledge. But as these circles turned to social questions they found themselves bewildered by 'the unanswered, fateful question of What to do?'[1] Late in 1871 the St. Petersburg circles attempted to answer this question by mapping out a programme of social action.

A first principle on which they agreed was an emphasis on social and economic rather than political reform. This emphasis was already established among the intelligentsia, inherited in part from Proudhon. It became the explicit policy of the *Chaikovtsy* at a secret meeting in December 1871 of Chaikovsky, Mikhailovsky, and a small group of leading students and intellectuals. Drawn together to formulate a political programme for the Chaikovsky circles based on Lassalle's *Essence of a Constitution*, the group soon concluded that political reform was not the first order of priority.

An analysis of our situation led to the one and inevitable view that without a serious material base or (in other words) without the conscious participation of the wide popular masses, there is not and cannot be any way out of our impasse. In order to create this base [one must now] bring into the struggle our many millions of peasants and workers.[2]

In order to bring these many millions into the struggle the *Chaikovtsy* decided to: (1) organize circles among, and disseminate knowledge to, the ordinary people, and (2) concentrate this activity initially among the industrial working classes. These principles of action were agreed on early in 1871 when Chaikovsky and Natanson had held a series of meetings at a country villa outside St. Petersburg. The authors whom they decided to distribute by legal and illegal means included Western socialists like Proudhon, Blanc, Lamennais, Lange, Lassalle, and Marx, together with a few other Western thinkers (Comte, Mill, Spencer) and Russian radicals like Chernyshevsky and Lavrov. The printing and distribution of books

---

[1] Ibid., pp. 35–36.

[2] N. A. Charushin, *O Dalekom Proshlom*, Moscow, 1926, part i, p. 102. Those at the meeting in addition to Charushin, then an eighteen-year-old student, included the legal theorist, V. D. Spasovich, the economist and future contributor to the *Annals*, V. P. Vorontsov, and the professor of criminal law at the University of St. Petersburg, N. S. Tagantsev, at whose home the meeting was held.

was a particular interest of Natanson, who had been a librarian. When he was arrested late in 1871 (and Chaikovsky shortly thereafter) the impulse to disseminate knowledge lost its momentum, though it remained characteristic of radical activity throughout the seventies and eighties.

The idea of concentrating activity among the urban working classes was a new development in Russian radical thinking, largely produced by one influential book, V. V. Bervi's *Position of the Working Class in Russia*. First published in 1869 and reprinted in three editions before its proscription by the censorship in 1872, Bervi's book was probably the most widely read single work by the *Chaikovtsy*. They were deeply impressed by Bervi's conclusion that 'However great the sufferings of industrial Russia may be, it is nevertheless the most civilized part of our society. Nowhere does the worker separate himself even in these conditions from the possibilities of mental and moral development.'[1] This conviction in the possibilities of development lying within the working class prompted the *Chaikovtsy* to take their gospel of progress first to the workers. Begun among the workers in the Vyborg district of St. Petersburg early in 1872 by two nineteen-year-old students, N. A. Charushin and S. S. Sinegub, the movement reached its climax in the winter of 1872–3 when the pioneers were joined by Serge Kravchinsky (Stepnyak), Prince Peter Kropotkin, Sophie Perovskaya, Leonid Shishko, and a host of other famous figures in the history of Russian radicalism.

Widespread dissemination of knowledge, the formation of circles among the working class, and a constant emphasis on social over political demands—these were the main points in the unwritten plan of action of the *Chaikovtsy*. The years 1872–3 witnessed the enthusiastic implementation of these policies by the St. Petersburg circle and the growth of allied circles in Kiev, Moscow, Kherson, and Odessa. Most of these new groups maintained connexions with St. Petersburg, so that, by the end of 1873, the *Chaikovtsy* possessed a broadly-based movement— the most important anti-governmental force in Russia at the

---

[1] V. V. Bervi (Flerovsky), *Polozhenie Rabochago Klassa v Rossii*, St. Petersburg, 1869, p. 403. For the fate of his subsequent works in the 1871–2 period see L. Dobrovolsky, 'The Condemned and Destroyed Books of V. V. Bervi-Flerovsky', *Literaturnoe Nasledstvo*, Moscow, 1933, nos. 7–8, pp. 163–79.

time and the most widely-supported of all the intelligentsia's attempts to shape the radical movement around the institution of the *kruzhok* (circle).

For a movement attaching such central importance to the spread of knowledge, the question of what journals were read is of particular significance. The rise of the *Annals* as Russia's leading radical journal and of Mikhailovsky as its leading philosopher exactly paralleled the rise of the *Chaikovtsy* as the dominant movement in the same radical circles.

The sudden emergence of the *Annals of the Fatherland* as the unchallenged spokesman for the radical intelligentsia surprised even its editors. The journal had fallen into disrepute in the sixties, and as late as November 1867 Pisarev had described it as a 'decaying corpse . . . in which the worms will soon have nothing left to eat'.[1] Yet it was so rapidly revived under Nekrasov and Eliseev that Pisarev himself became a contributor within six months of his statement. From 1867 to 1870 it increased in circulation from 2,000 to 8,000 copies per month— the largest circulation attained up to that date by a radical journal in Russia.[2] In the words of one of the most active figures in the seventies, '*The Annals* held almost universal sway over the minds of the epoch. Its influence was enormous. An entire generation, the energetic and combative generation of the seventies, considered *The Annals* to be practically its own organ.'[3]

The *Annals* owed its success primarily to the fact that its editors (Nekrasov, editor-in-chief; Saltykov, *belles lettres*; and Eliseev, publicistic section) were revered former members of the *Contemporary* and pioneers in the journalistic endeavours of the sixties. But the staff of the *Annals* exercised a direct and personal as well as indirect and ideological influence on the Chaikovsky circles.

Mikhailovsky himself had been called in for the important policy meeting of December 1871, and important links were

---

[1] Letter to Shelgunov in N. V. Shelgunov, *Vospominaniya*, Moscow-Petrograd, 1923, p. 170.

[2] B. P. Kozmin, *Zhurnalistika 70kh i 80kh Godov*, Moscow, 1948, p. 6. The highest circulation attained by *Sovremennik* had been 7,000 and by *Russkoe Slovo*, 4,000. M. V. Lemke, *Epokha Tsenzurnykh Reform (1859–65)*, St. Petersburg, 1904, p. 192 note. Conservative journals had higher subscription lists, but not proportionally larger reading publics since single copies of radical journals were often used by an entire circle.

[3] O. V. Aptekman, *Zemlya i Volya 1870kh Godov*, Rostov, 1907, p. 23.

concurrently established by two men who began working on the *Annals* in 1869, A. N. Englehardt and S. N. Krivenko.

Englehardt, who had been one of Eliseev's protégés on the moral idealist wing of the *Contemporary*, had long used his country estate as a meeting-place for radicals; and, when the *Chaikovtsy* moved their informal headquarters out of St. Petersburg in the spring of 1871, his estate became the centre of operations. Krivenko represented the equally wealthy, but more deeply committed younger element in the *Chaikovtsy*. After completion of his course at the St. Petersburg Military Academy, he turned his back on his past, went to work as an unskilled industrial labourer, and in the spring of 1869 joined the staff of the *Annals*. At the same time, he began an active association with the *Chaikovtsy* in St. Petersburg; and in 1871 he returned to his native Kazan, where he was a pioneer in establishing communal circles among the workers and peasants.

In addition to these important direct links with the *Chaikovtsy*, it should be pointed out that during 1871–2 both of the principal theorists of the movement, Lavrov (from abroad) and Bervi, had followed Mikhailovsky in moving from the *Week* to the *Annals*, where they published their principal articles on social questions. By 1872 the journal that had from the beginning possessed the creative writers whose popularity was highest among the young radicals—Saltykov, Nekrasov, and Uspensky —had won over as collaborators the most influential social theorists as well.

Mikhailovsky was hired to work on the bibliographical review section—the traditional medium for introducing radical ideas from the West and one which was of particular importance to the Chaikovsky movement. Since his collaborator on the bibliographical section, Nicholas Kurochkin, was simultaneously working for the *Spark*, Mikhailovsky acquired from the beginning almost complete control of this section.

His tireless dedication to his work and his moral earnestness soon earned him a unique reputation on the journal. As early as 1870 Nekrasov spoke of Mikhailovsky as 'the most gifted of our new writers',[1] and for almost every summer of the early

---

[1] 'Without a doubt a bright future lies before him. Besides his undoubted talent he is knowledgeable, very energetic, and hard working. . . .' Unpublished letter to Kraevsky in A. Faresov, 'Mikhailovsky', *Ist. V.*, 1904, no. 3, p. 1034.

seventies Mikhailovsky was a visitor at Nekrasov's villa in Chudovo. Mikhailovsky also accompanied Nekrasov and Eliseev on visits abroad to Kissingen in 1870 and 1873. As one who drank and said little, Mikhailovsky appears to have served the loquacious and heavy-drinking poet as a trusted companion and even, at times, as a moral confessor.[1]

With his long beard, his deep blue eyes, *pince-nez*, and gentle manner, Mikhailovsky soon stood out as a kind of trusted elder among the young radicals. No longer attired in the outlandish dress of the sixties, Mikhailovsky wore a studiously simple costume including 'a Proudhon-like blouse of unbleached sackcloth and a leather belt in place of a sash'.[2] So intense was his involvement in the life of the journal that his associates came to regard him as an ascetic. Whenever friends called on him in his flat there were invariably books piled up to the ceiling.[3] Another writer recalled that 'I did not dare go up to Nicholas Konstantinovich's writing desk; it was as if it was not a table, but an altar on which he celebrated his holy rites'.[4] 'Hardly a year had passed', remarked Skabichevsky, the journal's literary critic, 'before he had become the soul of society at all our youthful meetings.'[5]

True to the high calling of 'the man of journalism', Mikhailovsky devoted his time almost exclusively to the *Annals*. One of the least known and last to join the regular staff, Mikhailovsky soon became its most diligent member. The principal literary figures on the *Annals*, Saltykov, Uspensky, and even Nekrasov, kept up a wide range of outside activities; Mikhailovsky's colleagues on the 'publicistic section', Kurochkin and Krivenko, had interests in the provinces which took up much of their time. Even such full-time collaborators as Eliseev and Demert concentrated their efforts on their own columns ('The Internal Review' and 'Our Social Affairs' respectively) rather than on the journal as a whole. Mikhailovsky alone devoted his time almost exclusively to the *Annals*. Typical was his reaction early in 1871 to a suggestion by Kurochkin and another friend that he participate in a new journal dealing with the problems of

---

[1] *Lit. V.* I. 72–85; K. Chukovsky, *Nekrasov*, Leningrad, 1926, pp. 42–43.
[2] *Uspensky v Zhizni*, p. 129.
[3] A. M. Skabichevsky, *Vospominaniya*, p. 274.
[4] V. V. Timofeeva in *Uspensky v Zhizni*, p. 115.
[5] Skabichevsky, *Vospominaniya*, p. 273.

Russia's newly-opening East. Mikhailovsky questioned the morality of spreading one's interest over several journals and declined on the grounds that 'my patriotism to *The Annals* would not permit it'.[1]

Not only was Mikhailovsky *de facto* director of the bibliographical section and author of many of the anonymous reviews in each issue, but he wrote additional articles in the belles-lettres section of the journal and helped in the management of its finances as well. Through his consecration, industry, and assumption of thankless responsibilities, Mikhailovsky became by the early seventies the most indispensable figure on the august staff of Nekrasov's journal.

Narodnik Socialism

The positive beliefs of the Chaikovsky circles were the same ones which had been developed by Eliseev's group on the *Contemporary* and reasserted after 1868 by Mikhailovsky and the *Annals*: a faith in human progress and in the moral idealism of the individual.

It is not therefore surprising that the socialism which the Russian radicals combined with this world-view in the 1869–72 period was essentially the deeply moralistic socialism of the French revolutionary tradition. When socialism had first come to Russia in the 1830's, it had been the 'utopian' socialism of contemporary France; and, although the favour with which individual socialists were regarded varied widely over the next three decades, the Russian radicals never lost their sense of basic attachment to the French tradition. The two socialists whose influence was most pronounced inside Russia in the late sixties were those whom Mikhailovsky was translating and popularizing, Blanc and Proudhon. Louis Blanc was regarded by the *Chaikovtsy* as the father of modern socialism. Author of the formula 'from each according to his abilities, to each according to his needs', Blanc preached a socialism that appealed to sentiments of justice and brotherhood. Even more permeating

---

[1] I. I. Yasinsky, *Roman Moey Zhizni*, Moscow, 1926, p. 90. Yasinsky was the principal organizer, and Uspensky and Shelgunov the principal radicals lending support to this short-lived venture. Other collaborators on the *Annals* who declined to participate did so because of lack of interest.

than the influence of Blanc, however, was that of Proudhon, who was admired for his moral passion and his belief in the mystic force of 'the people' as bearer of the new social order.

By venerating the authority of the French socialist movement, Mikhailovsky and his contemporaries unconsciously committed themselves to opposing the major rival faction in the First International: the German Social Democratic movement of Karl Marx and Ferdinand Lassalle. For Mikhailovsky and his radical followers accepted the two major articles of faith that separated the socialism of Proudhon from that of Marx and the German movement:

1. The belief that the final appeal for socialism must be based on subjective choice and moral ideals rather than objective necessity and material facts.
2. The conviction that socialism opposed the institution of the state and should not work through political institutions even as a temporary expedient.

Support was almost unanimous among Russian radicals in the seventies for the preference Mikhailovsky expressed in 'What is Progress?' for 'practical' rather than 'metaphysical' socialism. The Russian radicals abroad sided almost to a man with the French Proudhonists and later with Bakunin in their struggles with Marx in the late sixties and early seventies.[1] But the radicals within Russia did not participate in this quarrel. So great was their certainty that the new 'third age' was about to dawn that the differences between various socialisms did not concern them. Indeed in the early seventies, Mikhailovsky simply fitted the distant figure of Karl Marx into his own world-picture and added him to his list of socialist saints.[2] The latent conflict between subjective and objective socialism did not arise inside Russia until the mid nineties when the optimism and idealism of the populists had been substantially weakened.

Mikhailovsky disregarded the metaphysics of Marx in

[1] Only one Russian radical collaborated with Marx in incriminating Bakunin and expelling him from the First International; and this figure, Nicholas Utin, later left the radical camp altogether to become a supervisor of mines in the Urals.

[2] Marx sensed the irony of the situation. When he learned of the Russians' plans to translate *Capital*, he called it 'the irony of fate that the Russians with whom I have fought for 25 years . . . have always been my patrons . . . [and now are] the first foreign nation to translate *Capital*'. Marx, letter of 30 September/12 October 1868, *Letters to Dr. Kugelmann*, London, 1934, p. 77.

introducing him to the Russian audience, for he had found in
Capital a moral position which attracted his deepest admiration—
opposition to the division of labour. Mikhailovsky's 'formula of
progress' had expressed a similar opposition, and his first discussion of Marx's great work, in January 1870, was little more
than a recapitulation of Marx's discussion of the dehumanizing
effects of specialization.[1] Mikhailovsky, and the narodnik radicals after him, defended Marx as a fellow moralist, who shared
their belief that labour was the source of value and was inevitably oppressed in capitalist society. There was, none the less,
a hint of antagonism in Mikhailovsky's review in April 1872 of
the first Russian edition of *Capital*:[2]

You are snorting (*fyrkaete*) at freedom, when with us it only exists
in embryo. . . . You criticize Darwin, Comte, western science and
philosophy while we don't have any. Strictly speaking, there is,
please, a fair share of truth in your snortings, but not for us. Maybe
freedom has been a fraud in Europe, but it hasn't defrauded us
because we haven't had any yet.[3]

Mikhailovsky did not question Marx's basic analysis, but only
its application to Russia:

Your place is not in Russia, but in Europe, and here you are only
interfering and fighting with windmills. . . . Our place is in Russia.
We not only do not scorn Russia, but we see in its past, and still in
its present, much on which one can rely to ward off the falsities of
European civilization.[4]

Thus, Marx's analysis of the painful process of gestation
which socialism was undergoing in the capitalist West increased
the passion with which Mikhailovsky sought to by-pass the
capitalist stage and forge a special path for Russia:

The ideas and interests with which he struggles are still too weak
with us for their rumblings to mean danger. But they are already

[1] I. 169–74.
[2] The translation of the first volume of *Capital* was completed by two young
friends of the *Chaikovtsy*, Herman Lopatin and Nicholas Danielson, in 1872, after
Bakunin had given up his attempt at a translation in the late sixties (and Lavrov's
son-in-law, Negreskul, gave up a concurrent attempt at a translation of the *Critique of
Political Economy*). Until this translation of *Capital* was completed Marx was not as
well known in Russia as Lassalle, whose speeches and writings had been published
in a two-volume Russian translation by Zaitsev in 1870, and in an abridged
Ukrainian translation by the Kievan *Chaikovets*, V. K. Debagory-Mokrievich, in
1872.   [3] X. 2.   [4] X. 3, 9.

strong enough for us to be obliged to consider soberly what the consequences would be of their further development. That is why we say that Marx's book has appeared as *apropos* as it possibly could have.[1]

In the course of 1872 Mikhailovsky began to give the idea of a special path the form which would become standard among radicals in the seventies. In January, in the first issue of a new column, 'Literary Notes', Mikhailovsky insisted that Russia could find its own path to socialism. The column attracted informal warnings from the censorship which were largely responsible for its suppression until August and for his extensive use of pseudonyms throughout the rest of the year. His April review of *Capital* was published under a pseudonym, while in May he wrote an anonymous article praising the work of a young Polish apostle of popular ownership and decentralized government.[2]

In August Mikhailovsky's column reappeared with an attack on the advocates of capitalist development in Russia. The occasion for this article—one of his most widely read and influential —was the publication of the proceedings of the first meeting of Russia's newly founded capitalist promotion society: 'the All-Russian Union of Producers, Manufacturers, and People Interested in the Industries of the Fatherland.' Mikhailovsky attacks these men for seeking to lead Russia along a discredited path, since 'reason and moral feeling did not influence the economic development of Europe'.[3] These qualities can and must be brought to bear on Russian development, Mikhailovsky argues in a famous passage:

The working question in Europe is a revolutionary question; there it demands the *transfer* of the tools of labour into the hands of the worker, the expropriation of the present proprietors. The working question in Russia is a conservative question; here only the *preservation* of the means of labour in the hands of the worker is required, a guarantee to the present proprietors of their property. . . . Guarantee

---

[1] X. 10–12. The earlier call for a special path in Shelgunov's proclamation of 1861 (*supra*, p. 47), had been, coincidentally, largely inspired by the picture of English society presented in Engels's *Position of the Working Class in England*, which Shelgunov had introduced to the Russian reading public in articles in the *Contemporary* from September through November 1861.

[2] X. 535–50. Mikhailovsky was reviewing a work by Gregory Simonenko, *Government, Society, and Law from the Point of View of Popular Ownership*, Moscow, 1870.   [3] I. 693.

them simply what is their own and the Russian working question
is solved.[1]

Mikhailovsky was not opposed to industrial development as
such; he merely wished to preserve communal forms of ownership which the government should protect if necessary.[2] Russia,
in Mikhailovsky's view, had a higher *type* of society than the
countries of Western Europe and should preserve it while
moving to the higher *level* of social productivity which prevailed
in the West. Thus, he criticized the apostles of capitalist development for their moral indifference to the fate of the commune. In particular he attacked Russia's most distinguished
advocate of *laissez-faire*, Count Orlov-Davydov, who had suggested during the summer of 1873 a rapid proletarianization
of the peasantry in the overall interest of the nation. Mikhailovsky's column of December 1873 appeared as an open letter to
Orlov-Davydov whom he accused of being a revolutionary
since 'revolution is the antithesis of *evolution*, the seeking to change
the guiding roots of a society's life rather than to develop them
further'.[3]

Once again, Mikhailovsky's kinship with Proudhon is striking
in the priority assigned to the moral question of fair recompense
to labour over the economic question of increasing total productivity, and in the importance attached to preserving the pre-
capitalist social structure: the ideal of a conservative revolution.
His stylistic use of paradox resembles that of Proudhon's *Système
des Contradictions*; and in an article on Marx in his column of
January 1873 he echoes Proudhon's accusation that 'the national
wealth of the free traders is the poverty of the people'.[4] Thus, it
was as a passionate Proudhonist that Mikhailovsky sought to
lead the radicals' attack on the Russian apologists for capitalism,
drawing from Marx only those ideas which lent substance to
his own moral outrage.

As early as April 1869 Eliseev used Marx's castigation of
Bentham in attacking Antonovich and Zhukovsky, his former
colleagues on the *Contemporary* who had joined forces with the
bourgeois liberals on the *Herald of Europe* (*Vestnik Evropa*):

The arch-philistine, that insipid, pedantic, leather-tongued oracle

---

[1] I. 703.   [2] I. 703–5.   [3] I. 943.
[4] I. 834, Proudhon, in turn, had taken the idea from Sismondi. See P. J. Proudhon, *De la capacité politique des classes ouvrières*, Paris, 1924, p. 105.

of the ordinary bourgeois intelligence of the nineteenth century. . . .
With the dryest *naïveté* he takes the modern shopkeeper, especially
the English shopkeeper, as the normal man.[1]

In April 1871 Mikhailovsky began a more sustained attack
on Zhukovsky's defence of free capitalist development. For
Mikhailovsky, Zhukovsky failed to see that 'the distribution of
wealth is every bit as much a part of science as the study of
production and accumulation'.[2] Mikhailovsky defended Marx
from Zhukovsky's criticism of the labour theory of value, accusing the latter of neglecting the moral end to which Marx was
dedicated by 'pompous' preoccupation with 'mathematical
analysis' of the economic means.[3]

The path to socialism which Mikhailovsky envisaged for
Russia lay not in economic developments on the Western model,
but in the moral sense of the Russian intelligentsia. All attempts
to link socialism with a materialistic philosophy were rejected
by Mikhailovsky, who relied largely on the arguments used by
the German socialist and neo-Kantian philosopher Albert
Lange in his monumental *History of Materialism*. First published
in 1866 and widely read in Russia during the early seventies,
Lange's work contended that, although materialism must be
the working philosophy of the natural scientist, a scheme of
values unashamedly based on 'the standpoint of the ideal' must
be introduced into any discussion of human problems. Mikhailovsky recommended to his readers the works of Lange, and of
his close philosophical relative (and Marx's *bête noire*), Eugene
Dühring, flatly declaring that 'at least as far as I know there
are no writers in Europe closer to the truth than these two'.[4]

Clearly Mikhailovsky's understanding of socialism as well as
his appreciation of Marx was based on a world-view of moral
idealism unaffected by Marxist metaphysics. By the time he
had fully formulated his own philosophy in the late seventies,

[1] G. Z. Eliseev, *Vospominaniya*, in *Shestidesyatye Gody*, Moscow, 1933, p. 372 and
notes pp. 562–3; from Karl Marx *Capital*, London (Blaisher), 1920, p. 622 and
note.
[2] IV. 142.
[3] IV. 173. Yu. Zhukovsky, 'Karl Marx and His Book on Capital', *V.E.*, 1877,
no. 5; answered by Mikhailovsky, 'Karl Marx Before the Court of Yu. Zhukovsky',
O.Z., 1877, no. 11 (wrongly dated 1887 in IV. 165). For detailed discussion of the
controversy see A. L. Reuel, '*Kapitala' Karla Marksa v Rossii 1870kh Godov*, Moscow,
1939, pp. 86–118.
[4] See *Note H*, p. 190.

he had already begun to identify Marx philosophically with the hated classical economists of England:

Despite all his tendentiousness Marx does not bring into the theoretical part of his studies any ethical or moral moments. He stands firmly on the abstract ground of [Adam Smith's] hypothetical man. . . .[1]

His attitude was that of the young populists, for, as one of the most active of them later observed:

Only the purely economic teachings of Marx on the value of labour and his views on the relationship between capital and labour were widely propagated in the seventies.

The men of the seventies held in their hearts a hate for the exploitation of labour by the capitalist and without hesitation recognized the liberation of labour as one of the first problems for any progressive program. Further than that the knowledge of Marx did not go; and no one in the seventies recognized him as the father of scientific socialism. The youth of that time even after reading *Capital* continued to base their outlook on what is now called utopian socialism. . . .[2]

Rejection of the West

In forming his social philosophy during the early seventies, Mikhailovsky developed as a corollary to his faith in a special path for Russia, a firm antagonism to the prevailing pattern of social development in Western Europe. Although his own social ideas came almost exclusively from such Western thinkers as Proudhon, Spencer, Mill, and Marx, Mikhailovsky emphatically turned his back on Western society, echoing the famous sentiment of Peter Chaadaev, the most Western-oriented of all the early intelligentsia: 'Nous avancerons plus rapidement que les autres parce que nous sommes venus après eux.'[3] As the populist movement moved towards a climax in 1873, Mikhailovsky dramatized his faith in Russia's unique potentialities by resolutely refusing to follow the classical radical pattern of leaving Russia to direct activity from abroad.

[1] I. 430.
[2] S. F. Kovalik (Starik), 'The Movement of the Seventies at the time of the Great Trial of the 193', *Byloe*, 1906, no. 10, pp. 5–6.
[3] P. Ya. Chaadaev (in a letter of 1835 to A. I. Turgenev), *Sochineniya*, i. 187.

Mikhailovsky's antipathy to Germany was rooted in his early rejection of Hegel's 'Berlin state philosophy' and reinforced by personal experiences in the summer of 1870. Mikhailovsky had journeyed to Kissingen with Nekrasov and was appalled by the chauvinism accompanying the mobilization for the Franco-Prussian War. In articles for the September and October issues of the *Annals*, Mikhailovsky singled out Germany as the greatest threat in Europe to his Proudhonist ideal of tolerance, evolutionary progress, and loose federation. Beginning with a note of nostalgia for the time of Diderot and Voltaire, when men 'fought for freedom of thought and tolerance against routine, tradition, and fanaticism',[1] Mikhailovsky goes on to say:

> I am writing these lines in Germany in early August. Around me I hear patriotic speeches of Germans on the unity of Germany. . . . Does this ever-recurring idea of the unity of Germany represent a progressive principle? . . . The profound and original mind of Proudhon . . . insists that this very unification of Germany and of Italy runs counter to the federative principle and is in essence retrogressive.[2]

With the steady German approach on Paris in the autumn and winter of 1870, the spectre of Bismarck's Germany assumed awesome proportions for Mikhailovsky, who expressed his growing Germanophobia in an important article 'Count Bismarck', which appeared in February. His view of the German Chancellor is contained in a quotation from Proudhon, placed at the top of the article:

> On n'admettait plus, en fait de société et de gouvernement, ni religion, ni droit, ni science; on croyait à l'art. Et les masses y inclinaient: elles y ont, au fond, toujours incliné. Produit d'une haute ambition, mélange d'habileté et d'audace, voilà ce qui est pour elles le génie politique. Insensiblement le pouvoir s'était fait artiste; encore un peu, il tombait dans la bohème.[3]

Bismarck represents for Mikhailovsky a frightening new phenomenon: the first purely practical politician to appear on

---

[1] V. 10. He distinguished the Germany of Lessing and Kant from that of Bismarck, X. 247–9.   [2] V. 15.

[3] VI. 71–72. Mikhailovsky gives as his source the *Contradictions politiques*. The citation is not contained in either volume of the *Système des contradictions*, but both the substance and the style make it almost certainly a genuine citation from Proudhon.

the European scene, recognizing no standard of values apart
from the exercise of power. Mikhailovsky does not damn him
with epithets such as 'feudal' or 'reactionary'. In Mikhailovsky's
view Bismarck, unlike earlier European tyrants, 'does not know
or want to know either feudal or non-feudal principles',[1] but
only the principles of exercising power.

The rise of Bismarck's Germany presented a double threat.
On the one hand, of war, since 'the idea of German empire is
the idea of world monarchy'.[2] On the other hand there is the
more insidious threat that 'in several decades, "Prussian Civilization", so attractive to some of our publicists, will have made
over the world in its own image'.[3] Nevertheless, Mikhailovsky
does not lose faith in progress. Bismarck is seen only as the last
gasp of a vanishing age:

These men of the past become drunk with their own success;
their audacity knows no bound. . . . But this is the strength before
death of the dying elements in our midst. Autumn flies before their
death, as is well known, are exceptionally active. Not long before the
collapse of the Roman Empire, the emperors began to call themselves Gods. Metaphysics on the eve of its death brought forth a
Hegel.[4]

Mikhailovsky's articles, along with Bakunin's celebrated
pamphlet of May 1871 'The Knouto-Germanic Empire
and the Social Revolution', established the general hatred
of Germany which was to prevail among the narodniks.
Bakunin and the narodniks would also follow Mikhailovsky
in mixing anti-semitism with Germanophobia. After visiting
Vienna in the summer of 1873 to review the International
Exhibition for the *Annals*, Mikhailovsky extended his condemnation to the Austro-Hungarian Empire. He saw hope only
for non-Germanic Hungary, which, 'although still dominated
in economic affairs by Jews, still lives in its own political
past and future'.[5]

English society presented for Mikhailovsky another road-
block in the way of progress. In a series of articles on evolutionary thought in 1870, Mikhailovsky began the standard
tendency of Russian radicals to equate social Darwinism with
contemporary English life. In his 'What is Happiness?' of

[1] VI. 98.   [2] VI. 110.   [3] VI. 111.
[4] VI. 104.   [5] II. 517.

March and April 1872, Mikhailovsky challenged the utilitarian philosophy of John Stuart Mill which had so stimulated him in the sixties. In Proudhonist fashion he finds 'a whole system of contradictions' behind the façade of English freedoms, including the fact that this land of the greatest wealth also has the highest suicide rate.

His most serious point is that under the English system 'reason and moral feeling were not brought to bear on economic development'.[1] The English he calls 'contemporary epicureans' just as the Germans are 'contemporary stoics'. Each represents a new 'Scylla' or 'Charybdis' to be avoided, since those who preach material self-interest degrade human personality just as much as those who preach blind acceptance. His attacks on *The Herald of Europe*, the Russian apologist for English liberalism, were no less forceful than his attacks on Russian proponents of German philosophy and statecraft.

Deepening disillusionment in France was also felt after the suppression of the Paris Commune and the establishment of the Third Republic. For Mikhailovsky and his contemporaries this was the greatest shock of all. Indeed, it was not until the spell cast by the home of revolutions was finally lifted in the early seventies that the radicals were psychologically able to create a movement of their own, free from the belief that salvation would ultimately come from the West.

Mikhailovsky's colleague, Saltykov, has given the best testimony of the intensity with which the radical intelligentsia followed developments in France in the early nineteenth century:

In Russia—and not so much in Russia as in Petersburg—we existed only physically. Spiritually we lived in France . . . every episode from the social life of France concerned us vitally, made us rejoice or suffer. . . . We instinctively turned to France. Not, of course, to the France of Louis Philippe and Guizot, but to the France of St.-Simon, Cabet, Fourier, Louis Blanc, and particularly George Sand. From there, the belief in humanity came to us; from there, the certainty burst upon us that 'the golden age' lay not behind, but before us.[2]

---

[1] I. 693. Cf. the influential article by V. V. Bervi, 'England, the Contemporary Carthage', *Delo*, 1872, no. 3.

[2] M. E. Saltykov, 'Beyond the Frontier', *Izbrannye Sochineniya*, Moscow-Leningrad, 1940, p. 30.

Disillusionment with France began after the failure of the revolution of 1848, and was deepened by the bourgeoization of French society under Napoleon III. Saltykov wrote that during this period 'Paris had already ceased to be the light of the world and made herself into a "treasurehouse of women's fashions and delicate condiments" '.[1] Nevertheless, the will to believe in France did not die; and as Proudhon's ideas and influence grew in the 1860's, hope that 'the real France' might once more assert itself gained momentum in Russian radical circles. This hope lay in part behind the decision of the new collegium of the *Annals* to journey abroad to Paris in the spring of 1869. Nekrasov and Eliseev (followed later by Saltykov), sought to recruit the 'Parisian correspondents' which were still indispensable to any radical journal in Russia. They gained the collaboration of Mikhailovsky's former colleague, Bartholomew Zaitsev, and of an eminent French editor and author of *Le Génie de la Révolution Française*, Charles-Louis Chassin.

In 1869 and 1870 interest was growing once more in French developments. The early *Chaikovtsy* were reading Mikhailovsky's translation of Proudhon's *De la capacité politique des classes ouvrières* and a new history of the French working-class movement by another radical journalist.[2] A short-lived new journal, *La Marseillaise*, was even being set up by a group of St. Petersburg students in direct imitation of a French radical journal of the same name.[3] When in March 1871, news reached St. Petersburg that revolutionary insurgents had taken over Paris, a new wave of exhilaration swept through the intelligentsia, a feeling that 'France had once more remembered herself'.[4] It was assumed that a large number of Russian and Polish exiles in Paris were participating in the movement.[5]

Nowhere was the story of the Commune told with more sympathy than on the pages of the *Annals*. In May 1871 Mikhailovsky's French-educated brother-in-law, N. E. Pavlovsky,

[1] M. E. Saltykov, 'Beyond the Frontier', *Izbrannye Sochineniya*, Moscow-Leningrad, 1940, p. 391.

[2] A. K. Sheller-Mikhailov, *Proletariat vo Frantsii*, St. Petersburg, 1869.

[3] Modelled on the journal of Henri Rochefort, the author of the highly regarded attack on French bourgeois society, *Les Français de la décadence*, Paris, 1866, and including among its founders Nicholas Danielson (Nikolai-on), Marx's principal Russian correspondent.

[4] Saltykov, op. cit., p. 393. Cf. Lavrov, *Narodniki-Propagandisty*, p. 32.

[5] See *Note I*, p. 190.

praised the Commune in Proudhonist language for its defence of 'the principle of federalism in its eternal struggle
throughout French history with centralism'.[1] Articles by Zaitsev
and Chassin, the regular correspondents of the *Annals*, and information supplied to the *Annals* by Lavrov, the most active of
all Russians in the Commune, kept the editors fully informed
of the situation in Paris.

As Mikhailovsky's colleagues looked with increasing scrutiny
at the story of the Commune, however, a growing sense of
futility and disillusionment came over them. A sense of elegaic
sadness began to be reflected in Nicholas Kurochkin's poem,
'The Steam Guillotine', in July 1871, in a subsequent series of
articles 'On the Ruins of Paris' and in translations from Victor
Hugo's *L'Année Terrible*.[2] This disillusionment was deepened by
the trip made to Paris late in 1871 by Uspensky and Pavlovsky
on behalf of the *Annals*. The only thing left to praise in Paris was
the memory of the communards, to whose place of martyrdom
in the Tuileries Uspensky made a pilgrimage. 'I stood for an
hour on that square, as if I were mad or in a stupor; my legs
seemed to have taken root in that place where so many died.'[3]

Mikhailovsky's own disillusionment in France was not, however, rooted solely in the failure of the Commune. He had in
fact rejected its Jacobin excesses and expressed greater sympathy
for the middle position of Louis Blanc, who avoided the 'furies
of both Paris and Versailles'.[4] What shocked Mikhailovsky was
the violence of the reaction and the moral poverty of the
society which was rising on the ruins of the Commune. For
him as for Saltykov the Third Republic became 'a republic
without ideals—without a passionate idea'.[5]

As late as August and September 1871 Mikhailovsky was
writing with sympathy that 'no one people has lived through
all that France has, and no one people could exhibit anything
that would not have been experienced by the French'.[6] But by
October of the same year he concluded that the land which

[1] Quoted in 'Nekrasov and the Paris Commune', *Literaturnoe Nasledstvo* (49–50),
Moscow, 1946, p. 402.
[2] M. Alekseev, 'V. Hugo in Russia', *Literaturnoe Nasledstvo* (31–32), Moscow,
1937, esp. pp. 883–8.   [3] See *Note J*, p. 190.
[4] *O.Z.*, 1871, no. 12, p. 204. This position was shared by Chassin, Paris correspondent for the *Annals*.
[5] Letter of 7/19 March 1876 to E. I. Yakushin, *Literaturnoe Nasledstvo* (13–14),
Moscow, 1934, p. 302.   [6] III. 20.

had given to Europe the vision of human progress, and the
thought of Voltaire, Comte, Blanc, and Proudhon had become
—in the words of the title of his article—the land of 'Darwinism
and the operettas of Offenbach'.

France was becoming like England, a land of 'liberalism and
the stock exchange', ruled by the jungle laws of survival of the
fittest. Offenbach's operettas were for Mikhailovsky signs of the
decadence and moral bankruptcy which any society given over
to social Darwinism would be bound to experience. As supporting evidence Mikhailovsky cites a verse from a light opera by
one of the 'vice-Offenbachs' on the Parisian scene:

> Demandez à monsieur Prud'homme
> Ce qu'il pense de mes talents,
> Il va vous répondre qu'en somme
> Ma danse est un signe du temps . . .[1]

Only as a 'sign of the times' can this senseless frivolity be understood. 'In olden times', Mikhailovsky sadly reflects, 'people
feared hell. Now the souls of the greatest sinners are doing the
can-can. . . .'[2] Just as he would later cite the music of Johann
Strauss as a symbol of Austrian decadence,[3] Mikhailovsky saw
in the popularity of Offenbach a final assurance that Paris had
ceased to be the 'light of the world'. Paris no longer looked at
'the *whole* man in *all* his many-sidedness' and was now only
'interested in the torso'.[4] Mikhailovsky was, moreover, horrified
that this same can-can was gaining popularity in St. Petersburg,
at places like the fashionable new cabaret, The Little Farmstead
(*Khutorok*). He shared the satirical sentiments of his friend Vasily
Kurochkin:

Molodaya zhena,	Young lady,
Ty *Chto Delat* vzyala?	Art thou reading *What to do*?
Eta kniga polna	That book is simply full
Vsyakoy gryazi i zla.	Of filth and evil too.
Bros zlovredny roman	Cast aside the lechery
V nem razvrat i porok	And vice of that romance
I poidem kankan	And come with me to the 'Khutorok'
Tantsovat v 'Khutorok'.[5]	Where the can-can we may dance.

---

[1] I. 394. This and other references from Hervé's *Le Petit Faust* raise the possibility
that Mikhailovsky may have accompanied Nekrasov and Eliseev to Paris in 1869,
since the operetta had been given only in Paris during the 1869 season.

[2] I. 419.   [3] II. 495-6.   [4] Quoted from Saltykov in V. 234.

[5] Quoted from *Iskra* in B. P. Kozmin, *Zhurnalistika 6okh gg.*, p. 51.

This decadence of Paris has historical parallels which Mikhailovsky draws in conclusion:

Was it not so when the Popes lived in incestuous relations with their mothers and sisters, and maintained brothels? Was it not so when Roman Caesars had public weddings with men? There have always been in society dying elements and these have always led debauched lives. This corruption is one of the sledge-hammers of history. If the comparatively unpretentious Offenbach can spread to all layers of society and at the same time to all corners of Europe, it is because we are going to have a great amputation. *Novum rerum mihi nascitur ordo.*[1]

This passage and several other articles aroused the ire of no less a figure than the Tsar, who issued in October one of his rare personal messages of disapproval to the Minister of the Interior. The Tsar's concern was well founded, for Mikhailovsky's expressions of disillusionment in the West were heralding the new emphasis on a special radical path for Russia. With the picture of France as the torch-bearer of human progress finally dispelled, the intelligentsia had come to feel that the unrealized social hopes of Europe had been passed on to them.

This sense of Russia's increased historical responsibility prevented Mikhailovsky from following the classical radical path of emigrating and organizing activity from abroad. Late in 1872 or early in 1873 Mikhailovsky received an invitation from Lavrov to join him in Paris as the leading collaborator on his new revolutionary journal *Forward* (*Vpered*). Lavrov outlined to Mikhailovsky his plans for the journal, which he hoped would unite the radical movement and co-ordinate its activities. Mikhailovsky's decision was not an easy one, and he may not have finally made up his mind when he left St. Petersburg in April 1873, since his letter declining the offer was not posted until he reached Vienna.

Mikhailovsky makes clear in his letter of response that he rejects Lavrov's unreconstructed belief in an international social revolution inspired and guided from the West.

I am not a revolutionary: to each his own way. The fight with the old gods does not occupy me, because their song is sung, and their fall just a matter of time. The new gods are far more dangerous,

[1] I. 422.

and in that sense worse. Looking on things in this way, I can even to a certain extent be in friendship with the old gods and thus write in Russia.[1]

The *émigrés* are out of touch with Russia's problems, Mikhailovsky contends, and cannot appreciate the responsibility he bears to the 8,000 readers of the *Annals* and many others who look to him for guidance. Consistent with his 'patriotism to the *Annals*' Mikhailovsky also refuses an alternative offer of partial collaboration: 'Either I will take the most intimate part in the journal or none at all.'[2] The abstract and theoretical cast of Lavrov's programme aroused Mikhailovsky's hostility:

> Give me your imperatives not in theoretical but in practical terms. In the meantime I will give you mine: 'Sit meekly and prepare yourself.'
>
> More cannot be said by a Russian socialist now. There is no radical socialist opposition in Russia now; it must be educated. . . . Japan and Turkey have gained constitutions; our turn must come. I don't know in what form the moment of action will come; I only know that it has not yet come, and that youth must meet it in the future not with Moleschott on their lips and not with toy communes, but with a real knowledge of the Russian people and with a full ability to separate the good from the bad of European civilization.[3]

The derogatory references to the materialist Moleschott and to the 'toy communes' are attacks on the traditions of Pisarev and Chernyshevsky respectively, giving notice that the age of the sixties is now past.[4] Indeed, by late 1873 Mikhailovsky had come to believe that a new day was dawning in Russia which would redeem the fallen West of Bismarck, Darwin, and Offenbach.

The 'Movement to the People'

By the spring of 1874, the narodnik faith had become so widespread that it gave birth to a mass social movement, the famous 'movement to the people' (*khozhdenie v narod*). The strange and convulsive *khozhdenie* has almost no parallel in

---

[1] X. 65.   [2] X. 67.   [3] X. 67.

[4] For another important proclamation that the iconoclastic age was past see Nekrasov's 1871 poem 'Recent Times', N. A. Nekrasov, *Izbrannye Sochineniya*, Leningrad, 1947, pp. 162–9.

modern history. It involved more than 3,000 young intellectuals who left their homes and studies in the spring of 1874 and ventured forth into every province of European Russia except Archangel in the north and the Caucasus in the south. The participants were mostly well-to-do students from St. Petersburg in their late teens or early twenties. About one-fourth of the total were women. With no organized leadership and inspired only by the ideas of Mikhailovsky's journal and the Chaikovsky circles, they moved out from the cities and university centres like a vast army of itinerant missionaries, dressing and working as peasants while evangelizing the peasantry with the gospel of socialism and progress. Almost every figure who was to play a significant role in Russian radicalism for the remainder of the century was active in the movement; and its identification with the *Annals* was made firm in the eyes of most radicals when the Tsarist authorities destroyed all copies of the May issue in a vain attempt to cut off the movement at its spiritual source.

In keeping with Mikhailovsky's advice to the *Chaikovtsy* in 1871, participants in the movement took little interest in political questions. Most merely preached passive resistance to governmental authority in order to dissociate themselves from the last of the *Nechaevtsy*, A. V. Dolgushin, who had called for a violent *Jacquerie* in 1873.

The immediate cause of the exodus was the disillusionment of the St. Petersburg *Chaikovtsy* with 'the possibilities of mental and moral development'[1] among the urban working class. Having concluded in the winter of 1873 that their efforts to build among the workers were fruitless, the young radicals turned to the country, confident that the village commune still provided 'the means for giving Russia an outstanding place in European civilization'.[2] Their ideal was 'to develop our *obshchina* in the sense of the communal working of the land and the communal use of its product, to make of the *mir* assembly the basic political unit of the Russian social order'.[3] Defence of the village commune was an *idée fixe* on the *Annals*; and

---

[1] V. V. Bervi, *Polozhenie Rabochago Klassa v Rossii*, p. 403.

[2] From the title of seven widely read articles by Bervi on the *obshchina* first published in 1870.

[3] From the inaugural manifesto of Lavrov's *Vpered*, 1873, no. 1, p. 9.

Mikhailovsky became one of its most vocal apoloigsts, even appealing in August 1872 for government interference to save the commune from destruction at the hands of private capitalists.[1]

Those 'going to the people' also followed Mikhailovsky's entourage in believing that the artel was the only just form of conducting business and trade. This institution was properly championed by the *Annals* since the journal itself was run along artel lines with both editorial authority and financial profits widely distributed among its editors. The artel was the institution with which the populists sought to bring the moral qualities of the *obshchina* into the world of trade and industry. Mikhailovsky and his colleagues criticized communal experiments that were too rationalistic,[2] or appealed to the profit motive rather than a sense of justice.[3] Consistently, Mikhailovsky insisted that communes and artels were not ends in themselves, but only useful aids in the 'struggle for individuality'.

Every social union—however sonorous or personally appealing its name may be for you—has only an abstract worth. It should be revered by you to the extent that it furthers the development of personality, guards it from suffering, widens the sphere of its pleasures. . . .[4]

Mikhailovsky and his journal also championed two other principal 'causes' of the young radicals: demands for cheaper credit and for popular education. Proudhon's plan for ending the 'leprosy of interest' by setting up 'people's banks' to offer credit at low interest rates was echoed in a number of articles in the *Annals*. Mikhailovsky's brother-in-law, Nicholas Pavlovsky, called for currency devaluation and a decentralized system of rural banks; Krivenko advocated a system of rural banks modelled on that with which the German agrarian socialist, Franz Hermann Schulze-Delitzsch, had opposed the centralized state socialism of Lassalle.[5] Skabichevsky, the literary editor of the *Annals*, had been one of the founders of the first major

[1] I. 703–6.
[2] S. N. Krivenko, 'Russian Popular Artels', *O.Z.*, 1874, no. 1.
[3] A. N. Englehardt, 'Dairy Co-operatives', *O.Z.*, 1872, nos. 2, 4, 5. Cf. Paul Apostol, *L'Artèle et la coopération en Russie*, Paris, 1899, pp. 141 ff.
[4] IV. 451.
[5] See the initial anonymous article on the subject in *O.Z.*, 1870, no. 2; Pavlovsky's article in *O.Z.*, 1871, no. 8; and Krivenko's in *O.Z.*, 1874, nos. 7, 11.

attempt to provide popularized education for the peasantry—
the so-called 'Sunday school' movement of 1859–62.[1] He, along
with Mikhailovsky and Demert, criticized the restricted enrol-
ment and narrow curricula of Russian schools, and helped influence members of the staff of the *Annals* to participate in the
campaign to make education more simple and accessible to the
peasantry. The publication of Tolstoy's controversial 'On
Popular Education' and of Mikhailovsky's subsequent columns
on the same subject[2] made the *Annals* the principal public
forum for this issue.

It is readily apparent that the social programme of the
narodniks was highly utopian. They did not—and in the
Russia of the 1870's could not—work through any political
channel. There was, indeed, no political side to their programme except in so far as the *obshchina* represented an institution for local self-government. Nor were their demands shaped
by a dispassionate study of economic facts. This was an age not
of political or economic calculation but of intense moral
idealism. Yet, as one of the most active radicals of the period
recalled: 'all seemed realizable and practical. The word "utopia" did not exist for us. . . .' The idea of avoiding political
agitation and seeking social regeneration directly seemed

the most suited to the conditions of Russian life; we have not had a
parliament, there is no point even talking of universal suffrage and
election of workers' deputies. However, in ancient Russia there had
existed popular rights such as Kostomarov described, artels about
which we read in Flerovsky, the *obshchina* which we knew through
Haxthausen, the works of Herzen, Bakunin, Shchapov, Yadrintsev,
and Posnikov. This *obshchina* was the prototype and at the same time
the germ of a just future organization of society.[3]

In spite of its disorganized nature and non-violent methods
the movement to the people represented such a deep challenge
to the existing order of things that the government treated it as
a revolution. Mass arrests began in the late summer; and by
the autumn more than 1,500 participants had been imprisoned
in thirty-seven provinces.[4] This decimation of the young

---

[1] Skabichevsky, *Vospominaniya*, pp. 117–19.
[2] *Infra*, p. 95.
[3] Vera Figner, 'The Student Years', *G.M.*, 1923, no. 1, p. 33.
[4] See the records of the Ministry of Justice as cited in L. E. Shishko, *Sotsialnye*

radicals effectively killed the movement. Yet many remained 'among the people', and many more would emulate the experiment of 1874 during the following three years. Indeed, the visionary hopes of the movement continued at a high ebb in the St. Petersburg circles of Mikhailovsky and his colleagues even after the initial wave of arrests in late 1874 and 1875. Particularly after the destruction of the May issue of the *Annals* participants in the movement sought to place themselves in closer personal contact with Mikhailovsky. Although he did not go among the people himself, his dacha on the outskirts of St. Petersburg continued to be a centre for many of the literary evenings, consultations with students, and intense discussions which characterized the period. Included among those who assembled during the summer of 1874 at Mikhailovsky's and Uspensky's villas were patrons and sympathizers as well as active participants in the movement. Mikhailovsky's friends from the dark days of 1866 were there: Demert, Minaev, and the Kurochkins, along with active young *Chaikovtsy* like A. I. Ivanchin-Pisarev and leaders of the rising reform movement in the zemstvos like I. I. Petrunkevich. Leading figures in the artistic world were frequent visitors: the painters, Repin and Yaroshenko, who were friends of Mikhailovsky and his brother-in-law; the cellist Davydov, who was head of the St. Petersburg Conservatory and a former teacher of Mikhailovsky's wife. Thursday nights were generally spent at Eliseev's and Fridays at Mikhailovsky's. In addition, some of the younger members of the staff met regularly during the day for tea, forming the so-called 'society of abstemious philosophers'.[1]

The connexion between these groups and the movement to the people was again dramatized when the police made an unsuccessful attempt to keep the September issue of the *Annals* from appearing. Far from moving to the defensive, Mikhailovsky and his colleagues were in this very month seeking to set up another publication 'to help spread the views of the *Annals*'.

Dvizheniya v 60kh i Pervoy Polovine 70kh Godov, Moscow, 1921, p. 86. Lavrov placed the figure of arrests outside St. Petersburg until November 1874 at 1,600 (*Narodniki-Propagandisty*, p. 235); but the figures from the third section files make it doubtful that the number of arrests (including St. Petersburg) could have been much greater than 1,500. Franco Venturi, *Il Populismo Russo*, Turin, 1952, ii. 966.

[1] Skabichevsky, *Vospominaniya*, pp. 328–32; P. I. Weinberg, 'The Literary Dinners', *Ist V.*, 1908, no. 1.

They considered founding a new journal to be called the *Russian* (*Rusak*) and buying a minor journal, the *Petersburg Leaflet* (*Peterburgsky Listok*), before effectively taking over the *Stock Market Journal* (*Birzhevyya Vedomosti*) late in 1874.[1]

The columns of the *Annals* in the final months of 1874 shone forth with an optimism which mirrored the spirit of the intelligentsia during the high tide of the movement to the people. At the same time the monthly dinners of the editorial staff of the *Annals* had become major occasions, held in the Metropole Hotel to accommodate the large number who sought to attend. Annual dinners were held also on 15 November, Mikhailovsky's birthday and the day celebrated by Uspensky as a birthday. Mikhailovsky participated enthusiastically in these dinners and evenings, and rarely missed any of the student balls—the benefit dances which sought to raise money for needy students in St. Petersburg. He was admired for his simple yet aristocratic bearing—his kindly manner and courtly manner of dancing the mazurka—as well as for his sympathy with radical youth. Because he never seemed to identify himself entirely with any disputing radical faction he was admired by all of them. At one of the evenings he explained his personal philosophy to an admiring group:

> ... for myself I would like only one thing: a little plot of land and as many books as possible. I hope with time to arrange things à la Cincinnatus; I will buy my *desyatina* [a 2.7-acre plot], build a hut, dig myself a garden, and read all these Spencers, Darwins, and Huxleys in the original.[2]

During 1875 the *Annals* reached the zenith of its influence, while Mikhailovsky was enjoying the most productive single year of his journalistic career. His new column, 'A Layman's Notes', which began appearing in the January issue rapidly proved his most successful attempt to give voice to the views of the idealized simple man. At the same time, his contacts with the major creative figures of Russian art and letters were becoming even more extensive.

[1] See *Note K*, p. 191.
[2] *Uspensky v Zhizni*, p. 136. See also Skabichevsky, *Vospominaniya*, pp. 272–5. Skabichevsky suggests that Mikhailovsky drank more and was more of a ladies' man than other memoirists, but adds that he was 'from head to toe a full-fledged gentleman', p. 273.

Mikhailovsky acted as the liaison figure with Tolstoy when the latter gave up the writing of *Anna Karenina* as 'repulsive and disgusting' in March 1874 and agreed to write for the *Annals*. Tolstoy insisted that 'no disagreement would be possible' with the *Annals* which he had come to consider superior to the *Contemporary*.[1] Mikhailovsky was also in sympathetic touch with Dostoevsky, who in January 1875 began publishing his new novel, *A Raw Youth*, in the *Annals*. As early as February 1873 Dostoevsky had called Mikhailovsky's critique of *The Possessed* a 'new revelation'; and in July 1873 he wrote of his debt to Mikhailovsky and the *Annals*:

I cannot forget Mr. N. M. of *The Annals of the Fatherland* and my debts to him. . . . With all my soul I affirm that this is *one of the most sincere publicists* that there could ever be in St. Petersburg.[2]

Enamoured with the new movement, Dostoevsky resigned from the editorship of the conservative *Citizen* (*Grazhdanin*) early in 1874, and in April agreed to publish his next work in the *Annals*.

While writing *A Raw Youth* late in 1874, Dostoevsky appears to have become converted to Mikhailovsky's view that the *Nechaevtsy*, which Dostoevsky had caricatured in *The Possessed*, were not representative of the radical camp. Whereas he had originally intended to write his new novel about the *Dolgushintsy*, the last imitators of Nechaev whose trial had taken place in July 1874, the final draft pays only incidental attention to this group and provides a generally sympathetic picture of the radical camp. His frequent sympathy with utopian social views in *A Raw Youth*, 'The Diary of a Writer', and such subsequent stories as 'The Dream of a Ridiculous Man' and 'The Heavenly Christmas Tree'—all reflect more a narodnik than an Orthodox, conservative understanding of human society.

Even Turgenev, the third and most removed from the Russian scene of Russia's great novelists, established close connexions

---

[1] *Lit. V.*, I. 200; V. E. Maksimov (Evgenev), *Nekrasov v Krugu Sovremennikov*, pp. 71–82, esp. 76. He remained in close collaboration with the *Annals* until the summer of 1875. Not until his own populist experiments had conclusively failed in 1876 did Tolstoy return to *Anna*, which, though published in Katkov's *Russian Herald*, revealed continued preoccupation with narodnik themes in the character of Levin.

[2] A. S. Iskoz (Dolinin), *V Tvorcheskoy Laboratorii Dostoevskogo*, Moscow, 1947, p. 152. See also ibid., pp. 63–64, and V. 434.

with the *Annals*, largely through Vasily Kurochkin and Uspensky, who had gone to Paris in December 1874. He arranged with Uspensky to conduct a series of 'literary and musical matinées' to aid exiled Russian students in Paris, contributed some of his own money to narodnik causes, and wrote an introduction to a book by Uspensky's wife for participants in the 'movement to the people'.[1] As in the case of Tolstoy and Dostoevsky, the movement became an important literary subject—indeed the theme of his last novel, *Virgin Soil*.

Thus, belief in the people—of which Mikhailovsky was a high priest, the *Annals's* holy writ, and the young *Chaikovtsy* the evangelists—cast its spell over the creative imagination of Russia's greatest novelists: the anarchist Tolstoy, the Orthodox Dostoevsky, and the cosmopolitan liberal Turgenev. In 1875 the Russian intelligentsia was united as it had never been before by a deep common faith: the social philosophy of Russian populism.

[1] *Ocherki i Rasskazy iz Zhizni Prostogo Naroda*, St. Petersburg, 1875. On Turgenev's link with the radicals, see *Uspensky v Zhizni*, pp. 567–8 notes, and Lavrov, *Narodniki-Propagandisty*, p. 69 note.

VI

THE FIRST MYTH:
BELIEF IN 'THE PEOPLE'

T HE causes for the great unrest of 1874 are not easily found. Politically, neither autocratic power nor the strength of the nobility was increasing in the early seventies. Economically, there had been seven years of increasing material prosperity, marred by a partial crop failure in 1873, but by no major famines; and the European recession of the mid seventies had left Russia virtually unaffected. Moreover, there was no central high command for the radicals and no coherent system of organization. To understand why they went out among the people by the hundreds, one must look within the collective psyche of the intelligentsia, to the visionary concepts which inspired the movement.

As the narrative reaches the climactic mid-point of the seventies, it is particularly important to consider in some detail the first of the all-pervasive myths of the period, the 'idea of the *narod*'. The mystical faith in the superior wisdom and sanctity of the people is preserved in the names *narodnik* and *narodnichestvo*, which became widespread for the first time during this decade. Whether evolutionary or revolutionary in outlook, reformers of the period followed Mikhailovsky in rejecting Nechaev's cold statement that 'to love the people means to lead it by grapeshot'[1] in favour of a visionary faith in 'the people'.

The Narod as an Idea

Whether they spoke of *das Volk*, *le peuple*, *il popolo*, or the *narod*, European thinkers living in the shadow of the French Revolution felt irresistibly compelled to introduce into their social philosophies 'the people' as a kind of regenerative life force in history. Like so many ideas first formulated in the

---

[1] Quoted in Kozmin, *Tkachev*, p. 156.

West, this romantic belief was taken up by Russians with even greater intensity than by its originators.

The Slavophils first gave to the word *narod* the peculiar appeal that it would retain for the Russian intelligentsia. From German romantic philosophy they brought into Russia in the 1840's and 1850's the contrast between the spontaneous truth of the people and the abstract, impersonal truths of bureaucrat and pedant. *Narodnost* maintained for the Slavophils something of the meaning of 'nationality', which it had carried when first used in Count Uvarov's famous governmental formula of the 1830's: Autocracy, Orthodoxy, and Nationality (*narodnost*). But they also thought of *narodnost* in its more untranslatable meaning of 'spirit of the people'. In the years immediately after the Crimean War Slavophilism faded away as a coherent body of thought, but the concept of *narodnost* commended itself to two new groups of Russian social thinkers. On the one hand the new ideologists of the right—Katkov, Fadeev, Ignatev—developed a chauvinistic belief in the supremacy of the nation (*narodnost* as nationality); on the other hand there began to appear among the radicals a new faith in the unspoiled simple folk of Russia (*narodnost* as 'the spirit of the people').

The populists derived their 'idea of the people' not so much from the mystical German romantics beloved of the Slavophils as from French thought—the revolutionary anti-enlightenment tradition which was rooted in Rousseau's glorification of the 'noble savage'. Whether one attributes more to Rousseau or to his interpreters, the idea of an 'internal light' and a 'general will' did represent a fundamental break with the tradition of the *philosophes*. Thinkers in the age of reason had seen the universe as an understandable whole, illuminated by an all-pervading sun—the light of the enlightenment. In contrast, the new romantic idea of an internal light, which the individual possessed merely by virtue of being himself, made man into a self-sufficient totality.

Only as a corollary of this metaphysical assumption about the divinity of man can the romantic belief in 'the people' be fully understood. To be sure, much of the belief was rooted in compassion for real men and women. But, just as Rousseau's idea of a 'general will' did not necessarily correspond with the will of any specific people, so the concept of 'the people' in romantic

social thought is never completely identifiable with any concrete group of persons. The 'voice of the people' became the
new force which would resolve contradictions and make a social
philosophy possible for those rebelling at all authority but their
own.

Intertwined with the romantic idea of the people was a
revolutionary new egalitarianism the seed of which was again
planted by Rousseau. As the natural state of affairs was thought
to be complete equality, the rise of inequality among men was
seen as the primary cause of evil. Thus the struggle for social
reform was synonymous with the destruction of inequality. The
conflict with the spirit of the enlightenment is again striking.
The age of reason had accepted the inequality of man by
recognizing that some were more fit to read the pattern in the
carpet than others, while in Rousseau there is an implicit distrust
of the expert, something of the indignation felt by the citizen
of Geneva towards the aristocratic *élite* of Paris.

This metaphysical belief in the people with its passionate
egalitarianism was introduced most forcefully into French
socialist thought by Proudhon—like Rousseau a 'French provincial'. In his journals of the late forties, *Le Peuple*, *Le Représen-
tant du Peuple*, and *La Voix du Peuple*, he attacked all rival
socialists who allotted a special place to *élites*. After 1848, as his
views came to dominate French socialist thought, his rough
plebian egalitarianism spread. Not only *élites*, but institutions
of all sorts were to be overthrown in order to liberate the people.
Above all, constitutions and the shibboleths of bourgeois democracy were to be opposed.

Proudhon's romantic concept of 'the people' was carried into
Russia by two great admirers of Proudhon and pioneers of
Russian radicalism: Bakunin and Herzen. They, like Proudhon,
were 'provincials' who had come to the Mecca of revolution in
the late forties, and had found an explanation for the débâcle of
1848 in the failure of the revolutionaries to link themselves with
the elemental power of the people. Herzen, who collaborated
on Proudhon's *La Voix du Peuple* after the failure of the revolution in Paris, gave testimony to the way in which Proudhon
helped inspire in him a saving faith in the people—above all,
the unspoiled peasantry. Contrasting Proudhon's Besançon with
civilized Paris, Herzen wrote:

In this landscape there is something mighty and austere, resolute and morose; gazing at it, a peasant boy grew up and was formed, the descendant of old country stock, Pierre Joseph Proudhon. And indeed one may say of him, though in a different sense, what was said by the poet of the Florentines:

'E tiene ancor del monte e del macigno.'[1]

In the dark years after 1848, it was his faith in the power of the unspoiled Russian people to realize the unfulfilled social hopes of the French tradition which Herzen later claimed saved him 'from moral ruin'. In a letter to Proudhon's friend Michelet in 1851 Herzen produced what may be termed the first clear manifesto of Russian populism.[2] On the pages of his illegal journal, the *Bell*, Herzen coined in the early post-Crimean period the two main slogans of populism: 'to the people' (*v narod*) and 'land and liberty' (*zemlya i volya*).[3]

Throughout the sixties, even among the most coldly iconoclastic members of the 'young generation', there was a ripening desire to make 'love for the people' more than a platitude. Even Bartholomew Zaitsev, one of the leading debunkers of the age, wrote admiringly of a radical predecessor that:

Love towards the people and feeling for them was not an empty sound as in 'men of principles' and not a mystic abstraction as in the platonic courtiers of the people, but a live and active feeling.[4]

If a key moment were to be selected for the transition of a belief in the people into a social phenomenon, it would be the summer of 1871, when the repression of the Paris Commune had dashed the last hopes for salvation from the West. It was then that Uspensky retired to the country to re-examine his world-outlook and rebuked himself 'for not having loved the people, for writing about them as if they were pigs'.[5] At the same time, Saltykov wrote to an old friend that:

In the word 'people' one must distinguish two meanings: the historical people, and the people as a famous idea . . . it is to the

---

[1] A. I. Herzen, *My Past and Thoughts*, London, 1924, iii. 155. For Proudhon's influence on Herzen, see Labry, *Herzen et Proudhon*, pp. 55–111; on Bakunin, see B.-P. Hepner, *Bakounine*, pp. 201–14.

[2] *My Past and Thoughts*, vi. 210–48.   [3] *Sochineniya*, xvi. 73.

[4] Quoted from V. Zaitsev, 'Belinsky and Dobrolyubov', *R.S.*, 1864, no. 1, in V. Ya. Yakovlev, *Aktivnoe Narodnichestvo*, p. 22.

[5] 'New Material on Uspensky', *K.A.*, 1941, no. 3, p. 147.

second that I have always felt an affinity, and all of my work is full of this feeling.[1]

This 'narod as an idea' rapidly came to dominate the imagination of polemic as well as creative writers of the *Annals*. Mikhailovsky played a major role in propagating this new idea. His 'Literary and Journalistic Notes' of the 1872–4 period come closer than any other writings of the time to expressing the narodnik philosophy. 'Serve the Russian people, abjure every personal interest in the interest of the people', Mikhailovsky urged in the first of these columns.[2] In the second he complained that:

The word 'popular' seems to me to be used in vain everywhere; our education is called popular although so far it is only shared by the middle and upper classes . . . our health is called popular, although medical help almost never reaches the simple people; finally, even credit is called popular although it is given only on deposit of more movable and immovable property than the people have. . . .[3]

In serving the people, Mikhailovsky warns that one must avoid the path of the bourgeois press in Paris and St. Petersburg:

Servir le peuple, c'est la théorie et le prétexte pour les journalistes vendus à la bourgeoisie; se servir du peuple, c'est la pratique et le profit.[4]

Bourgeois liberals can never understand 'the people', for they think in terms of the West; and 'in Western Europe, after the colossal development of divergent, mutually conflicting interests, it is far more difficult than with us to clarify one's understanding of the people'.[5]

Russia's backwardness can be turned to her advantage because she alone is in a position to understand

the very simple and deeply true view that the people, in the present meaning of the word, is the union of the labouring classes of society. To serve the people means to work for the good of the working people.[6]

---

[1] Quoted from a letter of Saltykov to Pypin in V. 189.   [2] I. 651.
[3] I. 655–6. Quoted from Prince A. I. Vasilchikov, an aristocratic and prolific populist theorist writing in *The Week*.
[4] I. 661. Quoted from an attack on *Figaro* by the Polish-born French radical, Krzyzanowski (Lacroix).   [5] I. 659.   [6] I. 659.

Although 'the people' was thus defined as 'the labouring class of society', it became more than any mere conglomeration of workers; it became for Mikhailovsky a kind of divine will active in history, in the service of which lay social regeneration and personal fulfilment.

Serving the people above all you serve no privilege, no exclusive interest, you serve simply labour, and as a result, incidentally, your own self.[1]

In January 1873, Mikhailovsky rejects Dostoevsky's idea that suffering was a natural attribute of the Russian people, recognizing at the same time that the burden of suffering borne by the Russian people deepens one's responsibility to them.

We realized that the consciousness of an all-human truth and all-human ideals has been given to us only thanks to the eternal sufferings of the people. We are not guilty in these sufferings; we are not guilty even in that our upbringing was at their expense, just as a rich and fragrant blossom is not guilty in absorbing the best sap from the plant. But, while recognizing this role of a blossom from the past as something fated, we do not wish it in the future.

His heritage from the immoral past places the privileged nobleman in a position of indebtedness, if not actual guilt, before the people.

We have come to the conclusion that we are debtors of the people. . . . We may quarrel over the extent of the debt, over the means of liquidating it, but the debt lies on our conscience and we long to discharge it.[2]

By early 1873 Mikhailovsky had formulated the doctrine of expiation before the narod, which was to be put into practice so dramatically the following year.

Early in 1874 Mikhailovsky began to insist that contemporary radicalism was basically different from that of the sixties. Unlike the iconoclasts of the sixties, Mikhailovsky saw much that was positive in the visionary generation of the forties. He praised and even compared to Proudhon Turgenev's Rudin, a romantic literary character frequently ridiculed by the men of the sixties.[3] In April, on the eve of the movement to the people, Mikhailovsky insisted that the men of the sixties must be set off

[1] I. 659.   [2] I. 868.   [3] II. 620-2.

from those of the seventies. He inveighed against linking 'the *raznochintsy* and the repentant noblemen under one sobriquet as "men of the sixties" or "new men" '.[1] The men of the sixties sought to remake society rationally, imposing their demands on the world into which they came. The repentant nobleman, on the other hand, feels the demands that the world makes upon him. He seeks social reform because it appeals not to his reason, but to his sense of moral responsibility:

> When the chasm of serfdom and all of the old order of Russian life was opened up clearly before us in all its terrifying ugliness there appeared in society an inescapable need for self-denunciation, for self-punishment, for penitence.[2]

This obsession of the 'repentant nobleman' not only took many of them out among the people in this same spring of 1874, but it created in many more the vicarious interest in ethnography, in popular fables and poems, and in village life and provincial *patois*, which were so characteristic of the period. Behind it all lay the tacit belief in the living truth of the people *vis-à-vis* the syllogisms of philosophers and bureaucrats. Simple popular themes (often treated in popular language) were the exclusive interest of the most famous creative writers of the seventies. Gleb Uspensky, Saltykov, Sleptsov, Levitov, Naumov, Karonin, Nefedov, the Kurochkins, Polonsky, and Vovchok.

Nearly all of these largely forgotten writers for the *Annals* were in sympathetic touch with participants in the movement during the summer of 1874, often using Mikhailovsky's dacha as a meeting-place. These writers conditioned an entire generation of readers to expect that the only legitimate subject of literature was the typical *muzhik* or villager engaged in some typically Russian situation of pathos, humour, or tragedy. On the pages of the *Annals* and, to a lesser extent the *Cause*, the *Spark*, and the *Week*, they created a whole body of literature that spurned the *salons* of St. Petersburg and the vagaries of the 'superfluous man' and glorified the spontaneous existence of the Russian people, who had not yet tasted the bitter fruits of civilization.

In September 1874 Mikhailovsky began his own apotheosis

[1] II. 648.   [2] II. 648.

of the common man in a new column, 'From the Diary and Correspondence of Ivan the Forgetful' (Ivan Nepomnyash-chago). Closely modelled on the social satire of Saltykov, this column appeared for the remaining months of 1874, and irregularly thereafter until March 1877. Through this 'Aesopian' form, Mikhailovsky offered his own views on contemporary affairs. As a 'layman' (*profan*) or as 'Ivan the Forgetful' with his 'advice for beginners to forget', he professed to offer truer guides to social conduct than 'Ivan the liberal' or 'the learned people'. This tendency to glorify the non-expert went so far as to bring forth in 1876 an anonymous column in the *Annals* entitled 'Sketches of a Fool'.

Thus, the 'narod as an idea', to which Mikhailovsky and the writers of the *Annals* felt such an irresistible attraction, was far more than simply the people as an object of compassion. The narod was a life-giving force for social regeneration; the unspoiled layman or fool was its spokesman; and the writer faced an awesome responsibility before it. As one of the leading poets of the age said:

Pisatel, esli tolko on	The writer, were only he
Est nerv velikogo naroda	The nerve of the great people,
Ne mozhet byt ne porazhen	He could not be but defeated
Kogda porazhena svoboda.[1]	If freedom were vanquished.

Mikhailovsky in his columns of the mid seventies remained 'a nerve of the great people'; but the best statement of the essentially lyric myth of the people was left, appropriately, by a poet: Mikhailovsky's friend and colleague, Nicholas Nekrasov. In one of the last poems before his death late in 1877, Nekrasov wrote:

Serdtse svobodnoe —	The free heart
Zoloto, zoloto	Is gold, gold—
Serdtse narodnoe!	The heart of the people!
Sila narodnaya,	The people's strength,
Sila moguchaya —	The mighty strength
Sovest spokoynaya,	Is a tranquil conscience,
Pravda zhivuchaya![2]	An undying truth!

---

[1] Ya. P. Polonsky, quoted in D. N. Ovsyaniko-Kulikovsky, *Istoriya Russkoy Literatury*, Moscow, 1911, iii. 494.
[2] N. A. Nekrasov, 'Rus', *Izbrannye Sochineniya*, p. 324.

Critical Populism

The emotional appeal of the 'idea of the narod' became so excessive in the wake of the movement to the people that Mikhailovsky felt compelled by the late seventies to redefine his position as 'critical *narodnichestvo*'.

The essence of Mikhailovsky's critical outlook was contained in an article of December 1873: 'Idealism, Idolatry and Realism.' He distinguished the practical idealism to which he subscribed from (1) crude realism, which by its nature is only descriptive and thus devoid of ideals, and (2) pure idolatry, which creates not ideals to be served, but idols which are worshipped to relieve one of the very responsibility of service. Thus, despite his semi-mystical concept of the narod, Mikhailovsky never viewed his own attitude as one of idolatry, of uncritical 'worship of the plain folk'.

Such idolatry was present, however, among many of the 'repentant noblemen' whose passion for expiation generally exceeded their practicality in helping the peasantry. Typical of this uncritical populism was an economist at the University of St. Petersburg who spent a decade doing research on the village commune, and even from his death-bed suggested to a young writer:

> Let us go to the village. . . . Let us gather together all who believe in the people. . . . Only there amidst the great people in the village, in the *obshchina*, can salvation and reason be found.[1]

Mikhailovsky shared this feeling to some extent, and added to it an element of Proudhonist anti-intellectualism in his columns of the 1874–7 period. He even expressed on occasion a longing for self-annihilation in the super-reason of the narod:

> Oh, if I could drown in that grey rough mass of the people, dissolve irrevocably, preserving only that spark of truth and ideal which I succeeded in acquiring for the sake of that same people. Oh, if only all of you readers were to come to the same decision, especially those whose light burned brighter than mine and without soot. What a great illumination there would be, and what a great historical occasion it would make! unparalleled in history![2]

[1] V. S. Prugavin, quoted in V. G. Korolenko, *Vospominaniya o Pisatelyakh,* Moscow, 1934, p. 81.   [2] III. 707.

Nevertheless, Mikhailovsky rebelled against any consistent doctrine of effacement before the wisdom of the people, such as Tolstoy was setting forth in the late seventies. Mikhailovsky insisted that in serving the people one must distinguish the 'interests of the people' from 'the voice of the village'.[1] He criticized Tolstoy's ideas on popular education for catering too much to the ignorance of the peasantry. He saw in Tolstoy's idea that the Russian peasant was morally superior to other people 'the poison of deceitful patriotism, bogus idealization of the people, national conceit, etc.'[2] He felt that Tolstoy was shirking his true responsibility to society by making an idol of the masses: 'In the people there lie deposits of great spiritual strength which need only a push. This push can be given only by us, representatives of "society". More cannot be done, but we are obligated to do this much.'[3]

Thus, for Mikhailovsky, the repentant nobleman must keep his 'spark of truth and ideal' intact while sinking into the 'rough grey mass'. His most biting polemics of the mid seventies were directed against two romantic narodniks who failed to keep this spark alive: P. S. Chervinsky and I. I. Kablits. In a famous outburst against Chervinsky, who had consistently glorified 'Russian life with all its ordinary practices', Mikhailovsky declared:

Upon my desk stands a bust of Belinsky which is very dear to me, and also a chest with books by which I have spent many nights. If Russian life with all its ordinary practices breaks into my room, destroys my bust of Belinsky, and burns my books, I will not submit to the people from the village; I will fight. . . . And even if I should be overcome with the greatest feeling of humility and self-abnegation, I should still say at least: 'Forgive them God of verity and justice; they know not what they do.' For all that, I should still protest.[4]

In extending his attack to Chervinsky's colleague on the *Week*, Kablits, Mikhailovsky challenged the extreme anti-intellectualism of the emotional populists. In his article 'Woe not from the mind',[5] Mikhailovsky ridiculed Kablits's view that feeling (*chuvstvo*) was the true 'factor of progress' rather than

---

[1] III. 707.   [2] III. 327.   [3] III. 514.   [4] III. 692.
[5] *Gorya ne ot Uma*—a play with words on the title of Griboedov's play *Gorya ot Uma* (Woe from Wit—or Mind).

mind (*um*), asking why Kablits and his journal continued publishing if a feeling for the people was all that mattered. The
intelligent must, for the people's sake, maintain his critical facul-
ties in serving them, for his service is a matter of honour, not
of guilt. Guilt, in Mikhailovsky's view, requires self-chastise-
ment for atonement; while honour appeals to a man's free
response in accordance with his moral ideals.

Fortified with these beliefs, Mikhailovsky turned in the late
seventies to debate with the most formidable exponent of uncritical populism: a young novelist and contributor to the
Annals, N. N. Zlatovratsky. Zlatovratsky, whose house had
become a centre for many young students and journalists in
the seventies, blamed Russia's ills on her separation from the
freedom and dignity of communal life. In his stories, and in his
great work, *Ustoy* (The Basis), which was published serially
from 1878 to 1882, Zlatovratsky insisted that this tragic separation was in large measure the work of the intelligentsia. This
arrogant class claimed to serve the people, but refused to bow
down before the wisdom of popular institutions, the 'golden
hearts' of Russia.[1]

Mikhailovsky would not take up the pen against one of his
own contributors. But he attempted to delay the publication of
Ustoy,[2] and his heated debates with Zlatovratsky at literary
evenings became celebrated in radical circles.[3] Against Zlatovratsky, and many followers of Tolstoy who were among his
friends and supporters, Mikhailovsky reiterated his position that
the *obshchina* and artel were desirable only because of certain
moral qualities which they helped develop, not because of any
mystical affinity with the 'spirit of the people'.[4]

The growth of this cult of the narod in the late seventies
forced Mikhailovsky to look more deeply for the source of his
own values and ideals. In his debate with Chervinsky, Mikhailovsky had hinted at a deeper basis for morality than service to
the narod. In his 'Letters on Truth and Falsehood', which

---

[1] See N. N. Zlatovratsky, 'The Golden Hearts', *O.Z.*, 1877, nos. 4, 5, 8, 12.

[2] See note in N. N. Zlatovratsky, *Izbrannye Proizvedeniya*, Moscow, 1947, p. 828.

[3] V. G. Korolenko, *Vospominaniya o Pisatelyakh*, pp. 82–84.

[4] Nevertheless, Mikhailovsky was identified with uncritical *narodnichestvo* by the
pure positivists (as later by the Marxists). Leading the attack of the positivists was
P. A. Boborykin, whose *Le Culte du peuple dans la Russie contemporaine*, Paris, 1883,
was later attacked by Mikhailovsky in *Lit. V.* I. 346–50.

began to appear in November 1877, he clearly affirmed for the
first time a belief in transcendent truth. Mikhailovsky did not
define this *pravda*. Yet he felt that it must have existence in and
of itself, for 'without it, it is impossible to live: that is, to live
as a human being rather than some kind of pig'.[1] He felt that
truth must be distinguished from metaphysical systems. His
Proudhonist hatred of systems, and the intensity of his belief in
the value of the individual personality caused him ultimately
to reject the 'idea of the narod' and all other concepts but that
of truth itself as the source of value for man.

In his articles on 'The Fight for Individuality', Mikhailovsky
had already developed a sociology which evaluated all social
groups from the viewpoint of service to the individual. In
articles of August and September 1878, on 'The Utopia of
Renan and the Theory of Personality of Dühring', he goes still
farther in deploring any state of affairs where 'the idea of
personality is sacrificed on the altar of some higher aim'.[2] He
specifically rejects slogans like 'the goal of nature', 'the mission
of history', 'the wealth of nations', and 'the honour of the
government'. 'These idols demand sacrifices, feast on human
bodies, surfeit themselves on human blood, but their followers
and creators label them gods.'[3] In one of his 'Letters on Truth
and Falsehood', he states conclusively: 'All mental, all psychic
processes perfect themselves in personality and only in personality. It alone feels, thinks, suffers, and desires... personality
can never be sacrificed for anything: it is holy and inviolable.'[4]

Mikhailovsky's profession of belief in truth as an ontological
concept was thus the direct result of his concern for the dignity
of human personality. For philosophic support he leaned on
Lange and the neo-Kantians.[5] Mikhailovsky's assertion of a *sui
generis* moral truth was a revolutionary one in Russian radical
thought. Equally revolutionary was his insistence on separating
subjective or moral truth from scientific truth. In elucidating
his doctrine of the 'two-sided truth', Mikhailovsky followed the
neo-Kantians in insisting that subjective and objective truth
were in no way contradictory or mutually exclusive. The truth
one finds in man's highest moral ideals does not conflict with
the truth one finds by 'looking fearlessly into the eyes of reality'.[6]

[1] IV. 405. [2] III. 219-20. [3] III. 230.
[4] IV. 451-2. [5] *Lit. V.* I. 291-5. [6] I. v.

In Mikhailovsky's view both kinds of truth should be goals of progressive thought, and both were contained in the Russian word *pravda*:

> Every time that the word *pravda* comes into my head I cannot help but be enraptured with its wonderful inner beauty. Such a word does not, it seems, exist in any other European language. It seems that only in Russia verity (*istina*) and justice (*spravedlivost*) are designated by one and the same word and are fused, as it were, into one great whole.[1]

Pravda was thus above, and yet related to, the world of men. It could only be defined negatively, as the opposite of *nepravda* (falsehood) or *krivda* (crookedness); yet for Mikhailovsky, 'truth in this wide meaning of the word has been the aim of my searching'.[2]

Thus, Mikhailovsky fitted his belief in the narod into a broader ethical theory during the mid seventies. In his 'critical populism' the people were not to be served out of a feeling of guilt and worshipped as an idol. They were to be served from a sense of honour, where the mind rather than the emotions would determine the course of action. Above all, the repentant nobleman must go to the people not empty-handed, but with the ideal of truth. Nothing less than truth—with its objective appraisal of natural events and its moral imperatives in human affairs—could be worthy of the 'holy of holies', the individual human personality.

[1] I. v.   [2] I. v.

VII

THE TURN TO REVOLUTION

By the time Mikhailovsky had fully articulated his social philosophy, a new revolutionary impulse had largely obscured the evolutionary *narodnichestvo* of the early seventies. Mikhailovsky would remain the benevolent friend and revered counsellor of all radicals. But in the second half of the decade he was faced with the new and difficult problem of defining his attitude toward the less peaceful form of narodnik belief which reached its climax in the assassination of Alexander II on 1 March 1881.

The Stimulus of War

The turn to revolution in the late seventies was in good measure precipitated—as in 1905 and 1917—by participation in a war.

The news in the early autumn of 1875 that Serbian bands had risen up against the Turks in Hercegovina had an electric effect on the radical camp. Fully a year before the Pan-Slav expansionism of Katkov and Ignatev became epidemic within Russia, a large number of Russian radicals went to the aid of their rebelling brother Slavs.[1] Revolutionary ardour was aroused among the Bakuninist *émigrés* and extremist groups in Southern Russia. But even the St. Petersburg radicals were enamoured with the cause of the rebelling Southern Slavs.

An anonymous article in the *Annals* of November 1875 complained that sympathy for the oppressed Slavs was being suppressed 'even more in Europe than in Russia, which in most of its sympathies and antipathies seems to be always waiting for the signal'.[2] The following month Uspensky set off to Belgrade from Paris to investigate and report on the situation for the journal. Mikhailovsky set the tone for the radical support of the Serbs in his 'Layman's Notes' of July 1876, when he urged approval of their cause as that of oppressed fighting oppressor

---

[1] See *Note L*, p. 191.   [2] *O.Z.*, 1875, no. 11, p. 110.

rather than Orthodox Slav fighting Turk. Indeed, Mikhail-ovsky could not keep from entertaining, however briefly, the idea that the uprising might provide a new 'popular' source for social redemption. Throughout the second half of 1876 he voiced 'great hopes' for the Slav cause, asserting that under present circumstances 'to destroy Turkey means to resolve the social question'.[1]

However, support for the Balkan insurgents was becoming at the same time the chosen cause of the Russian right. War was declared by Russia on 12/24 April 1877; and, as Russian troops rolled toward Constantinople, both the popular basis for the insurrections and the radicals' vision of a loose Slavic federa-tion were engulfed by a wave of Great Russian expansionism.[2] Thus, early in 1877, at the very moment when the Russian armies were reaching the height of their success, the radicals on the *Annals* began to sound a note of disillusionment. Mikhailovsky began to speak in the past tense of the fight for the liberation of the Slavs; and throughout the spring he expressed his growing opposition to 'pathological nationalism', and particularly to Suvorin, editor of the *New Time*, who, like Katkov during the Polish rebellion, had left a cosmopolitan liberal position for a retrogressive but popular chauvinism. In May Eliseev criticized the glorification of war by the chauvinist press: 'It is necessary to be either a great romantic or a very small philosopher . . . to find in war as war any moral uplift for society.'[3] The tale of dis-illusionment among the volunteers for the war was eloquently told in stories by Uspensky and by a talented young admirer of Mikhailovsky who had himself been a volunteer, Vsevolod Garshin.[4]

Mikhailovsky's brief infatuation with the cause of Slavic revolution and federation was dramatized in his story 'In the Interim' by the character of N. D. Dalmatov, who gave his lands to his serfs even before emancipation and lived as a manual labourer among the southern Slavs before being killed during the uprising in Hercegovina in January 1875.[5] Mikhail-

---

[1] III. 886.   [2] See *Note M*, p. 191.   [3] *O.Z.*, 1877, no. 5, p. 116.
[4] See especially G. I. Uspensky, 'Not Resurrected', *O.Z.*, 1877, no. 2; and V. M. Garshin 'Four Days', *O.Z.*, 1877, no. 10.
[5] IV. 272–3. There is no evidence of any exact historical parallel for Dalmatov, despite the intimations of D. N. Ovsyaniko-Kulikovsky, *Istoriya Russkoy Intelligentsii*, part ii, p. 86, note.

ovsky had begun to deviate slightly from the straight and narrow path of critical *narodnichestvo*; he was sowing the seeds of his own partial *rapprochement* with the revolutionary trends of the later seventies. The sense of impatience and frustration which would give impetus to this new movement was in good measure a by-product of the Balkan disillusionment. As one volunteer put it in explaining his own turn to terrorism: 'We thought that instead of freeing a foreign country, one should rather think of freeing Russia.'[1]

The Turn to Terror

As the old Bakuninist dream of a Slavic federation passed away like Bakunin himself in 1876, many disillusioned young radicals returned from Switzerland and from the Balkan wars to Russia—and particularly to St. Petersburg—to further their revolutionary ends. Mikhailovsky and his followers were to become deeply infected with this revolutionary influx. Under its influence, Mikhailovsky was to see, and indeed encourage, the forces of opposition inside Russia turning from their earlier, pacific approach to the new revolutionary *narodnichestvo* of the late seventies.

Typical of these new arrivals of the late seventies were the so-called 'Caucasians', who preached immediate insurrection on the pattern of the old peasant rebellions. Although they deliberately used Stenka Razin's term 'gangs' (*shaika*) to describe their circles, they came to St. Petersburg as professing believers in the narodnik ideology. As one radical who came from Kiev in 1875 to spur Russian radicalism into more revolutionary activity explained, the insurrectionists consciously repudiated the tradition of Nechaev, 'never having the slightest fondness for Jacobinism, and being against all kinds of centralisms, hierarchies, agents, etc.'[2] The best historian of the populists

[1] Pokhitonov, as quoted in Vera Figner, *Memoirs of a Revolutionist*, London, 1929, p. 93.
[2] Leo Deutsch, *Tvorchestvo Bakuninizma*, Berlin, 1922, p. 167. 'The Caucasians' (*Kavkaztsy*) were so called because of the prevalence of Georgians in the original 'gang' in Zurich. Most of the group returned to Russia under Dzhabadari, but some went with Chikoidze to help found the journal the *Worker* (*Rabotnik*) in Geneva. The Moscow 'gang' is best known as 'the fifty' after the court proceedings against them, the 'Trial of the Fifty' in 1876. See I. S. Dzhabadari, 'The Trial of the Fifty', *Byloe*, 1907, nos. 8–10.

observed of the turn to revolution: 'They began to concern themselves with improving methods of activity among the people, but never went on to examine the very principles on which their activity was based.'[1]

Accepting as they did a romantic faith in the people, many insurrectionists established ties with Mikhailovsky and St. Petersburg *narodnichestvo*, often through Ukrainians on the *Annals* like Krivenko and Vovchok. Mikhailovsky's growing admiration for the extremists was caused primarily by the leadership that they were taking in defending the honour of those who had 'gone to the people' and were now being brought to trial. Mikhailovsky's interest probably began as early as 1875, when two of his closest friends, Uspensky and Ivanchin-Pisarev, visited Kiev and lent their moral support to an extremist circle dedicated to liberating imprisoned radicals. He must also have been aware of the activity of Mark Natanson, an old friend and one of the original *Chaikovtsy*, who had drawn together late in 1875 a group known as the 'Northern Revolutionary Narodniks'.

Throughout 1876 the ranks of these 'revolutionary narodniks' were swollen by arrivals from the south. Their activities were climaxed by a mass demonstration of more than 2,000 on 6 December 1876, in front of the Kazan Cathedral, at which the principal speaker was a twenty-three-year-old contributor to the *Annals*, George Plekhanov. The programme of Natanson's group was steeped in the narodnik mystique. Natanson described their function as 'inscribing on a revolutionary banner the ideals already ripe in the consciousness of the people'.[2] The words that they did in fact inscribe on their red banner in the Kazan Square were the familiar *Zemlya i Volya*, which became thenceforth the name applied to the revolutionary narodniks.

Mikhailovsky did not actively join the new *Zemlya i Volya*, just as he had not personally gone among the people. But he soon came to be in as close touch with the new movement as he had been with the old, for only *Zemlya i Volya* was rising to the defence of the imprisoned radicals. It was discovered after Mikhailovsky's death that he had kept a private diary of the principal speeches and events of the political trials of the period. He visited some of the *Chaikovtsy* in the Peter and Paul Prison before

---

[1] V. Ya. Yakovlev, *Aktivnoe Narodnichestvo*, pp. 199–200.
[2] Quoted by V. N. Figner, *Memoirs*, p. 52.

the trial of 'the 193' began. Among those to whom he talked was a southern revolutionary, Yury Govorukha-Otrok.[1] When this figure became an informer and betrayed many of his fellow prisoners, Mikhailovsky was so shocked that he began to draw up plans for a novel that would centre on such a 'careerist' traitor.

By the time of the trial in September 1877 the assimilation of the southern tradition into *narodnichestvo* had been completed and the *Zemlyavoltsy* had become active in both the provinces and the capital. Concurrently, Mikhailovsky found himself in a better position than ever to be of service to the narodnik cause. For, with the illness and death of Nekrasov late in 1877, Mikhailovsky was formally appointed co-editor of the *Annals*. Since the other co-editors were devoting little time to their editorial tasks (Eliseev being in bad health and Saltykov spending much of his time abroad), Mikhailovsky became in effect editor-in-chief of the journal.

One of his first actions was to expand the 'new books' section, which had been his favourite vehicle for veiled radical propaganda since the sixties. He brought in a number of young radicals to work on this column: his long-time friend, A. I. Ivanchin-Pisarev; a young narodnik revolutionary, M. A. Protopopov; and George Plekhanov, the hero of the Kazan demonstration and a student at Mikhailovsky's old alma mater, the St. Petersburg Mining Institute. In January 1877 he published in the new books' section an article by the leading defendant in the trial of 'the 193' and a recent convert to terrorism, Nicholas Morozov.[2]

Thus, Mikhailovsky gathered around him a new group of

---

[1] S. Sinegub, *Zapiski Chaikovtsa*, Moscow-Leningrad, 1929, pp. 192, 201. Govorukha-Otrok's subsequent career would seem to justify Mikhailovsky's judgement of him. After early release from prison, he worked first for the conservative Kharkov journal, the *Southern Edge* (*Yuzhny Krai*) and then for Katkov's *Moscow News* (Sinegub, p. 318 note 93). Only a few fragments of the proposed novel *The Career of Oladushkin* (*Karera Oladushkina*) were ever published, in *Russkiya Vedomosti*, 1885, 1893, 1899.

[2] Although the article is actually signed 'N. Morozov', Kolosov attributes it to Protopopov (X, L). In either case, the very appearance of this signature in Mikhailovsky's section of the journal indicates at least a measure of sympathy with the terrorists.

For the activities of *Zemlya i Volya*, which profited greatly from the arrival in St. Petersburg in May 1877 of the Odessan revolutionary, Alexander Zhelyabov, see E. A. Serebryakov, *Obshchestvo Zemlya i Volya*, London, 1912, esp. pp. 48 ff.

radicals, imparting his moral idealism to these and the many others who sought him out at his editorial desk. Consistently he sought to dissuade them from pessimism by presenting 'the possibility of a new approach'[1] based on 'the ideas of truth and justice found in Dühring and Lange'.[2]

The moral ideals and narodnik social ends of Mikhailovsky's position had never specifically precluded a resort to more revolutionary means. In his famous article of September 1872 he affirmed that 'the basic principles of Russian life do not demand a revolution, changing the direction of their tendencies. Only the development of these principles is demanded.' But, he had added even then: 'Whether there will be in addition barricades or not is a matter of indifference—in the sense that it does not affect the conservative character of the Russian labouring question.'[3] 'Barricades' might thus be sanctioned if the end in view were not a revolution, but the defence of a moral social order. This doctrine was used by Mikhailovsky in February 1878 to justify Vera Zasulich, one of the first of the new terrorists to be brought to trial.

Zasulich had attempted to kill Trepov, the police commissioner of St. Petersburg, in January 1878. Her trial was watched with keen emotional interest by St. Petersburg radicalism, for Trepov had deeply alienated the student world the year before by subjecting to a series of cruel beatings a young organizer of the Kazan demonstration who had refused to remove his hat in the presence of police interrogators. When Zasulich was acquitted on 31 March 1878, she was borne out of the court by a jubilant crowd of students—away from a re-trial which was to have been held on new charges.

This event so excited Mikhailovsky's imagination that he turned for the first time in his career to the illegal press to give full expression to his sentiments. On 1 April he published a brochure or 'flying leaflet' (*Letuchy Listok*) at the press of a short-lived new radical journal, the *Basis* (*Nachalo*).

'March 31 will be forever a memorable day in Russian history', he wrote, 'On that day, society, "selected society" in the words of the *Moscow News*, first came to see the heroism of

[1] V. G. Korolenko, *Polnoe Sobranie Sochinenii*, St. Petersburg, 1914, i. 373–4.
[2] N. S. Rusanov, 'The Politics of N. K. Mikhailovsky', *Byloe*, 1907, no. 7, p. 129.
[3] I. 736.

the young who are perishing in prison and exile.'[1] A more bellicose attitude towards the government is now justified, Mikhailovsky contends, for 'an abyss has opened up between government and society'. Since the government sanctions the policies of men like Trepov, Mikhailovsky concedes that terrorism may be a necessary form of action.

While Mikhailovsky was reluctantly granting the necessity of terrorism, the young insurrectionists were eagerly practising it. Strategic terrorism had begun earlier in 1878 when the Kievan terrorists formed an executive committee to direct their struggle against the police.[2]

When, in November 1878, *Zemlya i Volya* drew up a co-ordinated programme and founded an illegal journal, they condoned terrorism not just as an occasional expedient, but as a general policy—assigning a special 'Disorganization Group', charged to assassinate selected officials, dynamite trains, and free political prisoners.[3]

Mikhailovsky's columns of 1878 reveal a partial acceptance of the anti-intellectual attitude which was characteristic of the insurrectionist tradition. Unlike Lavrov, Mikhailovsky did not continue to believe that critical thought was the ultimate moving force of history.[4] He would not let it call in question the moral ideals of populism. Indeed, Mikhailovsky directed some of his most caustic polemic against two men who were casting just such aspersions on narodnik ideals in his 'Letters to Learned People' in 1878.

The 'learned people' whom Mikhailovsky attacked were two professors of civil law, P. P. Tsitovich of Kharkov and B. N. Chicherin, formerly of Moscow. Each had committed the unforgivable sin of attacking the institution of the *obshchina*.[5] Mikhailovsky's June letter was addressed to Tsitovich, his July letter to Chicherin; his August–September article in praise of

---

[1] *Rev. St.*, 7. See also the attack on the passive populism of the *Week* for neglecting the Zasulich trial in his April 'Literary Notes', IV. 538.

[2] Terrorism in Kiev, as in most other centres, was initially designed largely to combat the system of informers and agents-provocateurs by means of which the police sought to break up the radical *kruzhki*. See 'From the Archives of Leo Tikhomirov', *K.A.*, 1924, no. 6, pp. 144–5.

[3] See *Note N*, p. 191.   [4] See *Note O*, p. 192.

[5] Tsitovich in *Novye Priemy Zashchity Obshchinago Zemlyavladeniya*, Odessa, 1878; and Chicherin in 'Russian Dilletantism and Communal Landholding' (co-author: V. I. Gurrier), in *Sbornik Gosudarstvennykh Znanii*, St. Petersburg, 1878.

Dühring can be considered a final salvo at the 'learned people'. In all these articles Mikhailovsky criticizes those who claim objective truth for public law, arguing that supremacy belongs to the internal moral law, to what Dühring called the 'sovereignty of the individual'. This distinction between legal and moral rightness was the perennial defence of the Russian radical on trial. Mikhailovsky's attack on the morality of the law (and his adoption of Dühring's explanation of the origins of law in repression and negation) thus provided philosophical reinforcements for an established radical outlook.

During the course of the summer Tsitovich took up Mikhailovsky's weapon and wrote a spirited rebuttal, his 'Reply to the Letters to Learned People'. Tsitovich defended the academician as a more valuable citizen than the radical *intelligent*, and scoffed at the latter's talk about 'new principles' and 'life-giving water'. In Tsitovich's view, both the *obshchina* and the radical intelligentsia itself had outlived their usefulness; the intellectuals were only projecting their own confusion into society, vulgarizing the search for truth by insisting on 'science for the layman', and breaking down 'the discipline that has been imposed on that beast known as the simple man'.[1]

Tsitovich's pamphlet underwent six reprintings and created added interest in the controversy. Mikhailovsky's eagerly awaited counter-attack was, however, of such an extreme tone that he was first cautioned by Saltykov, then warned informally by the censorship not to print it. Not until December, therefore, was a more restrained second 'Letter to Tsitovich' published, beginning with an unmistakable allusion to the earlier unpleasantness.[2]

During the unusually severe winter of 1878, the 'disorganization group' became increasingly active and finally attempted to assassinate the Tsar on 2 April. This incident—the first attempt at Tsaricide inside Russia since the Karakozov affair thirteen

---

[1] P. P. Tsitovich, *Otvet na Pisma k Uchenym Lyudyam*, Odessa, 1879, p. 35.

[2] 'Pardon the delayed response. I do not consider it either necessary or convenient to recount why it is delayed, and only ask you to believe that it is not so out of any wish on my part.' IV. 620. Although never published, the original article was read and circulated among the young revolutionaries. See Kolosov, 'Mikhailovsky in the Eighties', *Byloe* (Paris), 1909, nos. 9–10, p. 35. Tsitovich had the last word, however, in his spirited final attack on the narodniks, *Chto Delali v 'Chto Delat?'* (What they did in 'What to Do?'), Odessa, 1879.

years earlier—prompted the non-terrorists in *Zemlya i Volya*,
led by Plekhanov and Popov, to call for a general meeting to re-
establish unity of purpose among the group. The Tsar had
empowered a special commission under the Minister of Imperial
Domains, P. L. Valuev, to investigate and uproot subversion.
Envisaging a repetition of the 'white terror' after the Karakozov
affair, the young revolutionaries sought to close ranks against
the government. At successive gatherings at Lipetsk and
Veronezh in June 1879, a new revolutionary organization was
formed. Headed by a twenty-three-man executive committee
which included many southern agitators, the organization
represented the final wedding of the romantic insurrectionist
tradition with the slogans of *narodnichestvo*.[1]

It was almost inevitable that Mikhailovsky should be sought
out by the new organization. His fame had grown rapidly
throughout the seventies, and a heavily subscribed complete
edition of his works had begun to appear in 1879. At least four
of his journalistic protégés—Annensky, Ivanchin-Pisarev, Lesevich, and Protopopov—had been engaged in the preliminary
talks planning *Narodnaya Volya* during the spring of 1879. For
these men and for many others in the movement, Mikhailovsky
was a kind of a patron saint, his office a kind of shrine. They felt
like young V. G. Korolenko, later one of Russia's most famous
men of letters and then active in the preliminary discussion of
Narodnaya Volya. Korolenko felt 'something throbbing within
my chest' in February 1879, when he first met Mikhailovsky
'with his tempestuous blonde hair and his grey eyes'.[2] A whole
series of young radicals sought Mikhailovsky's counsel early in
1879; and a young student, A. P. Pribyleva-Korba, contacted
him formally on behalf of *Narodnaya Volya* to enlist him as an
editor of the organization's proposed journal. 'Mikhailovsky
listened to me with great interest and thanked me for showing
trust in him', she recalled. He agreed to work on the publication.[3]

---

[1] The leading figures on the executive committee were Mikhailov, Morozov,
Zhelyabov, and Tikhomirov. For details see Figner, *Memoirs*, pp. 62–85; and
David Footman, *Red Prelude, a Life of A. I. Zhelyabov*, London, 1944. *Narodnaya
Volya* is properly translated as 'the People's Will'; but *volya* also carries the meaning
of 'freedom'.   [2] V. G. Korolenko, *Sobranie Sochinenii*, ii. 283.
[3] A. P. Pribyleva-Korba, *Narodnaya Volya—Vospominaniya o 1870kh i 1880kh
Godov*, Moscow, 1926, p. 85.

Thus, by the summer of 1879, the new revolutionary forces had united among themselves and gained the collaboration of Mikhailovsky. The terrorist impulse which rose to dominate *Narodnaya Volya* was to encounter two main forces of opposition within the radical camp: first, from Plekhanov, who, through his short-lived protest group, *Cherny Peredel* (Black Redistribution),[1] was then the spokesman for the orthodox populist emphasis on the primacy of social and economic goals; second, from Mikhailovsky and the critical narodniks, who favoured political action rather than terrorism. This second group could not, however, dissociate itself from *Narodnaya Volya* even when it turned extremist. Mikhailovsky, who had flirted with revolutionary activism and anti-intellectualism in 1878, agreed in the summer of 1879 to co-operate with *Narodnaya Volya*. Despite the sincere attempts he was to make throughout the rest of 1879 to steer *Narodnaya Volya* away from extremism, he returned again to endorse terrorism in the critical winter of 1880–1.

A Political Programme

Ideologically, *Narodnaya Volya* was full heir to the romantic belief that truth lay in 'the will of the people', and happiness in giving up 'all that is personal for humanity'.[2] Such an uncritical outlook was bound to annoy Mikhailovsky, and his differences with the executive committee were outlined on the pages of its publication. Mikhailovsky's argument with the committee was centred on the broad strategy and aims of *Narodnaya Volya* which were, for the first time within the narodnik movement, primarily and frankly political. In the course of the debate Mikhailovsky became the first major populist inside Russia to insist on the need for a constitution and a parliamentary arena for their struggle.

The political aims of *Narodnaya Volya* were the overthrow of the Tsarist government and the establishment of a popularly elected constitutional government. The organization felt 'that

---

[1] Plekhanov's group was in fact more a splinter defection from the powerful *Narodnaya Volya* than a major schism as it is often represented. The ideological content of *Cherny Peredel* was purely narodnik and did not reflect the influence of the Marxism to which Plekhanov would later turn.

[2] N. Morozov, 'In the Name of Brotherhood', *G.M.*, 1913, no. 8, p. 87.

the people's will should make itself the sole source of law';[1] and, although it was to sponsor the assassination of the Tsar and nearly one hundred other officials, the periodical *Narodnaya Volya* condemned the assassination of President Garfield in the U.S.A.

In a country where personal freedom makes honourable ideological struggle possible, where the free will of the people determines not only the laws, but the personality of the governors—in such a country political murder as a means of struggle is an example of the very same spirit of despotism that we are seeking to destroy in Russia.[2]

There was, nevertheless, an inherent conflict between the visionary democratic ends of *Narodnaya Volya* and the sordid terroristic means it sanctioned. It contended that on certain occasions political assassination represented 'a duty to which the citizen must sacrifice himself, his feelings, and even the feelings of other people'.[3] As this concept of duty came to dominate the thinking of the executive committee, Mikhailovsky became estranged from its programme; for in the late seventies, his critical populism was leading him to develop a less extreme outlook.

As early as 1873, in his letter to Lavrov, Mikhailovsky had stated that Russia must eventually have a constitution.[4] But the idea that a constitution was a prerequisite for, rather than a result of, reform did not come until well after the repression of the movement to the people and the social unrest of the Turkish war. In 1877 he began dissuading some of his young admirers from revolutionary agitation in the countryside. He brought Ivanchin-Pisarev back from insurrectionist agitation in Yaroslav by urging that he begin working for a political programme among radicals in St. Petersburg: 'Without a constitution one cannot fight in Russia . . . throw aside your pilgrimage into the village and busy yourself with the organization of the political fight. . . .'[5]

In his illegal pamphlet in the spring of 1878 praising Vera Zasulich, Mikhailovsky called for a constitution and a

---

[1] *Literatura Sotsialno-Revolyutsionnoy Partii 'Narodnoy Voli'*, Paris, 1905, p. 867.
[2] Ibid., p. 401.   [3] Ibid., p. 903.   [4] X. 70.
[5] A. I. Ivanchin-Pisarev, 'From Reminiscences of N. K. Mikhailovsky', *Zavety*, 1914, no. 1, pp. 104–5.

legislature in the form of a *zemsky sobor*, insisting that the time
had come to put the government into the hands of society as a
whole. Moreover, Mikhailovsky suggested that if no such
popular selection of representatives for a national assembly
were permitted, 'committees of public safety' should be formed
throughout the country to rival the official bureaucracy.[1]

Thus Mikhailovsky was one of the first radicals to advocate the
political goals which became the novel feature of the *Narodnaya
Volya* programme. In the pages of the periodical, *Narodnaya
Volya*, Mikhailovsky opposed those who had lost sight of these
political ends in their enthusiasm for the terrorist means of
struggle.

In drawing up the very first issue, this conflict between the
extremists and Mikhailovsky arose. For, despite an initial decision to submit the issue to Mikhailovsky for editing and comment, the dominant terrorist group on the executive committee
insisted that Mikhailovsky should not be empowered to make
any changes in the text. They feared the possible introduction of
a more moderate and gradualist approach. As a result, the
terrorist article by Tikhomirov, *Delenda est Carthago*, was printed
as written, and an article which Mikhailovsky submitted from
his summer retreat at Kislovodsk was rejected.[2]

The second issue of the periodical *Narodnaya Volya* (20
November 1879) highlighted even more sharply the conflict
between those primarily concerned with waging the terrorist
struggle and those chiefly interested in the political ends of the
struggle. The leading article paid tribute only to 'the eternal
slogans of the popular movement' and to the utter destruction
of the state machine. It refused to discuss practical political
questions; as one of Morozov's associates later explained: 'We
did not want to bind the people. We believed that once they
had been given the chance to work out their own destiny, they
would arrange things far better than we could even imagine.'[3]

Against this romantic, anarchist outlook, which dominated
the executive committee, Mikhailovsky directed his first
'Political Letter of a Socialist'. The letter, which appeared in
the same issue bearing a false Geneva postmark and 'greetings

---

[1] *Rev. St.*, pp. 7 ff.   [2] See *Note P*, p. 192.
[3] L. E. Shishko, quoted in Kolosov 'Bakunin and Mikhailovsky in the Old
Narodnichestvo', *G.M.*, 1913, no. 5, p. 65.

from the land of Rousseau', developed the altogether new idea
in populist thought that political freedoms are prerequisites for
the struggle with autocracy. Mikhailovsky admits that in
Western Europe political freedoms have been only formal, and
that liberal constitutions were in part responsible for the rise of
the hated bourgeoisie. But he argues that it does not follow that
the struggle for social and economic progress *cannot* be conducted in the political arena. The granting of a constitution
could not, in Mikhailovsky's view, give to the bourgeoisie in
Russia any more power than it already possessed. The pressing
problem is not the killing of this or that official, but the effective
overthrow of autocracy itself.

Revolutionary people are counting on a popular uprising. This
is a matter of belief. I do not share it. But even from the viewpoint
of the believer I ask: When is a popular uprising more likely? When
at the summit of the political order there sits the distant semi-myth-
ical Tsar, in whom the unenlightened people out of habit still
believe—or when the country is ruled by elected people, ordinary
people, without any mystical eagle?[1]

He goes on to challenge the emotional insurrectionism of the
Narodnaya Volya programme, which he had not been permitted
to modify:

The prejudice against political struggle has been nursed along
throughout all Russian history, training us to live not in the practice
of the present from which autocracy drives out all honourable
activity, but in the future with theories and fantasies. I repeat: the
most worthy people, the salt of the Russian earth, are infected with
this malady. The time has come, and already for some time now, to
get over it, to understand that political nepotism is profitable only
to enemies of the people. A constitutional régime is the question of
tomorrow in Russia. This tomorrow will not bring a resolution of
the social question. But, really, do you want to fold up your hands
tomorrow? Are you really tired of fighting? Believe me, even the
most unified popular revolution, if it were possible, would not permit
you to rest on your laurels, but would demand a new exertion, a
new struggle. Live a century, struggle a century![2]

[1] *Literatura Narodnoy Voli*, p. 90.
[2] Ibid., p. 91. The last slogan, which was often repeated by radicals (*Vek zhivi,
vek boris*), is a variant on the standard Russian proverb for 'live and learn' (*Vek
zhivi, vek uchis*).

In the third issue (1 January 1880), the difference between
Mikhailovsky and the executive committee became even more
striking. The anonymous leading article reaffirmed the
Bakuninist doctrine that 'reform can only have the character
of revolution. . . . We, revolutionaries, in our most utopian
of plans, have always regarded the people as the supreme
managers of their own fate, continually placing their will
higher than all our ideals.'[1] The basic tone of the issue was well
summarized in the citation with which one of the articles
began: 'Society has only one necessary relationship to government—to put it to death.'[2]

Against this categorical rejection of the political struggle,
Mikhailovsky insisted in his second 'Political Letter of a Socialist' that terrorism 'contains nothing socialistic in it'. It does not
avoid the political struggle, but merely conducts it in an un-
profitable fashion. 'Neither Geiking nor Kropotkin should be
killed, but the idea of autocracy', he urges in direct criticism of
two assassinations recently carried out by the executive committee. The *Narodnaya Volya* editors and terrorist theoreticians,
Morozov and Tikhomirov, felt obliged to put in a footnote saying:
'We do not fully understand the author's viewpoint on political
assassination. In any case we do not assume responsibility for
his opinion.'[3] Mikhailovsky goes on to plead with the *Narodovoltsy* to concentrate on their positive demands for a constitution
and a popular assembly. He argues against suicidal revolutionary martyrdom:

I see my unhappy fatherland! A white shroud of snow lies on thy
fields and meadows. Ice clogs thy rivers, ponds, and lakes. . . .
But here life is beginning to shine forth. It is the Russian revolution.
Clearer, clearer burns its consecrated flame, melting away the
shroud of snow and . . . . Deceived! These people can only die and
do not want to live.[4]

So insistent is Mikhailovsky on launching an effective political
struggle that he suggests, for the first time in the radical camp,
a united front with moderate reformist elements. The elements
which Mikhailovsky had in mind were not the classical liberals

---

[1] *Literatura Narodnoy Voli*, pp. 155-6.
[2] Quoted from the former Communard, Edouard Vaillant, in ibid., p. 180.
[3] Ibid., p. 172 and note.   [4] Ibid., p. 173.

on the *Herald of Europe*, but the reformers in the provincial zemstvos who had suddenly, late in 1878, become numerous and articulate.[1]

These 'zemstvo liberals' were largely professional men from the provinces. Their sudden appearance on the scene seemed to offer renewed hope that some sort of span might be built across the gap which had come to separate the radical intelligentsia from all other reformers in Russia.

In late 1879 Mikhailovsky represented the focal point for all hopes of uniting the two camps. Mikhailovsky had enlisted as contributors to the *Annals* two of the principal zemstvo liberals, Dragomanov and Ziber; the leader of the movement, Ivan Petrunkevich, was an old personal friend. After failing in his bid for a united front with the *Zemlyavoltsy* in December 1878, Petrunkevich conferred with Mikhailovsky in April 1879. He was unsuccessful in gaining Mikhailovsky's active co-operation at that time,[2] but he may have planted in Mikhailovsky's mind the idea of a *rapprochement*. For in his second 'Political Letter', Mikhailovsky declared:

> Union with the liberals is not to be feared if you approach them honourably and, without cant, explain to them your sacred motto: 'land and liberty'. They will come to you and not you to them. In the practical struggle it is stupid not to profit from unions, however haphazard and temporary. And I confess to you that I think many liberals are much closer to you than you think. They would be still closer if they clearly understood the peculiarities of Russian life.[3]

Indeed, these special Russian circumstances make the prospects for social progress through a popular assembly greater than elsewhere. Mikhailovsky cites the American Homestead

---

[1] The Tsar had unconsciously called the zemstvos back to life as organs of reform, by indicating, in proclamations of August and November 1878, that he was counting on zemstvo support both in combating terrorism and in forming plans for 'gradual development through the peaceful, legal method'. A series of radical political demands by zemstvo leaders and the formation of a 'league of zemstvo constitutionalists' soon followed. See I. P. Belokonsky, 'The Zemstvo Movement', *Byloe*, 1907, no. 4, pp. 234–8.

[2] According to Petrunkevich, Mikhailovsky 'believed in our personal sincerity, but not in the success of our project and could not sympathize with it because now the people need land, not a constitution . . . '. V. Ya. Yakovlev, *Iz Istorii Politicheskoy Borby v 70kh i 80kh gg. XIX veka*, Moscow, 1912, p. 399, note 1. Uspensky rejected in similar terms a parallel overture from Victor Goltsev of the Tver Zemstvo.

[3] *Literatura Narodnoy Voli*, p. 174.

Law as an example of social gain through legislation and a vindication of 'the principle of ownership of land by the farmer'.

How much easier to implement this principle in our country, where it lives not only in the soul of the people, but in the conscience of every decent and intelligent man.[1]

Thus in this second and last 'Political Letter' Mikhailovsky confirmed his new-found belief in the necessity of a political struggle and reasserted the independence of his critical *narod-nichestvo*.

Mikhailovsky v. Loris

By the autumn of 1879 it became clear that Mikhailovsky's *alter ego* was rebelling at the idea of *rapprochement* with liberal reformism. His dacha was raided by the police in the summer;[2] and on the night of 13 October he was found at a clandestine meeting of St. Petersburg students, most of whom were *Narodovoltsy*.[3] In his 'Literary Sketches' of November Mikhailovsky denounced the moderate reformist outlook of fashionable society, and particularly the renegade radical, Suvorin.[4] He attacks the 'wavering' and 'ideal-lessness' of liberalism, and, in particular, the liberal critic Eugene Markov, who had accused the narodniks of enforcing a narrow 'party spirit' (*partiinost*) in literary criticism.[5] In his December column Mikhailovsky expresses renewed admiration for Proudhon's rejection of political parties and programmes.

The growth of government sponsored reformism also struck him ill, for two of the leading participants in this 'official liberalism' were Chicherin and Tsitovich, the 'learned people' whom he had attacked only the year before. Chicherin had become the principal contributor to the official *Collection of Government Knowledge (Sbornik Gosudarstvennykh Znanii)* and had begun to establish close contacts with the Tsarist court. Chicherin's interest in expanding the functions of the zemstvos may have put the kiss of death on the zemstvo movement for Mikhailovsky, who was

---

[1] *Literatura Narodnoy Voli*, p. 175.   [2] IV. 978–81.
[3] *Literatura Narodnoy Voli*, p. 137 note.   [4] IV. 816.
[5] IV. 817–18, 820, 826. Terms like 'ideal-less' and 'party spirit' have of course become familiar through subsequent Soviet usage. Note also the use of the term 'enemy of the people' in the first issue of *Narodnaya Volya*. See *Literatura Narodnoy Voli*, pp. 32–33.

deeply apprehensive of Chicherin's organic concept of the state.[1] Having attracted the government's attention with his spirited replies to Mikhailovsky, Tsitovich was given the editorship of a new semi-official weekly, the *Shore (Bereg)*, designed to introduce 'official liberalism' into the intellectual arena of St. Petersburg. The very existence of such a journal was viewed as an affront to the intelligentsia, and when it failed in 1880, Mikhailovsky tartly commented that Tsitovich's journal was well named, for 'he was indeed a little fish out of water, unhappily washed up on the *Shore*'.[2]

By early 1880 a sense of crisis and impending change was clearly in the air. Three attempts had been made on the life of the Tsar since the terrorist campaign began, and the bewildered Tsar was receiving advice and criticism from all quarters. When the *Narodovoltsy* set off a large explosion within the very confines of the Winter Palace on 4 February 1880, Alexander realized that his indecision would have to end. One week after the attempted assassination he appointed a distinguished provincial governor, Count Michael Tarielovich Loris-Melikov, to head a special commission to restore order and investigate possible reforms.

A hero of both the Crimean and Turkish wars, Loris seemed to possess the aura of a national figure above faction and self-interest. As a friend of Nekrasov and a successful governor-general of Kharkov, where he had won the confidence of the local zemstvos while suppressing terrorism, he appeared to be a logical figure for winning over the milder reformist elements of the intelligentsia into the camp of 'official liberalism'. Yet, from the beginning, all parties tended to distrust this part-Armenian outsider; in the St. Petersburg of 1880 standing aside from party conflicts brought suspicion and contempt rather than respect and trust.

By December 1879 the Kharkov branch of *Narodnaya Volya*

---

[1] The *émigré* radicals became permanently estranged from the *émigré* leaders of the zemstvo movement at about this same time, and for the same reason—because the zemstvo leader (Dragomanov) was on too familiar terms with Tsarist officials (particularly Peter Shuvalov, former head of the Third Section). Mikhailovsky's animosity towards Chicherin is almost exactly paralleled by the split which developed abroad between the narodnik journal, the *Common Cause (Obshchee Delo)* and Dragomanov's the *Free Word (Volnoe Slovo)*. See V. Ya. Yakovlev, *Iz Istorii*, pp. 389–91.

[2] IV. 900.

had begun to speak of 'the wily double-meaning policy of Loris-Melikov'. His stern prosecution of the Kharkov terrorists was not resented so much as his use of 'semi-liberal phrases', which are so saccharine in tone that 'noble ladies cannot speak of this "angelic soul" without tears of emotion in their eyes'.[1]

The initial actions and announcements of Loris's 'Dictatorship of the Heart' may have raised many radical hopes to expect more than any man could have accomplished.[2] But whatever Loris had done, it is unlikely that he could have appeased the sense of desperation that was rising within *Narodnaya Volya* at the time of his accession to power. On 18 January the organization's press had been found and confiscated, and on 3 February its 'ambassador' to the revolutionary movements of Western Europe, Leo Hartmann, was arrested in Paris by the French government at the personal request of the Tsar. For weeks thereafter it was rumoured that 19 February—the twentieth anniversary of the emancipation edict—would be the date for some concerted counter-attack by the revolutionary forces. The appointment of Loris just a week before this date was viewed by many of the revolutionaries as a calculated move to deflate their zeal at this critical time.

The anniversary passed without incident, the Tsar remaining within the Winter Palace while a crowd of some 6,000 gathered expectantly outside. However, when Loris appeared on the streets the following day, an attempt was made on his life by I. O. Mlodetsky, a young Polish student acting on his own initiative. Mikhailovsky and his associates did not condone such random terrorism; but they did look, in this period of renewed social expectations, for official action which would transcend mere reprisal. Accordingly, one of Mikhailovsky's young protégés, Vsevolod Garshin, wrote a letter to Loris on 21 February condemning terrorism, but beseeching Loris to pardon Mlodetsky as a sign of moral greatness and the first step in the creation of a new social order. Two letters and a visit could not

---

[1] *Literatura Narodnoy Voli*, p. 203.

[2] Loris dismissed two ministers who had been symbols of reaction, Dmitry Tolstoy (Education) and General Greig (Finance), and agreed to curtail the activities of the Third Section. The result of the latter, however, proved to be merely the transfer of all police affairs into the Ministry of the Interior (under V. K. Plehve), the weakening of the independent powers of the judiciary, and, consequently, a lessening of the chances for acquittal of suspected revolutionaries.

dissuade Loris from sanctioning the hanging of Mlodetsky after a harrowing parade through St. Petersburg on 29 February.[1]

By rejecting Garshin's entreaties, Loris cut off the last avenue —however improbable—that might have led to a reconciliation with the radical intelligentsia. His activities in Kharkov had already won the enmity of the extremists; his harsh reaction to the Mlodetsky affair now guaranteed him the opposition of Mikhailovsky, who took the lead in attacking Loris.

In an anonymous 'Towards a Characterization of Loris-Melikov', which appeared on 1 June 1880,[2] Mikhailovsky spoke of 'the fox's tail and the wolf's mouth' of Loris—a metaphor that was to be echoed in subsequent radical propaganda. The 'fox's tail' was cunningly wagged when Loris spread initial hints of impending reforms. But from his very first movements the count showed that he also had a 'wolf's mouth' by ordering the execution of Mlodetsky.[3] Loris becomes 'an Asian diplomat' who is as cruel as he is clever. The way in which the press allows itself to be deceived by the fox's tail particularly distresses Mikhailovsky: 'Let Europe know what a liberal Asiatic is, how adroitly he is able to puff up his miserable handouts. . . .'[4]

Loris's policy of sternly repressing the revolutionary movement could hardly avoid affecting many who were not terrorists; it is not unlikely that the arbitrary arrest and deportation to Siberia of N. F. Annensky, one of Mikhailovsky's young writers on the 'New Books' section of the *Annals*, was responsible for further disillusionment with the intentions of the count. Mikhailovsky began secretly to see more of the extremists during the summer of 1880. 'You have a way of disappearing so that no trace of you can be found. No one knows anything about you', Saltykov wrote to Mikhailovsky on 28 June, apropos of his unprecedented absences from his editorial desk.[5]

The 'dictatorship of the heart' came to an end on 6 August, when Loris dissolved his special commission and became Minister of the Interior. Exactly a month later, Loris, in his

---

[1] See Garshin's letter and notes *K.A.*, 1934, no. 3, pp. 143–4. Garshin was living at the time with two other close associates of Mikhailovsky, Krivenko and Rusanov. See the latter's 'Literary Memoirs', *Byloe*, 1906, no. 12, pp. 50–53.

[2] In the fourth issue of the periodical *Narodnaya Volya*, which had assumed the name *Listok Narodnoy Voli*.

[3] *Literatura Narodnoy Voli*, p. 247.   [4] Ibid., p. 249.

[5] M. E. Saltykov, *Pisma, 1845–1889*, Leningrad, 1924, p. 179.

new capacity, summoned a personal conference with leading journalists for the announced purpose of reaching an understanding which would permit abolition of the censorship. Once again, the radicals assumed that more was involved than Loris had intended. They were annoyed when no discussion of broader issues was countenanced, and when Loris parried all questions with appeals to trust in his good intentions. Challenged to commit himself on a specific issue by one of Mikhailovsky's old friends, Loris finally lost his temper and threatened arbitrarily to shut the questioner's journal.

Mikhailovsky saw in this performance a vindication of his theory of wolf and fox; for, while Loris promised freedom of the press, he was at the same time quite willing to issue capricious threats of closure. In an article for the journal *Narodnaya Volya* on 20 September, Mikhailovsky expressed disappointment, although he could hardly have been surprised, at the failure to invite *Narodnaya Volya* to the meeting. He rebuked Loris for contending that 'paradise is found only in his own, the count's, good intentions'.[1]

Mikhailovsky was probably the only man with sufficient stature among both legal and illegal publicists to serve as a bridge between the reformists and the revolutionaries. But, despite his own critical outlook, Mikhailovsky declined to do so, and ended by putting aside his earlier social philosophy to gratify his passion for immediate social justice. The final words of his report on the September meeting with Loris were an ominous prelude to the accelerated terrorist programme of late 1880 and early 1881: 'Brothers! You have been seeing paradise in your dreams! It is time to wake up.'[2] Paradise must come about on earth, not in dreams; the Tsarist bureaucracy must be annihilated, since it cannot be won over.

Even his legal 'Literary Notes' reflect this new revolutionary impulse. He came out in December against those who 'recommend waiting as a political principal, a programme. Fifteen years ago those might have been reasonable words. Now they are behind the times.'[3] At the same time he utilized his position of prominence among journalists in St. Petersburg to the advantage of the radical cause. He used the Wednesday gatherings

[1] *Literatura Narodnoy Voli*, p. 280.
[2] Ibid., p. 281.   [3] IV. 1019.

at his house, which had become fashionable occasions among the intelligentsia, for obtaining information and governmental material for *Narodnaya Volya*.[1]

With Mikhailovsky joining in the call to arms and aiding the revolutionary forces, it was plain that all hope of moderation had gone from the radical camp. Accordingly, between October 1880 and March 1881, three more attempts were made on the life of the Tsar, with the last succeeding in killing him on 1 March 1881. A final irony lay in the fact that the murder occurred just two days before the distrusted Loris was to present the Tsar with a draft constitution which he had been secretly preparing since January.[2] The political concessions which Mikhailovsky had sought in his 1879 'Political Letters' might have been substantially granted but for the terrorist blow, which Mikhailovsky helped to bring on with his own turn to revolution late in 1880.

Extremism had triumphed in the narodnik camp, and it would bring forth its extremist counterpart in the government. With the assassination of the Tsar, his son Alexander III succeeded to the throne, haunted by the fate of his father and dominated by his reactionary tutor, Constantine Pobedonostsev. From his post as procurator of the synod, Pobedonostsev would play the leading role in forging the policy of 'freezing-up' Russian society which prevailed during the fourteen years of Alexander III's reign. It is not likely that Mikhailovsky alone could have provided a bridge between the illegal revolutionaries and the legal reformers to prevent this triumph of reaction. But it is important to realize that in the crucial months of 1880, Mikhailovsky consciously gave up trying. He did not follow the logic of his own critical narodnik position built up against the pacifists of the *Week* in 1876 and against *Narodnaya Volya* in 1879. Sensing the imminence of social change, he ceased calling for moderation. He had succumbed to the belief which lay at the very heart of *narodnichestvo*, faith in the possibility of a messianic transformation of society.

[1] A. I. Ivanchin-Pisarev, 'Reminiscences of N. K. Mikhailovsky', loc. cit., pp. 115–16. Since he is the only memoirist mentioning this, it is not probable that Mikhailovsky engaged in much of this rather dangerous practice.

[2] P. E. Shchegolev, 'From the History of the "Constitutional Murmurings"', 1879–81', *Byloe*, 1906, no. 12, pp. 261–87.

VIII

THE SECOND MYTH: THE VISION OF A 'TRUE CHRISTIANITY'

THE populists cannot be understood solely in terms of the externals of what they did and said. It is not enough, for instance, merely to say that they believed in the *obshchina* and the artel and idealized the French radical tradition and the American federation. For one may still ask: whence came the vision of a better society from which all of these beliefs were derived? Nor is it enough merely to catalogue the Western thinkers who influenced the Russians. For the prior problem remains: whence came the deep sense of historical expectation and moral longing which made the Russians turn to a study of these thinkers with such unique intensity? Having examined in some detail what Mikhailovsky and his colleagues did and what they read, attention must now be turned to the vision which lay behind it all. One must look for the essence of their faith, without which the bewildering profusion of their works may always remain incomprehensible.

No inner understanding of this impassioned movement of secular protest is possible without an appreciation of its deeply religious basis. Viewed in the context of a society that had known no renaissance or reformation and was indeed just emerging from the social and religious world of the Middle Ages, populism can be said to represent for Russia a unique form of protesting, if not Protestant, Christianity. Indeed, close examination reveals the unmistakable imprint of Christian ideas on the moral and historical outlook of the narodniks. The forms of schismatic Christian dissent still prevalent in Russia produced an impact as did the more general nineteenth-century idea of 'a new Christianity', a religion of humanity to be based on Christian morality without Christian metaphysics. Russian populism was in truth such a 'new Christianity', in which the Jesus of the New Testament provided the hope of glory for men who no longer looked to Him for the means of grace.

Sectarian Roots

In discussing the men of the seventies on the eve of the movement to the people, Mikhailovsky had said that they could only be understood as a kind of religious sect: 'precisely a sect, because here were all the characteristic signs of sectarians: sincerity, formalism, fanaticism, reticence, and a strict but narrow logic.'[1] A close examination of the movement reveals that there were deep internal links as well as external similarities between populism and the sectarian religious traditions of Russia.

Sectarianism in Russia was largely the product of the great religious schism (*raskol*) which began in the seventeenth century and lived on as a movement of moral and political protest to the rule of the Romanovs. The 'Old Believers', as they came to be called, refused to accept the new Greek ecclesiastical reforms which the Tsars were introducing into the Church in the mid seventeenth century. After being condemned as heretical in 1666, they came to view themselves as the defenders of the true organic Christian community against the new Caesar (Tsar), the 'false pretender' to a throne reserved only for Christ. Consistently and well into the nineteenth century, the schismatics and other related sects kept alive in the popular imagination this dichotomy between the old, undefiled Christian community and the perversions of the anti-Christ in authority.

The schismatic tradition was also characterized by periodic bursts of apocalyptical expectation. There was indeed an almost apostolic succession of sectarian groups: the old ritualists, the 'priestless ones', the 'dwellers by the sea', the Theodosians, the Philipists, and finally in the thirties and forties of the nineteenth century, the 'people of Christ', the 'runners', and the 'wanderers'. Each group separated itself from the main body of sectarians to preserve the all-important original cause of keeping alive the 'true Christianity', undefiled by compromise with the ways of the world and constantly prepared for the second coming of Christ. This dual belief in a true Christian community uncompromised with temporal authority and in the imminent fulfilment of world history was present as well in other forms of Christian dissent (which had a common development with, though not actual origin in, the Russian schism)

[1] II. 647–8.

such as the 'milk drinkers' (*Molokane*) and 'wrestlers with the Spirit' (*Dukhobortsy*).

Thus, up until the Crimean War, there was a continuous and vital tradition of protest among large sections of rural Russia—believing alike in the need for a truer communal Christianity and in the imminence of a new age in history.

The sectarians traditionally made their converts from within the Orthodox community; and nowhere were the ideas of the sectarians studied with greater interest and intensity than in the seminaries of Russia in the mid nineteenth century. In the decade after Crimea the radical camp became infused with the visionary ideas of the sectarians through the strikingly large number of radical leaders who were either sons of priests or educated for the priesthood. The most important single channel through which sectarian ideas entered the radical tradition was provided by Mikhailovsky's lifelong friend, Gregory Eliseev.

Eliseev was educated in the finest theological academies of Kazan and Moscow, and in the late forties, he became a professor of church history at the Kazan Academy. During his early researches on the spread of Christianity in Russia he became oppressed by the failure of the land-owning classes to see the moral message of Christianity, and in 1852 he published a brochure which marked his turn from theology to social radicalism: 'On the Life of the Privileged Classes in Russia, On the Sad Life of the People, and on Serfdom.' Like the many who would follow him in this change, Eliseev saw no conflict between his early theological interests and his later career as a radical pamphleteer. 'My theoretical, religious world-outlook must have changed with the years,' he later wrote, 'but my moral world-view has remained the same. Those moral truths which I taught in sermons and set forth in my lectures to students . . . are the very same that I am setting forth and have in view in my internal reviews.'[1]

At the academy, Eliseev had become interested in the schismatics, and an admiration for the moral purity of their communities helped him decide to leave the seminary altogether. His influence made itself felt, in turn, on one of his pupils at Kazan, A. P. Shchapov, who became the first to work for a united front between the radicals and the schismatics. In 1859,

---

[1] Quoted from unpublished papers of Eliseev by Mikhailovsky in *Lit. V.* I. 445.

under the influence of Eliseev, Shchapov wrote a brochure, 'The Voice of the Old Russian Church on the Betterment of the Life of an Unfree People'—a work which eventually led to his expulsion from the seminary.[1] In 1862 he published his monumental work, *Zemstvo i Raskol*, and in the same year he arrived in St. Petersburg and began directing the attempt of the first *Zemlya i Volya* to co-ordinate their anti-governmental activity with that of the Old Believers. At the same time Herzen's *Bell* had been induced to print in London a special supplement, *The Popular Assembly* (*Obshchee Veche*), for distribution to the Old Believers through *Zemlya i Volya*. Edited by Ogarev, Kelsiev,[2] and an anonymous '*sektant*', the journal marked the beginning of a continuous effort throughout the early sixties by Kelsiev to organize the *raskolniki* for radical activity. In addition to Kelsiev, a bishop of the Old Believers came to London late in 1861 to establish contact with Herzen and Bakunin.

Meanwhile, the prevalence of ex-seminarians was becoming so widespread in St. Petersburg that the term 'seminarian' was becoming synonymous with 'revolutionary' and Nekrasov was referring to his staff on the *Contemporary* as 'my consistory'.

This early alliance between the radicals and the Old Believers was as short-lived as the *Bell* and the first *Zemlya i Volya*, both of which faded into oblivion after the failure of the Polish rebellion in 1863. The more extreme circles of the mid sixties were also under the influence of sectarian ideas, however.[3] The Ishutin circle, to which Karakozov belonged, was recruited almost entirely from a circle of Saratov 'seminarians' first drawn together by A. Kh. Khristoforov, another former student at the Kazan Theological Academy who had been expelled in 1861. This Saratov circle read Proudhon and the French socialists together with the New Testament and histories of Russian sectarianism. Ishutin confessed at his trial that he acknowledged only three masters: Christ, St. Paul, and Chernyshevsky.[4]

---

[1] A. P. Shchapov, *Sochineniya*, St. Petersburg, 1906, i. 1–15.

[2] *Supra*, p. 49.

[3] It must be remembered that influence flowed almost entirely in a one-way channel from the schismatics to the radicals. Kelsiev had little success in recruiting radicals from among the schismatics; and in 1864 the metropolitan of the Old Believers denounced 'the London atheists', thus sounding the first of many *raskolnik* rejections of collaboration with the radical intelligentsia.

[4] 'The Karakozov Attempt', *K.A.*, 1926, no. 4, p. 93.

Khudyakov, the effective leader of this group, had entitled his own radical testament of faith, written in Geneva earlier in the year, *For True Christians* (*Dlya Istinnykh Khristian*). In it he developed the standard sectarian contrast between an idealized community ruled only by Christian love and that of the new Caesar, the Tsar. As a student of early Russian history and religion, Khudyakov may well have been in touch with the leaders of the 'milk-drinker' sect, who published their 'Confessions of Faith of the Spiritual Christians' in Geneva in the same year.[1]

In the dark years after the Karakozov affair, the radicals turned with increased enthusiasm to a study of the sectarians. They studied not only *The Popular Assembly* and Shchapov's works, but Kelsiev's *Collection of Governmental Information on the Raskol*, and a new *émigré* journal by the *raskolniki*, *Truth* (*Istina*), which began to appear in Prussia in 1867. Some of the interest was, ironically, prompted by a series of articles in Katkov's *Russian Herald*, which expressed the fear that anti-autocratic forces might make use of the schismatics.[2] So much was written on the Russian dissenters in the *Annals* and the *Cause* from 1867 to 1870 that subsequent studies on the subject are dependent on these journals as primary sources.[3] Writers on the sectarians contrasted the brotherly atmosphere of their communities with the prevailing social order in Russia. They pointed out that sectarian leaders were chosen by the community rather than by the Tsar or the bureaucracy, and that the sectarians had sought above all to defend the rights of the local community. When some, like Shchapov, drew too radical a social message from their studies of the schism, they attracted warnings from the censor.[4]

The appeal of the *raskolniki* to the radicals of this period lay in their lofty moral idealism and their power to survive and flourish despite two centuries of persecution. They were, more-

---

[1] See *Note Q*, p. 192.

[2] N. I. Subottin, 'The *Raskol* as a Weapon for Anti-government Parties', *Russky Vestnik*, 1866, nos. 9, 11; and 1867, nos. 4, 5. Subottin later served as editor of the *Brotherly Word* (*Bratskoe Slovo*), a quarterly journal on the *raskol* which appeared intermittently from 1875 to 1915.

[3] See particularly Andreev, *The Raskol and its Significance in Russian Popular History*, St. Petersburg, 1870; and articles by Vishuyakov (*Nevsky Sbornik*, 1867), Kostomarov (*O.Z.*, 1869, no. 3), Filibert (*O.Z.*, 1870, no. 3), Atav (*O.Z.*, 1870, no. 4), and Stolov (*O.Z.*, 1870, no. 6).

[4] A. P. Shchapov, *Sochineniya*, i. 580 note.

over, seen as the guardians of the idealized old life against the empty and impersonal new. Like Avvakum, the original leader and martyr of the Old Believers, the narodniks felt a prophetic hate for 'the lovers of new things . . . who have fallen away from the truth'.[1] The truth-seeking intelligentsia shared Avvakum's feeling that *pravda*—the absolute, Platonic truth of the East— was being deflowered by irreverent and petty innovators. They shared as well Avvakum's distinction between the Tartar God, Mohammed, who taught domination and power, and Christ, who opposed these forces.[2]

The radicals saw in the schismatics representatives of the same 'True Christianity'—the Christianity of morals rather than metaphysics—of which they conceived themselves to be apostles. The positive social ethic of sectarian communities, where the only punishment was exclusion from their society, was contrasted with the repressive basis of Tsarist society. But the narodniks were most deeply influenced by the schismatics' belief that all spiritual truth can and must be realized on earth. A messianic belief in the coming kingdom of righteousness was, indeed, the most important single doctrine that the radicals took from the religious dissenters.

In the Old Believers' understanding of human history, the incarnation was not simply the unique redemptive event in an otherwise corrupt human history (as in the Augustinian view of history) or a cosmic redemptive force beyond the time process (as in Origen and the main stream of Eastern Christianity). The incarnation was for them the opening event of a new historical epoch, unique only in the sense that it was the first event to give man the possibility of uniting the human with the divine. Christ first lived the life of God-manhood; now this was a status available to all men who would reject the false gods and anti-Christs that appear in human affairs.[3] The belief that Christ had opened up the possibility of a new age in human history was

[1] *The Life of the Archpriest Avvakum by Himself*, London, 1924, p. 34.
[2] Ibid., p. 131.
[3] In the *raskolnik* chronology, two principal false pretenders to the throne of Christ had appeared: the Pope of Rome and the Tsar of all the Russias. The Pope had become anti-Christ by A.D. 1000 (shortly before the definitive East–West split) and the Tsar, in 1666 (when the Nikonian reforms were made requisite articles of faith in the Russian Church). Great significance was thus attached to the date, 1666; for it was the number formed by adding the apocalyptical number of the beast (666) to the date of the emergence of the Pope as anti-Christ.

transferred from the scattered sectarian communities into the centre of radical thought in St. Petersburg largely through the figure of Nicholas Chaikovsky, in whose circles the narodnik movement was born.

Chaikovsky had made several excursions out of St. Petersburg in the sixties into communities of schismatics and had been deeply impressed by their pacific and moralistic outlook. His experience among them may have helped turn his mind to a new sect among the intelligentsia of the early seventies devoted to the principle of 'God-manhood' (*Bogochelovechestvo*). This nameless sect had been founded by a friend of Chaikovsky and former seminarian;[1] its vision was one of *raskolnik*-like expectation of the kingdom of righteousness. It preached absolute selflessness and non-violence, declaring that the incarnation was but the first in a series of historical dispensations that would bring about the kingdom of heaven on earth. Although few of the *Chaikovtsy* actually joined their leader in espousing this new form of sectarian belief, the sense of historical expectation radiated out from him and accounted for his central place in the movements of the early seventies. So important was this sense of millennial expectation to Chaikovsky, that, after the movement to the people had been crushed, Chaikovsky left for America, where he became a leader among the Shakers—a sect also preaching that Christ was but the first in a series of new God-men, and that men should return to a 'take no thought for the morrow' existence, literally shaking in anticipation of the final coming.[2]

Turning from Chaikovsky, the practical leader of the movement to the people, to Lavrov, who provided the call to action, one finds that he was writing articles on the Mormons, Shakers, and other millenarian sects in America at the very time he was composing the *Historical Letters*.[3] These articles betrayed

[1] A. K. Malikov, who was also a member of the *Ishutintsy* and participated in an attempt to liberate Chernyshevsky before turning to found the new sect in 1870–1. His Orel estate was the centre of the movement and was visited by many of the *Chaikovtsy*. Malikov's role as prophet of the new religion produced the desired effect on his children, at least, who were reputed to inform visitors on arrival that 'Daddy is God'. M. Frolenko, 'From the Distant Past', *M.G.*, 1908, no. 7, pp. 96, 99. Cf. Frolenko, 'Chaikovsky and His God-manhood', *K. i S.*, 1926, no. 5.

[2] On the experiences of Chaikovsky in America, first in the utopian community in Kansas of V. K. Geins (William Frey) and then among the Shakers, see David Hecht, *Russian Radicals Look to America*, Harvard, 1947, pp. 196–216.

[3] See *Note R*, p. 192.

admiration for the sects considered; and it is possible that Christian sectarianism may have exerted additional influence on him through *Dukhobor* leaders, who were in exile at Vologda at the same time as he. In any event, shortly after his *hegira* to Paris in 1870, on the eve of the Paris commune and of the narodnik movement in Russia, Lavrov's writings have more the tone of Russian sectarianism than of dispassionate Western positivism. One need only consider the lines he wrote in 1870 for an occasion of no special significance on the positivist or revolutionary calendar, Christmas:

Messiya Istinny rodilsya	The true Messiah was born
Vsesilny Bogo-chelovek	The all-powerful God-man
On v mysli nashey voplotilsya	In our thought was he incarnated
On—pravda, bratstvo, mir—vo-vek!¹	He is truth, brotherhood, peace, eternally!

   The personal challenge in the *Letters* illustrates how the populists maintained the sectarian pattern of appeal to repentance and rebirth even when rejecting Christian belief. After appealing to man's sense of sinful responsibility ('What shall we do not to be responsible before posterity for new sufferings of humanity?'), Lavrov exhorts him to take up the mantle of faith ('Live according to the ideal that you have set before you as the ideal of the *developed man*'), holding out the promise of salvation to all ('Every person who thinks critically and is resolved to carry his thought into life can be an agent of progress').²

   As this sense of messianic expectation swept through the intelligentsia in the early seventies, the need began to be felt for a clear statement of the new Christ-like morality to be followed in anticipation of the apocalypse. Among those radicals who attempted to draw up the moral philosophy of the new religion were Bervi, with his *How One should Live by the Laws of Nature and Truth* (*Kak Dolzhno Zhit po Zakonam Prirody i Pravdy*) in 1873, and Kravchinsky, with his 1872 pamphlet *The Word of a Believer to the People* (*Slovo Veruyushchago k Narodu*).³ Among the groups that continued the idea of incarnating a pure Christian community in radical circles well after the fading of the God-manhood sect

---

¹ *G.M.*, 1916, no. 7/8, p. 142.
² P. L. Lavrov, *Istoricheskie Pisma*, pp. 92, 94, 107.
³ See V. V. Bervi, 'The Idea of a New Religion', *G.M.*, 1916, no. 2, pp. 82–91, and also his *Na Zhizn i Smert: Izobrazhenie Idealistov*, Geneva, 1877.

in the mid seventies was Natanson's 'Society of Friends' (*Ob-shchestvo Druzey*) inside the second *Zemlya i Volya* and Mikhailov's 'Christian Brotherhood' (*Khristianskoe Bratstvo*) within *Narodnaya Volya*.[1]

All these new religions and groups developed under the impetus of the messianism which persisted throughout the seventies. The radicals continued to find renewal through contact with religious sectarianism. This sense of religious mission and expectation also helped encourage many radicals to volunteer to aid the Serbs against their Turkish oppressors. One of the figures about whom many Russian and Serb radicals spoke was the Belgian, Jeanne Markus, who had spent a decade and a half (1860–75) in Palestine awaiting the second coming, but had left to fight in Hercegovina, convinced that the Serb cause was that of the New Jerusalem. Alexander Mikhailov, one of the most important of the *Narodnaya Volya* leaders, had spent late 1877 and early 1878, the months immediately before his revolutionary activity, living with a number of other radical leaders among the Old Believers in Saratov. Indeed the impact of millenarianism in general and of the Russian sectarians in particular remained decisive throughout the narodnik period. Even the materialist Chernyshevsky addressed an appeal from Siberia in 1879 on behalf of the Old Believers.[2]

Le Nouveau Christianisme

The radicals' vision of a new era had its roots not only in the sectarian traditions of Russia, but in the nineteenth-century West as well, Mikhailovsky, whose great interest was contemporary Western European thought, was a major channel for fortifying Russian radicalism with the belief of many Western thinkers that history was on the verge of a new 'third age' of which Christ was the harbinger and in which a new Christian morality would prevail.

This messianic concept of three ages of human history came into the Western world from the Bogomil-kathar heretics and received its first important exposition in the works of a twelfth-

[1] A. D. Mikhailov, *Pisma Narodovoltsa*, Moscow, 1933, pp. 222–4, and notes; Figner, *Memoirs*, pp. 57–58.
[2] N. G. Chernyshevsky, *Sochineniya*, Moscow, 1951, x. 518–22.

century Cistercian monk, Joachim of Flora. Joachim declared that history was divided into three successive ages: the age of the Father (of the Hebrew God, of oppression and *fear*), the age of the Son (which began with Christ, who through the atonement gave man *hope*), and the age of the Holy Ghost (in which the grace of Christ would be universalized and all would reign with God in *glory*). Although declared heretical, this idea lived on in varying forms among the Spiritual Franciscans and the medieval heretics. Two of these Western heretics were much admired by Mikhailovsky and his contemporaries: John Huss, celebrated for his martyrdom for Czech political and spiritual independence,[1] and Thomas Münzer, the Anabaptist leader whose struggle with the German princes was seen as a prototype of the Russian peasants' struggle with autocracy. Mikhailovsky, however, viewed Western Protestantism primarily as a political movement which betrayed the visions of the heretics. 'Luther was still a Pope'[2] in Mikhailovsky's view. The Western figures whom he viewed as proper heirs to the true Christian traditions of Huss and Münzer were not the 'philistine metaphysicians' of Protestantism, but the secular prophets of a new millenial concept of history, Proudhon and the French socialists.

Haunted by the unrealized hopes of the French Revolution, the nineteenth-century intelligentsia had revived the idea of three ages in history. Like the heretical Christians, they longed for a doctrine that would allow them to believe in an earthly realization of glory. The most famous, most original, and most intellectually satisfying of these new messianic theories of history was that of Hegel, for whom the new age was coming as the result of the inner processes of history. But the line of prophecy to which Mikhailovsky and the narodniks turned was that which came from St.-Simon, Michelet, and French radical thought of the early nineteenth century. This school stood apart from the

[1] Huss had been particularly celebrated among insurrectionists in the south. See the famous poem 'The Heretic' by the Ukrainian revolutionary poet Taras Shevchenko (*Byloe*, 1906, no. 6, pp. 2–5). By the sixties, Huss was also admired in St. Petersburg. See M. K. Lemke, *Politicheskie Protsessy*, pp. 5–7.

[2] III. 48. Condemnation was not extended, however, to Stundism, the indigenous Russian version of Lutheranism which was growing rapidly during this period. Among the radicals who lived among, and wrote warmly about, the Stundists were Ivan Kovalevsky ('Rationalism in the South', *O.Z.*, 1878, nos. 3, 5) and Serge Kravchinsky (*The Stundist Pavel Rudenko, Sobranie Sochinenii*, St. Petersburg, 1907, part i).

monistic consistency of Hegel because of a deep-seated conviction that the human personality was its own source of value and the ultimate arbiter of its own destiny. For them the new age would be ushered in by human beings elevated by moral ideals. Thus, the same function that the dialectic played in the messianic system of Hegel and Marx was assumed in the French school by the new ethic which would usher in the new third age of brotherhood. For almost all French radical thinkers, this new ethic was to be a purified Christianity. St.-Simon called it *Le Nouveau Christianisme*, in which 'everything is understood in this saying: "Thou shalt love thy neighbour as thyself." ' [1]

As early as the forties, St.-Simon replaced Hegel as the principal influence over both Herzen and Belinsky, and the subjective French approach began to predominate among the radical intelligentsia in Russia. Mikhailovsky had drawn his ideas from the French tradition, considering successively the theories of Vico, St.-Simon, Comte, and Louis Blanc, while rejecting that of Hegel and largely ignoring that of Marx. With Mikhailovsky, of course, the decisive influence was that of Proudhon, and the degree to which Mikhailovsky's contemporaries exceeded the men of the forties in passionate expectation almost exactly parallels the degree to which Proudhon's apocalyptical fervour exceeded that of previous French radicals.

Proudhon, who had long planned to write a vast study depicting Christ as a social reformer,[2] imparted to the 'new Christianity' its distinctly apocalyptical flavour:

C'est quand la civilisation nous apparaîtra comme une perpétuelle apocalypse et l'histoire comme un miracle sans fin; quand, par la réforme de la société, le christianisme aura été élevé à sa deuxième puissance, que nous connaîtrons la religion.[3]

... à l'Église militante doit succéder au dernier jour une Église triomphante, et le système des contradictions sociales m'apparaît comme un pont magique jeté sur le fleuve de l'oubli.[4]

---

[1] See *Note S*, p. 193.

[2] Proudhon gave up on the idea when Ernest Renan published his *Vie de Jésus* in 1863 and 'deflowered the idea' by painting Christ as a 'pure mystic'. Édouard Dolléans, *Proudhon*, Paris, 1948, p. 466. His notes were posthumously published as *Les Évangiles annotés par P. J. Proudhon*, Brussels, 1866. Mikhailovsky closely paralleled Proudhon in dislike of Renan as in opposition to Luther and praise of Münzer.

[3] P. J. Proudhon, 'Revolutionary Manifesto', from *le Peuple*, 2 September 1848, in Dolléans, *Proudhon*, p. 149. See also p. 41.

[4] P. J. Proudhon, *Système des contradictions*, ii. 530-1.

Just as St.-Simon had suggested that the 'new Christianity' should resemble the heretical sects of Europe and America,[1] so Proudhon in his final work had praised sectarian Christianity and proclaimed that

Jésus lui-même a annoncé qu'après lui viendrait un troisième personnage. . . . Ce paraclet, dont les apôtres attendaient la venue, que l'on a attendu de siècle en siècle, et sur lequel on a débité tant de rêveries, pourquoi ne dirais-je pas que nous en avons aujourd'hui la manifestation dans le mouvement régénérateur de la plèbe moderne?[2]

The idea of a new Christian age had appealed to Mikhailovsky from the time he first began translating Proudhon. Mikhailovsky was particularly concerned with refuting the then-fashionable idea that the ethics of the 'new Christianity' and the methods of the natural sciences were incompatible. As early as 1868 he asserted that 'Christian ethics say love and forgive; natural science say learn and understand. In essence they are saying one and the same thing.'[3] In refuting the applicability of the concept of the struggle for survival to human affairs. Mikhailovsky adopted the standard millenarian concept of a coming third age of 'universal survival'. The new age was made possible for Mikhailovsky by the advance in religious thought from the autocratic God of the Hebrews to the Christian concept of love. Indeed, through Christ God turned over to man the task of working out his own historical salvation, and voluntarily became—like the king of England—a constitutional monarch.[4]

Thus, Christianity played a decisive role for Mikhailovsky in opening up the possibility of the new age. As he said in a speech to a large assemblage of radicals in May 1872:

The ancient world knew nothing of the idea of personality. Man as something beyond fixed castes, layers, and nationalities meant nothing to antiquity. . . . Christianity gave a completely new characteristic to history. It brought forth the thought of the absolute worth of man and human personality. . . . Henceforth, for all peoples, in spite of delays, mistakes, and wanderings there is but one

[1] Henri de St.-Simon, *Œuvres*, xxii. 116.
[2] P. J. Proudhon, *De la capacité politique*, pp. 129–30.
[3] X. 473.
[4] I. 205.

goal: 'the absolute recognition of man, of human personality, and of its many-sided development.'[1]

Mikhailovsky followed Proudhon not only in insisting on the historical importance of Christ but in accepting the necessity of a new ethical Christianity. Mikhailovsky contended, in his 'Idealism, Idolatry and Realism' of 1873, that only a belief in 'the essence of religion' could equip man to combat the hypocrisy of the metaphysicians. For him this essence lay in a new purified Christianity, closely related to the heretical traditions of old. Sokolov, a close friend of both Mikhailovsky and Proudhon, first set forth a kind of apostolic succession of dissenters in 1866, in his *The Heretics*. Sokolov's book, which cited Proudhon and the French socialists as the true heirs to the traditions of the early Christians, was confiscated: when its author was imprisoned for seeking to undermine the religious basis of Russian society, Mikhailovsky visited him in prison.[2]

In his trial—one of the first involving radicals to be held under the newly instituted system of trial by jury—Sokolov set the pattern for the impassioned radical court orations of the seventies. 'The entire guilt of the heretic socialists', said Sokolov, 'consists in the fact that they seek the kingdom of God not in the clouds, but on earth. . . . Silence me if you find in my words any perversion of the commandment of Christ on love of neighbour. I know only that none of you love Christ more than I.'[3] Sokolov insisted that 'no coercive revolution can ever be successful', that he never proposed to 'thrust people into acting before goodness and truth . . . had ripened within them'.[4]

Throughout the seventies the New Testament was the major source of defence in the great political trials. More than 20 per cent. of the major radical figures brought to trial were former seminarians, and the influence of religious ideas was if anything

---

[1] I. 641. The speech was made to a meeting commemorating the bicentenary of the birth of Peter the Great.

[2] Sokolov later published this work abroad, *Die Abtrünnigen*, Zürich, 1872. Another book with the same Russian title (*Otshchepentsy*) was published in 1883 and also confiscated. Its author was A. S. Prugavin, a narodnik who became one of the greatest of all authorities on the schism after his exile from St. Petersburg in 1871 for radical activities. See G. I. Uspensky, *Materialy i Issledovaniya*, Moscow-Leningrad, 1938, pp. 228–9.

[3] V. Ya. Yakovlev, *Materialy*, pp. 149–50.

[4] Ibid., p. 150.

strengthened by the experience of prison.[1] Few defendants
seriously attempted to use their liberal rights of defence to
challenge the *facts* of their accusation. Like all genuine martyrs,
they sought only to vindicate the *ideals* in the name of which
they acted. The raised section in which the accused sat during
these trials became known as 'Golgotha'.[2] Even terrorists with
little religious background, like Zhelyabov, who directed the
assassination of Alexander II, declared in his defence that

... I deny Orthodoxy, although I affirm the essence of the teachings of Jesus Christ. The essence of his teachings was my primary
moral incentive ... all true Christians must fight for truth, for the
rights of the humiliated and weak, and, if necessary, even suffer for
them: this is my faith.[3]

Without being a martyr himself, Mikhailovsky felt a deep
veneration for the populists on trial. He visited Sokolov and
many other radicals in prison during the long and lonely period
in which they were waiting for formal court proceedings to
begin. He kept a private record of the great trials of the seventies,[4] and it was the trial of Zasulich in 1878 which made him
turn at last to the illegal press to express his sympathies.

In his semi-autobiographical 'In the Interim', Mikhailovsky
expresses his admiration for the society of justice and brotherhood of the early Christians and for their readiness for martyrdom. He recalls stopping transfixed at an art exhibition in St.
Petersburg before a famous painting of Nero preparing to burn
Christian martyrs. The executioners and Roman senators in the
picture symbolized for Mikhailovsky the Russian society of his
day; the Christian martyrs represented his young radical
friends.[5] The positive figure who showed the way to social redemption in the same story was significantly called Apostolov (of
the Apostles).

Despite his professed agnosticism, Mikhailovsky constantly

[1] Of the 425 major political criminals of the decade the two largest groups were
noblemen (147) and former seminarians (90). Franco Venturi, *Il Populismo Russo*,
ii. 966.
[2] S. Sinegub, *Zapiski Chaikovtsa*, p. 196.
[3] *Delo Pervogo Marta 1881* (intr. Leo Deutsch), St. Petersburg, 1906, pp. 6–7.
[4] E. E. Kolosov, 'The Social World-View of N. K. Mikhailovsky', *G.M.*, 1914,
no. 2, pp. 219–20. For a reproduced sample of Mikhailovsky's chronicle, see Kolosov, 'N. K. Mikhailovsky in the Eighties', *Byloe* (Paris), 1909, no. 9/10, p. 43.
[5] IV. 340–6.

wove citations and illustrations from the New Testament into
his works. Christ's teachings on human society were, indeed, the
highest ethical ideal for both Mikhailovsky and his associates on
the *Annals*. Typical of the group was Saltykov's declaration that
his early reading of the gospel stories

sowed in my heart the seeds of an all-human conscience and
brought forth from the womb of my being something solid and
personal thanks to which the prevailing tenor of life could not so
easily enslave me.[1]

The great expectations of the men of the seventies would have
been inconceivable in the adverse circumstances of the time had
they not passionately believed a new day to be dawning. This
belief was related to a conviction that the supreme ethical ideal
had been set for man by Jesus, the God-man. Illustrative of the
importance to the narodniks of their belief in a 'true Christianity', a new French-style ethical religion was an incident at a
New Year's party given by the Mikhailovskies for a host of
radicals in the mid seventies. As a climax to the meeting, the
poet Minaev proposed that everyone present should embrace
one another 'with agape à la Auguste Comte and Fourier'; that
they should exchange not a 'coarse physiological embrace' but
'the kiss of the cult of great and eternal ideas—liberty, equality,
and fraternity'. The group concurred, although some protested
that they were still unworthy and 'not yet fully dedicated to the
cult of great ideas, of God-manhood'.[2]

The narodnik faith was indeed a 'cult of great ideas', and the
greatest of these was the vision of a 'true Christianity', a utopia
ruled by a purified Christian morality. Such a vision was common to both the evolutionary populists of the early seventies
and the revolutionary populists at the end of the decade. Only
the 'idea-less' liberals on the one side and the calculating Jacobins
on the other failed to share it.

The Climax of 1881

So central to the thought of this period was this thirst for a
new, ethical Christianity that it is impossible to neglect it in
appraising the thought of any influential Russian thinker of the
period. Thus, for example, the most penetrating theologian of

---

[1] Quoted in G. Z. Eliseev, *Vospominaniya*, p. 386.
[2] *Uspensky v Zhizni*, p. 143.

the age, Vladimir Solovev, was deeply influenced by the radical movements of the seventies and may have taken the title for his famous 'Lectures on God-manhood' from the sect of the same name. The lesser known, but equally influential Nicholas Fedorov, bore even more decisively the messianic imprint. He went so far as to suggest that the new age would bring about the resurrection of the dead by wedding scientific knowledge with Christianity.[1] Tolstoy also formulated one of these moralistic religions, drawing inspiration from Russia's native traditions of religious dissent, and, particularly, from their belief in non-resistance to evil.[2]

Finally, if one considers two other non-radicals who were perhaps the greatest creative artists of the period, Modest Musorgsky and Fedor Dostoevsky, one finds an intense interest in both the messianic expectations of the Russian schismatics and the general idea of a new, ethical Christianity. Musorgsky spent almost the entire decade of the seventies studying about the Old Believers, while writing and rewriting the music for his opera, *Khovanchina*, the subject of which is the self-destruction of the *raskolniki* in protest to Imperial power. He chose the Old Believers as the subject of this 'popular musical drama', feeling that no other subject contained enough of 'mother Russia and all her simple-hearted truth'. *Khovanchina* represented not so much a work of art for Musorgsky as a striving to represent a new Christian order among men. In a letter of 1876 to a friend, who had asked him why *Khovanchina* was taking him so long to complete, he wrote:

Khovanchina is too big, too extraordinary a task. . . . I have stopped work—I have been thinking things over, and now and yesterday and for weeks back and tomorrow do nothing but think the one thought—to go forth as a conqueror and say to people a *new* word of friendship and love, *frank, single-hearted, and traversing the whole breadth of the Russian land*. . . .[3]

[1] On Solovev, see his 1878 *Lectures on God-manhood* (intr. and tr. Peter Zouboff, New York, 1944) and the work in which his apocalyptical views are best outlined, *Three Conversations on War, Progress, and the End of World History*, London, 1915. On Fedorov, the librarian at the Rumyantsev Museum in Moscow, see N. O. Lossky, *History of Russian Philosophy*, New York, 1951, pp. 75–80.

[2] See. J. W. Bienstock, *Tolstoy et les Doukhobors*, Paris, 1902, for Tolstoy's connexions with sectarians; and N. V. Reinhardt, *Neobyknovennaya Lichnost*, Kazan, 1889, for Tolstoy's connexions with the God-manhood sect.

[3] Quoted in Gerald Abraham, *Masters of Russian Music*, New York, 1944, p. 233.

Dostoevsky also combined a specific interest in the sectarians with the vision of a new Christianity. His own partial *rapprochement* with the narodniks in the mid seventies had been based on a realization, partly through Mikhailovsky's writing, that socialism need not be either atheistic or revolutionary.[1] His journal of the early sixties, *Time*, had been one of the first to popularize the beliefs of the schismatics in the popular press. His recurrent use of Christ-like figures, the holy idiot, the *yurodivy* (fool for Christ's sake), and finally the returning Christ of the 'Legend of the Grand Inquisitor' show how he developed the characteristic narodnik juxtaposition posed by Sokolov of spontaneous Christian love through freedom opposed by a nominally Christian social order of fear and authority.

The assassination of Alexander II on 1 March 1881 was a decisive milestone in the history of the Russian intelligentsia. The dramatic murder brought on the reaction that would effectively crush *narodnichestvo* as a social movement. At the same time, however, it precipitated a brief final flowering of messianic expectation. When the news came to him of the assassination, Mikhailovsky went immediately to see Tikhomirov and the other editors of *Narodnaya Volya* to draft a letter to the new Tsar, Alexander III. Although they sent the letter to Alexander just a little more than a week after killing his father, the *Narodovoltsy* seemed to expect that he might respond to their appeal for a 'voluntary turning over of supreme power to the people'.[2] They appealed to him to utter the word which would end 'the sad necessity of this bloody struggle'.[3] Indeed the attitude of the intelligentsia was not so much shock at the crime, although this was generally felt, as excitement at the unique opportunity that lay before the new Tsar—the chance for a redemptive Christian pardon of the six condemned assassins. He had the chance, as it were, to usher in the new age of Christian forgiveness with one apocalyptical stroke. This was the idea that had lain behind the impassioned, improbable plea for forgiveness of a would-be assassin that Garshin had addressed in 1880 to Loris-Melikov. In early March of 1881 Tolstoy issued a similar plea in a famous letter to the Tsar asking clemency for the condemned. In a dramatic lecture to his students during the trial, the young

---

[1] A. S. Iskoz, *V Tvorcheskoy Laboratorii*, pp. 151–6.
[2] *Literatura Narodnoy Voli*, p. 906.
[3] Ibid., p. 905.

theologian, Vladimir Solovev, urged that 'the Tsar as the representative of a people acknowledging the religion of beatitude, should and must pardon them'.[1] When Solovev repeated his statement after being challenged from the floor by a university official:

> Something indescribable took place in the hall. There was not only applause, but all were captured by a wave of exultation. Hundreds of hands were extended to the lectern. . . . Many had tears in their eyes. Some were weeping. Solovev had difficulty leaving the hall.[2]

Thus, three of the greatest creative minds of the period, though each was opposed to revolutionary agitation in general and to terroristic assassination in particular, had come to believe that only a freely chosen Christ-like act of moral greatness could resolve the moral frustration and spiritual striving of the narodnik movement.

Just as their own personal fate had been an incidental consideration to the defendants in the trial, so it was the possibility of bringing in a new moral order, rather than of acquitting the condemned for their own sakes, which was the basic concern of the intelligentsia. This thirst for the new Christianity was, however, not to be satisfied. Just as Loris had rejected Garshin, so Pobedonostsev dismissed Solovev from his chair of theology and kept Tolstoy's letter from the new Tsar.

The six were tried and hanged, but the sense of Socratic calm with which they faced death gave further testimony to the intensity of the narodnik faith in the coming age of brotherhood. Pobedonostsev had set in motion the forces which would crush the social movement that had been inspired by the vision of a new Christianity, but he could not crush the dream itself. It would weave its golden thread through the purple tapestry of Russian thought. Indeed, Pobedonostsev, the apostle of Byzantine absolutism, may have secretly shared the dream himself in his later years, when he left his position of authority in 1902 and turned to a reading and translation of Thomas à Kempis's *De Imitatione Christi*.

---

[1] I. I. Popov, *Minuvshee i Perezhitoe*, Leningrad, 1924, p. 75.
[2] Ibid., pp. 77–78. Cf. P. Shchegelov, 'The Event of 1 March, and Solovev', *Byloe*, 1906, no. 3, pp. 48–55; and A. Khiryakova, 'The Event of 1 March and Tolstoy', ibid., pp. 56–61.

Nevertheless, the accession to power of Alexander III early in 1881 marked the beginning of the end of the narodnik movement. It is perhaps significant that the early part of this same year should see the death of both Musorgsky and Dostoevsky, the two tortured artists of the narodnik period who had sought to have their work provide 'the new word of love' which the narodniks were seeking. By 1881 the lyric of the narodnik vision was turning imperceptibly into a lament. The demonstrators and agitators of an earlier day were being dispersed by the new Tsar's policies, and the largest crowds to be found were the lines of mourners paying final homage to these two great artists of the age as they were laid to rest not far from one another in the Alexander Nevsky graveyard.

IX

THE WANING OF THE OLD
TRADITION

THE Russia to which Alexander III fell heir was still an overwhelmingly agrarian state. To be sure, industrialization had taken place during the seventies, and the number of workers had grown steadily since the mid sixties. But the industrial worker still comprised only a microscopic portion of the vast seventy-six-million population of European Russia; and, despite a sharp growth in the urban population, small-scale craft industries still predominated.[1] The backbone of Russia was still the peasantry, which harvested the chief source of Russia's wealth, the wheat crop. The value of Russia's grain exports had quintupled in the two decades since 1860.[2] Russia's inefficient methods of agriculture had not yet been brought to light by competition with long-haul shipments from North America. Compared to the average size of holdings in Western Europe at the time and to the later size of holdings in Russia, the peasant household (*dvor*) was well off, with an average landholding of more than 35 acres.[3] The village commune in its many forms was still the principal juridical institution for the bulk of the peasantry. The great village fairs were still more important than the stock-markets of St. Petersburg as centres of commercial exchange.

At the heart of this vast, agrarian empire, the new Tsar was making a determined effort to end the indecision and conflicting policies that had marked his father's rule. He sought to suppress once and for all the ferment and unrest created by the radical intelligentsia. His consistent policy of repression throughout his reign, from 1881 to 1894, dealt the populist movement a series of blows from which it would never fully recover, though

[1] M. W. Kovalevsky, *La Russie*, pp. 93, 854; M. Tugan-Baranovsky, *Russkaya Fabrika v Proshlom i Nastoyashchem*, Moscow, 1938, pp. 253, 305.
[2] B. H. Sumner, *Russia and the Balkans*, p. 13.
[3] G. T. Robinson, *Rural Russia*, p. 97.

Mikhailovsky and his associates did regroup their forces for a final assault on autocracy in the early nineties.

The Triumph of Reaction

On 29 April 1881 Alexander III proclaimed in a manifesto that autocratic power was unchallengeable in Russia, thus destroying not only the narodniks' messianic expectations, but all hopes for the moderate administrative reforms which Loris had recommended and a majority of the Tsar's own Council of the Empire had endorsed. Alexander had fallen back on the arguments for theocratic absolutism advanced by his private entourage of tutors, Pobedonostsev and Count S. G. Stroganov. The principal ministers who had advocated reform—Loris-Melikov (Interior), Milyutin (War), and Abaza (Finance)—tendered their resignations, and the 'League of Zemstvo Constitutionalists', which had been so encouraged by developments in the late seventies, soon collapsed. A decisive blow was the replacement, in May 1882, of the new Minister of the Interior, Count Ignatev, by the hated Dmitry Tolstoy.

Thus, by mid 1882, the moderates in both the government and the opposition camps had been dispersed. Just as the government had been taken over by a determined clique of extremists, the only significant opposition force that remained in 1882 was the terrorist 'fighting organization', a small group within *Narodnaya Volya* which sought to organize revolutionary cadres within the armed forces. Repressive measures against the *Narodovoltsy* had been so successful that, by June 1882, one of the leaders of the 'fighting organization' (Serge Degaev) had been enlisted as a police informer and only one of the original twenty-four members of the executive committee (Vera Figner) remained out of prison and active inside Russia. Friends of the movement like Uspensky were sadly asking the sole survivor, 'What is Vera Nikolaevna going to do with us now?'[1]

Narodnaya Volya was not to die, however, without one final episode of ironic drama. At this very moment of irreversible defeat, a new opportunity was given to the remnants of the organization through a gross overestimate of their real strength by the 'Holy Brotherhood', a counter-revolutionary clique close to

[1] V. N. Figner, *Memoirs*, p. 130.

Alexander III. These autocratic extremists, apparently feeling that their own success must have been paralleled by extremists in the opposition camp, sought to open negotiations for a cease fire with *Narodnaya Volya* in the summer of 1882. One of the leaders of the Brotherhood, Count Vorontsov-Dashkov, broached the subject to one of Mikhailovsky's subordinates on the *Annals*, N. Ya. Nikoladze.[1] Agreeing that discussions were desirable, Nikoladze consulted with Mikhailovsky, who rapidly assumed the role of mediator-in-chief. In August Nikoladze went abroad carrying a secret letter, which presumably contained suggested terms of settlement from Mikhailovsky's closest associate at this time, Krivenko, to Tikhomirov, the head of the executive committee in exile. At the same time inside Russia, Mikhailovsky established contact with Vera Figner and arranged for a personal meeting with Vorontsov-Dashkov.

At the meeting in early October Vorontsov-Dashkov requested an immediate pledge from *Narodnaya Volya* to end political terror. In return, he promised to secure a general amnesty for political prisoners, freedom of the press, and permission for peaceful socialistic propaganda. To prove his sincerity, Vorontsov-Dashkov was willing to offer the immediate release of a prominent terrorist, Isaev; but the amnesty was not to be proclaimed until after the coronation of the new Tsar in May 1883, by which time the sincerity of the *Narodnaya Volya* pledge to renounce the terror would have been proven.

Mikhailovsky journeyed immediately to Kharkov to communicate this proposal to Vera Figner, under the pretext of visiting a bookseller. To his amazement the crippled *Narodovoltsy* rejected the offer. Figner was deeply suspicious of the proposals, recalling the duplicity of the government over similar promises in 1879,[2] and insisting that Nechaev rather than Isaev

---

[1] Vorontsov-Dashkov was a hero of the Turkish war and Minister of the Imperial Court. Nikoladze was a Georgian who had known Herzen abroad, worked for the *Contemporary*, and returned to Tiflis in the seventies to set up the *Tiflis Herald* (*Tiflisky Vestnik*) and sponsor several St.-Simonian projects such as the building of an aqueduct. He returned to St. Petersburg in 1881, worked on the *Annals*, and established contact with Vorontsov-Dashkov when he went to ask his permission to start another journal.

[2] The Third Section had extracted a full confession and list of accomplices from the terrorist Goldenberg by promising to grant social reforms in return. When he discovered that his action had only succeeded in betraying his comrades, he committed suicide.

be released by the government as an indication of their good intentions. The latter request indicates the extent to which the disintegrating *Narodnaya Volya* was breaking with the populist ideology and returning to the conspiratorial atmosphere of the late sixties.[1] Although Mikhailovsky still distrusted the government's 'fox tail', he saw nothing to lose in accepting the proposals. He pointed out to Figner the obvious fact that the organization was no longer in a position of strength and that 'you will lose nothing, while you stand a chance of gaining something'.[2]

Unable to allow for the possible sincerity of the government proposals and paralysed by the hopelessness of her own position, Figner gave no decisive reply to this unforeseen overture. While she hesitated, the final *coups de grâce* were being administered to *Narodnaya Volya*. More arrests, the destruction of the illegal printing press in Odessa, the failure of Nikoladze to reappear from Paris, and the eventual arrest of Figner herself on 10 February 1883, brought an end to the original *Narodnaya Volya* organization.[3] When the news reached Mikhailovsky that the last of the original executive committee had been arrested Uspensky burst out into tears and Mikhailovsky was so overcome that he gave up all work for several days.[4]

By early 1883 the main lines of the political reaction had been drawn. The moderate administrative reformers, constitutionalists, and federalists had been the first casualties; the extreme left had been eliminated next despite the eleventh-hour over-estimation of *Narodovoltsy* strength by the Tsar's advisers. The final element in Pobedonostsev's formula for destroying all forms of opposition to Tsarist power was the *pogrom*, which in the course of 1883 became a new means for redirecting the social unrest of the south and of the growing urban districts.[5]

---

[1] The idea of liberating Nechaev was mooted among the executive committee in 1881; but even throughout this period opposition to Nechaev remained dominant. See P. L. Lavrov, *Narodniki-Propagandisty*, p. 31 and note.

[2] V. N. Figner, *Memoirs*, p. 137. Cf. N. K. Mikhailovsky, 'Vera Figner', in his *Vospominaniya*, Berlin, 1906, pp. 7–8; 'Documents and Materials toward a History of the Conversation of the Executive Committee and the Holy Brotherhood', *Byloe*, 1907, no. 9, pp. 208–12; and I. I. Popov, *Minuvshee*, p. 105.

[3] See *Note T*, p. 193.   [4] I. I. Popov, *Minuvshee*, p. 86.

[5] Katkov and the chauvinistic press had always played up the participation of Jews in *Narodnaya Volya*; and when the Pan-Slav Ignatev became Minister of the Interior in 1881, anti-semitic demonstrations received official sanction. The

Meanwhile, reaction in the field of education had begun in March 1882 with the appointment of Count T. D. Delyanov as Minister of Education. Hand-picked by Pobedonostsev, Delyanov was the first minister since Uvarov in the thirties to have a clear concept of education as a form of civic discipline. He shared the apprehension in the Tsar's entourage at the rapid and disorganized growth in educational opportunities which had taken place during the seventies. Tsarina Mariya Fedorovna was of the opinion that the troubles in the Empire were directly related to the breakup of family life and could be solved largely by sending female students back to their homes. Pobedonostsev was worried by the undisciplined autonomy of the new provincial school system. Accordingly, restrictions were gradually applied on higher education for women;[1] central jurisdiction over provincial elementary education was given to Pobedonostsev and the synod;[2] and finally, in 1884, the elective principle was abolished in university administration.

Since one of the chief means of forcing the female intelligentsia back into their homes was the curtailment of scholarships for women, St. Petersburg student circles began in 1882 to sponsor student balls and 'evenings', both to raise money and to reassert the solidarity of the student body *vis-à-vis* the government. Mikhailovsky's presence was always sought by his young student admirers. Despite warnings from the authorities, he appeared in December 1882 at one of the most important of these evenings, the annual student gathering of the Medical-Surgery Academy. Called upon by the crowd to speak, Mikhailovsky stood up on a table and issued a clear appeal to resist the government

organized *pogrom* did not become widespread, however, until Pobedonostsev's power had been consolidated firmly in 1883. Author of the technique for diverting radical crowds into agitation against Jews was the Kievan official, Strelnikov, who was rewarded by Pobedonostsev with a position as special police commissioner for south Russia.

[1] The number of female students in higher educational institutions shrunk from a height of 2,000 in 1881 to a mere 144 in 1899. Nicholas Hans, *History of Russian Educational Policy* (1701–1917), London, 1931, p. 147. Although Dmitry Tolstoy had been strongly disliked during his period as Minister of Education (1867–80), the educational system as a whole had expanded greatly under him. Resentment at Tolstoy was primarily directed at his emphasis on the classics in school curricula.

[2] Ibid., pp. 154–64. So opposed was Pobedonostsev to all forms of student activity and organization that he even proposed in November 1882 that student agitators be impressed into military service—a suggestion that was not finally rejected until June 1883.

repression in the name of the narodnik faith. Mikhailovsky praised the medical profession for its down-to-earth service to mankind. Vocationally they were repaying their debt to the people, but Mikhailovsky warned them not to forget broader social issues in so doing:

In discharging this debt one should not forget about that other debt which is the debt of honour, and without fulfilment of which the first debt cannot be discharged in any real way. You must realize where every confining influence comes from that puts obstacles in the way, to block the true development of society and hold the people in ignorance.[1]

Mikhailovsky's refusal to remain silent in the face of events precipitated the final wave of repressive measures which struck at the very citadel of the narodnik faith, the radical journals. Reports of his speech to the student evening, together with reports from the police spy Degaev of Mikhailovsky's conversations with Vera Figner, led to his being ordered by Plehve to leave St. Petersburg in December 1882, and to remain under virtual house arrest in Lyuban.[2] The official pretext for this punishment was the anti-Tsarist tone of another of his speeches to students, delivered at the St. Petersburg Technical Institute. Even harsher measures would have been applied on Mikhailovsky but for Plehve's desire 'not to make him into a second Chernyshevsky'. The new policy was to avoid creating martyrs as the court trials of Alexander II had so often done, thereby strengthening rather than weakening the revolutionary cause.[3]

It was inevitable that the administration should become aware of the connexion between the *Annals* and the forces of illegal opposition. In January 1883 a strong warning was sent to the journal apropos of the appearance of Nikoladze's article, 'Gambetta and Louis Blanc'. For the same issue, Mikhailovsky sent from Lyuban the first of his new anonymous columns, 'Letters of an Outsider to the Editor of *The Annals*'. In these letters, which were Mikhailovsky's sole contribution to his

[1] Quoted by I. I. Popov, *Minuvshee*, pp. 97–98.
[2] See *Note U*, p. 193.
[3] See E. E. Kolosov, 'Mikhailovsky and the Narodnik Movement from the Second Half of the Seventies', *Kievskaya Mysl*, 1914, no. 28, pp. 3–4. Shelgunov, who also participated in the student demonstration at the Medical-Surgery Academy, was exiled to Vyborg at the same time.

journal during the last year and a half of its existence, he played back in reprise most of the major themes of his own narodnik ideology.

In the January column he informed his readers of his fate through the 'Aesopian' device of pointedly quoting passages telling a similar story. In February he launched another attack on Katkov and his right-wing daily, the *Moscow Herald*, complaining that now 'in place of an ideal one must have only an identity card'.[1] In July he distinguished his own position once more from the uncritical populism which failed to recognize any applicability to Russia of the ideas and experiences of the West. In September he paid tribute again to Belinsky and the traditions of the intelligentsia, and in the following month he criticized once more the sentimental populism of Yuzov and the *Week*. In January he discussed Dostoevsky with sympathy;[2] his 'letter' of March reaffirmed his faith in Russia's ability to profit by England's reckless advance into industrialization. Russia could still attain England's level of development without losing the moral basis of its own society and was thus better able than England itself to realize the dreams of English socialists like William Morris.[3]

The March issue of the *Annals* was the last ever to appear. The journal had been earmarked for oblivion by Pobedonostsev, and the discovery that Mikhailovsky and at least two of his subordinates had been closely connected with *Narodnaya Volya* offered an ample pretext for closure. On 3 January 1884 Krivenko and Protopopov were arrested and sent to Siberia. The officials chose to deny Mikhailovsky a similar martyr's fate; but, when his journal was shut by official decree in April, Mikhailovsky's anguish was equal to that of any exile. The announcement in the *Government Herald* referred to the journal as 'an organ which not only opened its pages to the dissemination of dangerous ideas, but had among its principal collaborators those belonging to the ranks of secret societies'.[4]

With this arbitrary action Mikhailovsky's bitterness at Dmitry Tolstoy and the 'Gatchina captivity' of the government

---

[1] V. 716.   [2] See *Note V*, pp. 193-4.   [3] V. 929-30.

[4] *Pravitelstvenny Vestnik*, 1884, no. 87, quoted in M. E. Saltykov, *Pisma*, p. 259 note. The *Cause* was also shut in May; and, although it reopened immediately, it became (and remained until its collapse in 1888) extremely conservative. Even Kraevsky's mildly liberal *Voice* was shut in 1884.

reached unprecedented heights. In an article which he wrote after the closing and gave to the revolutionary courier, Herman Lopatin, for publication in *Listok Narodnoy Voli* within Russia and the *Common Cause* abroad, Mikhailovsky declared of his beloved journal:

> It was almost the only organ of the Russian press in which, through the smoke and soot of the censor, there glimmered a spark of understanding of the problems of Russian life in all their vastness. . . . As long as the obstinate, stupid, and self-seeking administration does not give any legal place to the free representatives of the country, the Russian government will continue to fall lower and will finally collapse.[1]

But neither Mikhailovsky's acrimony nor the flood of protests that came from all over Russia[2] could deter the authorities. The old formula of 'Autocracy, Orthodoxy, and Nationality' had been reasserted in journalism and education as well as politics. Indeed, with the closing of the journal of Belinsky, Nekrasov, and Mikhailovsky, the narodnik era of Russian social history can be said to have ended. A final wave of arrests of the remaining *Narodnaya Volya* leaders and the collapse of *Listok Narodnoy Voli* later in the year were further milestones.[3] The narodnik faith did not die, but the fresh glow of optimism that had radiated through the seventies gave way to the lingering twilight of the late eighties and nineties.

Small Deeds

Confronted with systematic repression, the intelligentsia became oppressed by a feeling of frustration and unfulfilment. The belief in progress and a new moral order, which had given meaning to their personal sacrifices in the seventies, had largely vanished, and the late eighties became—to use their self-applied terms of abuse—an age of *beznarodnost* (without the spirit of the

---

[1] *Literatura Narodnoy Voli*, pp. 693, 695. Lopatin had returned to Russia from abroad in hopes of reconstituting *Narodnaya Volya* after the Degaev affair and enlisting Mikhailovsky to write the 'internal review' section on *Listok Narodnoy Voli*. E. E. Kolosov, 'Toward a Characterization of the World-View of N. K. Mikhailovsky', *G.M.*, 1914, no. 2, pp. 227–8.

[2] See B. P. Kozmin, *Zhurnalistika 70kh i 80kh Godov*, p. 15.

[3] See *Note W*, p. 194.

people), of *malie dela* (small deeds) in which service to the people continued on without any real sense of purpose.

The aimlessness of revolutionary activity in the age of 'small deeds' was illustrated by the confused student demonstrations in November 1886 on the twenty-fifth anniversary of Dobrolyubov's death; by an ill-conceived attempt to revive terrorism in 1887, in which Lenin's older brother was one of the leaders caught and executed; and by petty, internecine feuds among radicals abroad. Disillusionment was deepened later in the eighties when the former head of the executive committee of *Narodnaya Volya*, Leo Tikhomirov, publicly renounced revolutionary activity and returned to Russia.

A sense of futility was also growing among the evolutionary populists as the purely passive populism of the *Week* rose to predominance in the late eighties. The prophet of this new and unexalting 'cultural *narodnichestvo*' was Ya. V. Abramov, a participant in the movement to the people who had transferred his talents from the *Annals* to the *Week* after the closing of the former. In his writing of the late eighties he preached a kind of homely moralism that paid homage to 'the principles of the people' but avoided all broad controversial topics. This widespread tendency among the narodniks of the late eighties—*Abramovshchina* as it became called—could only depress those like Mikhailovsky for whom populism had been 'a cult of great ideas', a vision of social regeneration.

After the shutting of the *Annals*, Mikhailovsky was ordered to leave St. Petersburg and take up permanent residence at Lyuban. Although he returned during the winter of 1884 and intermittently over the next three years, Mikhailovsky was deeply saddened and could not bring himself to recommence his writing as readily as Abramov. In November 1884 he wrote to the editor of the *Russian News*—the only daily still at all respected by the narodniks—refusing an offer to collaborate: 'Fate has beaten me down . . . I live for nothing.'[1] His feelings of the time were well expressed at a literary evening of Mikhailovsky's old colleagues who had come to visit him in Lyuban. Uspensky read

---

[1] Quoted by Vladimir Rozenberg, 'N. K. Mikhailovsky on *Russkiya Vedomosti*', *Rus. Ved.*, 1914, no. 22, p. 3. Uspensky and Zlatovratsky had both agreed to contribute to the gazette; and Mikhailovsky eventually agreed to submit occasional articles, which he continued to do until 1890. On the *Russian News*, see Rozenberg, *Iz Istorii Russkoy Pechati*, Prague, 1924, pp. 73–76, 176–8.

as his selection Nekrasov's famous 'Knight for an Hour', with its fleeting dream of nobility and its lament upon waking:

> O mechty! o volshebnaya vlast
> Vozvyshayushchey dushu prirody:
> Plamya yunosti, muzhestvo, strast
> I velikoe chuvstvo svobody—[1]
>
> Oh dreams! oh magical power
> Which lifts up the spirit of nature:
> Flame of youth, courage, passion
> And the great feeling of freedom—

So moved were Uspensky, Mikhailovsky, and everyone else by the relevance of the poem to their own lives that most were reduced to tears, and Uspensky was unable to finish the reading.[2]

In these years of estrangement from his editorial desk, Mikhailovsky found solace only in this idea that brief moments of nobility had somehow redeemed an otherwise barren life. This is the moral of his short story, 'The Tale of Tavolgin', which was the first work published after the shutting of his journal and appeared in the summer of 1885 as the first part of his projected novel *Karera Oladushkina*.[3] The tale deals with a French youth whose bleak life is brightened only on a few brief occasions, including the moment when he is singing the *Marseillaise* just before being killed in the Franco-Prussian War. The emphasis in the story is on the rare moments of nobility, which made his life infinitely preferable to the temporal success of the 'careerist'. This message of consolation to the narodniks moved many of Mikhailovsky's readers and even brought him a personal letter of gratitude from an imprisoned *Narodovolets*.[4]

However much Mikhailovsky may have urged the narodniks to remain true to their spirit of nobility, he fell victim himself to the creeping paralysis of 'small deeds'. Although he deplored

---

[1] N. A. Nekrasov, *Izbrannye Sochineniya*, p. 79.

[2] *Uspensky v Zhizni*, p. 387. At another of these evenings, Uspensky moved his audience by opening his book, standing in silence, and then closing it and taking his seat. See V. Burtsev (V. B-va) 'Memoirs of a Citizen of Petersburg on the Second Half of the Eighties', *M.G.*, 1908, no. 11, pp. 170–6.

[3] *Russkiya Vedomosti*, 1885, no. 156. See E. E. Kolosov, 'The World-View of N. K. Mikhailovsky', *G.M.*, 1914, no. 2, pp. 218–20, 247–9 for discussion of the outlines and drafts of the work.

[4] Kolosov, 'The World-View of N. K. Mikhailovsky', loc. cit., pp. 222–3.

the petty and ignoble, he could not escape from them. During
this period of forced absence from his editorial desk, he began
for the first time since his youth to pay more attention to his
personal affairs than to his task as a 'nerve of the great people'.

Life with his second wife had not proven any more amicable
than life with his first. With Mikhailovsky absorbed in radical
activity, often exiled to Lyuban, and frequently travelling to
Moscow for medical treatment, Ludmilla Nikolaevna decided
in the early eighties to try living in a separate home in St.
Petersburg with their two young sons. When she left Mikhailovsky altogether in 1885 to elope with a mining engineer in the
Urals, the two boys elected to stay behind with their father.
Thus Mikhailovsky was cast in the domestic role of father and
tutor during the second half of the eighties. He early recognized
and encouraged the interest in dramatics which was shown by
his older son, Kolya, who was ten years old in 1885; but he enjoyed even more the companionship of his more intelligent
younger son, Mark, who even at the age of eight already resembled his father in appearance and love of books.[1]

At the same time Mikhailovsky was free again to take a wider
interest in the company of women. Even while married to
Ludmilla he had fallen in love with a young student while
visiting Moscow in the early eighties.[2] With Ludmilla gone,
Mikhailovsky became a close friend and confidant of several
members of the female intelligentsia including the doctor and
writer, E. K. Pimenova, and the young journalist, A. A. Davydova. He lived briefly with Davydova while in St. Petersburg
and flirted with a certain Yulia Petrovna Kashchenko while in
Kislovodsk visiting Davydova's husband, the director of the
St. Petersburg conservatory.[3] In the course of several visits to
this resort centre in the Caucasus, Mikhailovsky made new
friends through Davydov and developed an amateur interest in
mountain climbing. At the same time he began paying visits to
a number of personal friends outside of radical circles in St.
Petersburg: the painter Yaroshenko in Poltava, the novelist

---

[1] See *Note X*, p. 194.

[2] Mikhailovsky's first wife, Mariya Evgrafovna, had refused to grant him a
formal divorce on the grounds that 'I want to keep your name till death', and had
refused again when Mikhailovsky's infatuation with the Moscow student led him
to repeat the request, E. K. Pimenova, *Dni Minuvshie*, p. 141.

[3] Ibid., pp. 125–30; Nikolenko-Gilchenko, 'Memoirs', loc. cit., pp. 8–10.

Tolstoy at Yasnaya Polyana, and the editor and professor V. M. Sobolevsky at Klin.

Yet this increase in external activity only accentuated Mikhailovsky's internal sadness. Small deeds and limited horizons were no substitute for noble visions and great expectations. Most of his acquaintances served only to depress him, for they carried no new revelation. Tolstoy, for instance, with whom he developed for the first time a personal friendship during this period, outraged him with his doctrine of complete non-resistance to evil. 'This colossal misunderstanding', he wrote to Rusanov of Tolstoy's outlook in the summer of 1886, 'is possible only in such bleak times as we are living through.'[1]

The first new journal to present a serious claim of successorship to the *Annals* was the *Northern Herald* (*Severny Vestnik*), which was founded in 1885 by A. M. Evreinova, the first Russian woman ever to receive the degree of Doctor of Law. The *Northern Herald* soon attracted many of the former principal contributors to the *Annals*: Vorontsov, Yuzhakov, Uspensky, Korolenko, and Pleshcheev. It is not surprising that Mikhailovsky chose this journal when he decided in 1886 to affiliate himself once more with a monthly journal. For a little more than two years Mikhailovsky served as editorial advisor and leading contributor to the bibliographical section.

Although Mikhailovsky moved back to St. Petersburg, a sense of frustration remained with him. His irregularly appearing columns were devoted mainly to destructive criticism of the journals of Katkov and Suvorin, which were enjoying great popularity as a result of the new wave of chauvinism accompanying the Balkan crisis of 1885. He also attacked Gaideburov's the *Week*, with its *Abramovshchina* and 'cultural narodnichestvo', and, with less acrimony, Goltsev's moderate *Russian Thought* (*Russkaya Mysl*). Equally depressing to Mikhailovsky was the sudden rise of the sensationalist illustrated weeklies such as the *Pictorial Review* (*Zhivopisnoe Obozrenie*), and the *Field* (*Niva*), which soon attained an unprecedented circulation of 200,000. Shelgunov observed that these journals possessed bright covers but 'empty interiors';[2] and Mikhailovsky spoke for the radical

---

[1] N. S. Rusanov, 'N. K. Mikhailovsky in the Social Life of Russia', *G.M.*, 1914, no. 2, p. 24.

[2] Quoted in B. P. Kozmin, *Zhurnalistika 70kh i 80kh Godov*, pp. 40–47.

intelligentsia as a whole when he declared in the *Northern Herald* of November 1887 that:

A journal wishing to satisfy everyone—every taste—will never be more than a petty retailing establishment (*lavochka*), perhaps a very good one, but it will never be a journal in the lofty, responsible sense which we are accustomed to link with that word. . . .[1]

The overall tone of the *Northern Herald* was one of disillusionment and pessimism. No longer was it possible to speak of the ideals of 'popular' institutions without dwelling on the detailed and often sordid realities. The French naturalistic school was becoming popular in Russia and was imitated in many descriptive sketches of peasant life. As one writer pointed out in the *Northern Herald* of December 1887, the men of the eighties were crushed by the gap which had opened up for them between the ideal and the actual commune. On the one hand, there was still the idealized morality of the peasant and the democracy of the *mir*; on the other, there was 'the determination of each peasant to use everything just to buy vodka':

. . . these are the two tendencies, the Ahriman and Ormuzd of popular life, which continually struggle between themselves and produce such a maelstrom that it is difficult to tell which will emerge victorious . . . at the present time the bright water of altruism, truth, and good is more and more being engulfed by the dark torrents of venality, isolation, and egoism.[2]

During these sad years Mikhailovsky's apartment became the centre for the evenings of the *Northern Herald* circle. The man who best portrayed the sense of unfulfilled longing in this group and in the entire period of narodnik twilight was a young writer to whom Mikhailovsky was giving particular encouragement during this period, Anton Chekhov.[3] In Chekhov's great plays one finds both the comic aspect of the small deeds which filled up the lives of the men of the eighties, and the tragic sense of unaccomplished mission which paralysed their creative powers. Life was for the narodnik survivors of the late eighties an endless succession of petty activity redeemed only by that vision of

[1] Quoted in G. I. Uspensky, *Materialy*, p. 240.
[2] Ivan Keussler, 'The Village Commune and its Contemporary Possibilities', as quoted in K. R. Kacharovsky, *Russkaya Obshchina*, Moscow, 1906, p. 35 note.
[3] See *Note Y*, p. 194.

the good society which they no longer expected to see realized on earth.

There is nothing for it. We must go on living. . . . We shall live through a long chain of days and weary evenings; we shall patiently bear the trials which fate sends us . . . and when our time comes, we shall die without a murmur, and there, beyond the grave . . . we shall see all earthly evil, all our sufferings drowned in mercy which will fill the world. . . . [1]

The years at the end of the decade were among the saddest of Mikhailovsky's life. A series of deaths among his old friends came as a grim reminder that the personalities as well as the visions of the seventies were passing away. In 1888 Vsevolod Garshin, one of the most promising of the young writers on the *Annals*, committed suicide. In 1885–6 Mikhailovsky had seen in Garshin's work one of the few encouraging signs in creative art, but had been troubled by Garshin's fatalism and pessimism in describing the struggle between 'human dignity and the elemental process which makes man into a mere air vent (*klapan*)'.[2] Garshin's mental breakdown and suicide must have shown Mikhailovsky that, in yet another writer of great promise, the 'elemental process' had triumphed over the 'testament of faith and hope' of the seventies.

In the following year, the same mental depression struck Uspensky; his first mental attacks of 1889 foreshadowed the complete nervous breakdown which overtook him in 1892.[3] Also in 1889, both Saltykov and Chernyshevsky died, while a third of the original 'consistory' on the *Contemporary*, Eliseev, was stricken with an incurable illness which led to his death in January 1891. Shelgunov, with whom Mikhailovsky had become increasingly friendly in the late eighties, died in April 1892.

With these personal losses superimposed on the general atmosphere of 'small deeds', Mikhailovsky began to turn from the present to the past. *Sovremennost* (contemporaneity), which had seemed to hold so much promise for all radical thinkers since Crimea, had now been replaced by *zloba dnya* (the malicious

---

[1] Anton Chekhov, *Uncle Vanya*, in *The Cherry Orchard and Other Plays*, London (Chatto and Windus), 1950, p. 149.   [2] VI. 332.

[3] Uspensky was committed to an asylum in 1892, where he remained until his death in 1902, with Mikhailovsky a frequent visitor.

gossip of the day), the title of the most popular section of the new weekly journals. The column which Mikhailovsky agreed to submit to the *Russian News* in the late eighties no longer reflected the historical optimism of the seventies. In place of his earlier, confident social theories he now contributed only a series of 'chance notes'—the title of his new column.

These notes were largely filled with reminiscences about the great figures of the narodnik age, beginning with a series on Saltykov in 1889–90 and followed by memorials to Shelgunov and Eliseev early in 1891.[1] The death of the latter, Mikhailovsky's oldest friend, prompted him to begin writing his own memoirs,[2] and the confiscation of Eliseev's posthumously published memoirs in 1894 must have caused Mikhailovsky further grief. Overcome by the relentlessness of the reaction, the passing of the great figures of the movement, and the pettiness of small deeds, Mikhailovsky sought to summon up memories of things past. He turned to his memoirs and to the commemorative work of the literary fund, delivering the principal address in 1891 at the fiftieth anniversary celebration of the death of Lermontov.[3] Mikhailovsky was beginning to prefer what he remembered of the past to what he expected of the future.

The Final Flowering

Despite the discouraging atmosphere of the eighties, the creative potential of the populists had not been entirely exhausted. As the decade drew to a close, it became apparent that they were regrouping for what would be their final assault as a coherent group on the bastions of autocracy. All of the familiar components of narodnik radicalism were to reappear in this revival of the early nineties: a new 'thick journal', a new circle, a series of illegal brochures, the practical leadership of the indefatigable Mark Natanson, and the personal and ideological

[1] V. 137–304; V. 349–92 and VI. 947–55; and VI. 898–906. He also wrote a lengthy introduction to the first edition of Uspensky's works in 1888 (V. 77–138), and was an editorial consultant for the St. Petersburg publisher, F. F. Pavlenkov, who specialized in publishing the works of radical writers.

[2] They began appearing in March 1891 and were published during the next four years as a column 'Literature and Life' (in Goltsev's *Russian Thought* and *The Wealth of Russia*) and republished in two volumes in 1900 as *Literary Memoirs and The Contemporary Struggle*. [3] V. 303–48.

support of Mikhailovsky. Because of his long association with the aspirations of the radical intelligentsia Mikhailovsky was to be the central figure in this final flowering of *narodnichestvo*.

Mikhailovsky's increasingly critical attitude towards Chekhov in the late eighties and early nineties illustrated the growing determination of the surviving narodniks not to allow the creeping paralysis of Chekhovian melancholy to overcome them. In a series of reviews Mikhailovsky rebuked Chekhov for his pessimism and the large element assigned to pure chance in his stories. Chekhov became for Mikhailovsky an example of great talent without 'a guiding idea'. Mikhailovsky rejected Chekhov's 'pantheistic vision' which left men without the dignity which comes from the struggle to create a more moral society.[1]

The organ which pointed out the path along which this unsatisfied quest for social justice would be redirected was *Self-Government* (*Samoupravlenie*) which began appearing in Geneva in 1887. *Self-Government* was the first radical journal of the decade to dissociate itself categorically from terrorism and place all its emphasis on decentralizing power and securing popular representation in the government. In sharp contrast to the extremism of *Narodnaya Volya*, this journal insisted that legal agitation for political rights was a duty of all socialists and that the *obshchina* need not necessarily be the major buttress against capitalist development in Russia.[2] Mikhailovsky had already criticized his fellow populists for neglecting this question of political rights in his 'Political Letters' of 1879 and his article on the closing of the *Annals* in 1884. He was naturally attracted to the new journal and began an anonymous collaboration with the third issue in February 1889.

His first article was another of his periodic denunciations of 'careerist' defection from service to the people. Just as he had returned from a period of inactivity in 1868 to denounce Kelsiev for his celebrated renunciation of radicalism, Mikhailovsky returned into print in 1889 to attack an even more famous

---

[1] N. Klestov, 'Chekhov and Mikhailovsky', loc. cit., pp. 5–23.

[2] For the programme of *Self-Government*, which elicited letters of approval from Lavrov, Dragomanov, and even Plekhanov's Marxist circle, see *Samoupravlenie*, 1887, no. 1, pp. 2–4. On Mikhailovsky's collaboration, see Kolosov's notes in X. 1083–4. Mikhailovsky's friends, Krivenko and Uspensky, also collaborated on the journal as did his young admirer, the future Socialist-Revolutionary leader, Victor Chernov.

renegade from radicalism, Leo Tikhomirov—the leader of the executive committee of *Narodnaya Volya*, who had disowned his revolutionary past and returned with a full pardon to Russia in 1888. Mikhailovsky spoke with sadness of 'our former comrade' in criticizing Tikhomirov's *apologia* of 1888: 'Why I ceased to be a Revolutionary.' Mikhailovsky did not follow the fashionable line of accusing Tikhomirov of evil motives and insincerity. 'That is his personal affair, not of interest to us. Of general interest stands only the illusion of autocracy, sincere or insincere.' The Tsar, Mikhailovsky continued, may be stubborn (*samodurny*), but he is autocratic (*samoderzhavny*) only in name; Pobedonostsev rules Russia with the aid of Plehve, and 'police cover Russia as a shroud a corpse'.[1] In his second article for *Self-Government* Mikhailovsky reiterated his opposition to the idea that the Tsar could possibly be the centre of any movement for social betterment. Commenting on the miraculous escape of the Tsar from an accident on the Kharkov-Azov railroad, Mikhailovsky remarks that 'God may help the Tsars, but the people must help themselves'.[2]

But how were 'the people' to provide themselves with an alternative to Tsardom? *Self-Government* had provided a forum abroad for a preliminary discussion of the problems; but with the publication of the last issue in November 1889, the scene shifted back to Russia where narodnik activity was beginning anew.

Perhaps sensing the radicals' need for the familiar guidepost of a 'thick journal', Mikhailovsky became concerned in 1890 with finding an heir to the tradition of the *Annals*. He offered to lend support to a new journal begun by friends of Uspensky, which had promised 'not to serve as light relaxing reading like all the ideal-less, illustrated publications . . . [but rather] to pose those vital social and personal questions which are ripening in Russian society with each passing year but are not being answered, or even asked clearly and firmly'.[3] When, however,

[1] Quoted from *Samoupravlenie*, no. 3, in E. E. Kolosov, 'N. K. Mikhailovsky in the Eighties', *Byloe* (Paris), 1909, nos. 9–10, p. 41. On Tikhomirov's volte-face, see Vera Figner's introduction to Leo Tikhomirov, *Vospominaniya*, Moscow, 1927; and the more hostile portrayal in N. S. Rusanov, *V Emigratsii*, pp. 158–68.

[2] Kolosov, 'N. K. Mikhailovsky in the Eighties', loc. cit., p. 42.

[3] Quoted from the manifesto of *Gazeta Gattsuka* by G. A. Machtet and I. I. Rodzevich, in G. I. Uspensky, *Materialy*, p. 329.

Mikhailovsky found 'nothing ideological (*ideinogo*)' in it, he ceased collaboration.[1] 'Truly the situation of our rising writers is terrible', he wrote sadly in the summer of 1890, 'when the people directing our journals have no understanding of anything.'[2]

In January 1891 Mikhailovsky hinted at plans of his own for a new journal, urging a prospective collaborator in the optimistic tone of an earlier day to 'throw away melancholy and seek to engross yourself in work'.[3] By following his own advice, however, Mikhailovsky was arousing the suspicions of Durnovo, the new Minister of the Interior. Throughout 1890 he had been establishing closer contacts with workers' and students' groups in St. Petersburg. These groups sought advice from him and from Shelgunov, author of the original narodnik 'Proclamation to the Young Generation'. The occasion of the latter's death and funeral in the spring of 1891 brought forth a large and emotional demonstration of students and workers. Mikhailovsky's presence was seized on as a pretext for banishing him once more from St. Petersburg.[4] He had actually tried to pacify unruly elements at the demonstration, as Durnovo admitted in answer to appeals on Makhailovsky's behalf. 'But he just showed once again what a great influence he has over these easily excited youth and what might take place if he decided to use this influence in another way.'[5]

Thus, Mikhailovsky was forced to withdraw once again to his villa at Lyuban, where throughout 1891 he discussed with old narodnik friends like Uspensky, Krivenko, and Korolenko,

[1] Mikhailovsky, Uspensky, and Goltsev criticized both *Gazeta Gattsuka* and its successor the *Dawn* (*Zarya*) in a letter to the *Russian News* on 24 November 1890 (Uspensky, *Materialy*, p. 330). These three acted briefly in 1890–1 as a kind of triumvirate to combat the 'cultural *narodnichestvo*' of *Gazeta Gattsuka* and of Gaideburov's the *Week*. The three developed their ideas largely on the pages of Goltsev's *Russian Thought*, and found considerable support in the provinces, notably in the *Volga Herald* (*Volzhsky Vestnik*) in Kazan.

[2] V. Nikolenko-Gilchenko, 'Memoirs of N. K. Mikhailovsky', *Zavety*, 1913, no. 1, p. 15.   [3] Ibid., p. 19.

[4] E. V. Geshina, 'The Shelgunov Demonstration', *M.G.*, 1908, no. 11, pp. 27–29.

[5] From the answer to an appeal addressed by Durnovo's personal friend, Baroness Uekskÿll, the wife of a former ambassador and a literary patron of the narodniks, as quoted in E. K. Pimenova, *Dni Minuvshie*, p. 149. Mikhailovsky was exiled with Zasodimsky who had delivered the traditional eulogy at the grave of Shelgunov. For Mikhailovsky's influence on students in the late eighties and other of his attempts to dissuade them from violence, see B. A. Shchetinin, 'N. K. Mikhailovsky and Moscow Students', *Ist V.*, 1914, no. 3, pp. 948–54.

plans for a new monthly journal.[1] When Durnovo permitted him to return to St. Petersburg early in 1892, Mikhailovsky and his friends proceeded to take over and revitalize the monthly journal the *Wealth of Russia (Russkoe Bogatstvo)*.[2] Just as Nekrasov had given stature to the reformed *Annals* a quarter of a century earlier, Mikhailovsky was indispensable in establishing the reputation of this new journal.

As the only major radical survivor of the sixties and seventies, Mikhailovsky acted as a magnet to attract as full collaborators a host of populist theorists who had been contributing to a variety of journals: Vorontsov, Danielson, Ivanchin-Pisarev, Yuzhakov, and Krivenko. Former assistants on Mikhailovsky's 'new books' section in the *Annals* followed him to his new journal: Annensky, Korolenko, and Rusanov. Finally, just as the *Annals* had attracted not only the leaders of its major radical predecessor, the *Contemporary*, but the leading figure on the second most influential radical journal (Pisarev of the *Russian Word*), so the *Wealth of Russia* attracted not only the leaders of the *Annals*, but the most important survivor of the only other important radical journal, Stanyukovich of Shelgunov's the *Cause*. With such a consolidation of narodnik forces on a single journal, Mikhailovsky could identify himself once more with the high calling of 'a man of journalism'. Although he would never fully regain the enthusiasm of the seventies, Mikhailovsky played a vigorous role on the new journal, which carried the narodnik message on into the twentieth century.[3]

Meanwhile the revolutionary circle which was to provide the nucleus for the narodnik revival had formed at Saratov early in 1890 around the original *Chaikovets*, Mark Natanson. His group, composed largely of old narodniks just released from prison, was thoroughly opposed to the terrorism of *Narodnaya Volya*.

---

[1] For a sample of the reports sent by the local police to St. Petersburg on Mikhailovsky during his banishment see 'New Materials on Uspensky', *K.A.*, 1941, no. 3, p. 155 note.

[2] See *Note Z*, p. 195.

[3] The narodnik camp was further strengthened in 1892 by the founding of *God's World (Mir Bozhy)* 'a journal for youth and self-education' by Mikhailovsky's intimate friend, A. A. Davydova. Despite the presence of many Marxists on this journal (including Davydova's son-in-law, Michael Tugan-Baranovsky), its basic tone was narodnik. Its dominant figure (Angel Bogdanovich) was, like Mikhailovsky, active in 'The People's Right', and its relations with the *Wealth of Russia* remained close until Davydova's death in 1902.

They discussed with some of the old zemstvo leaders a new *modus operandi* for Russian radicalism. When confronted with the great famine of 1891–2, they began to set forth their views in a series of illegal pamphlets published in Smolensk: 'The All-Russian Devastation', 'Brothers-Comrades', 'A Letter to Hungry Peasants', and others. By early 1892 Natanson's group was in communication with radical centres in St. Petersburg, Moscow, Kharkov, Novgorod, and Perm, and in the spring Mark Natanson personally solicited Mikhailovsky's aid and advice.

Mikhailovsky agreed to write several pamphlets and to help edit a journal. Although the latter never materialized, Mikhailovsky published an important pamphlet, *The Free Word* (*Svobodnoe Slovo*), in January 1892 at the secret 'press of the young *Narodovoltsy*':

Governors-general, ministers, and governors have led Russia to the brink of an abyss. It is time to call on other people. Only the convocation of elected representatives of the land and a free debate on our present situation will dispell the inertia and mistrust in society . . . will call forth the enthusiasm of self-denial which has always saved Russia.[1]

Mikhailovsky was only reiterating the appeal he had long been making for a political struggle, but this time his views were to prevail, when the new group gathered in Saratov in the summer of 1893 to draw up a manifesto. Mikhailovsky went in person to participate in the meeting of more than 200 radicals, and his wisdom and kindly manner produced a profound impression on young and old alike. 'The relationships of the young to Mikhailovsky moved me a great deal', one of the older narodniks later recalled. 'In them could be found the genuine deep devotion of pupils to a teacher of life.'[2] Before returning to St. Petersburg, Mikhailovsky helped to draw up the manifesto which at last gave radical sanction to his contention that the demand for political rights need not mean renunciation of the economic and social goals of *narodnichestvo*.

The group's new name, 'the party of the Peoples' Right' (*Narodnoe Pravo*), dramatized its adoption of the classical narodnik juxtaposition between actual laws and true right.

[1] X. 72.
[2] O. V. Aptekman, 'The Party of *Narodnoe Pravo*', *Byloe*, 1907, no. 7, p. 195.

More clearly than any previous narodnik group the *Narodo-pravtsy* insisted that a whole new basis for justice was necessary—that 'the people's rights' were political as well as social and economic. 'Popular right includes in itself the conception of the right of the people to political freedom and the conception of its right to secure its material needs upon the basis of national pro-duction.'[1] A new political order was now for the narodniks the *sine qua non* of further social progress—'the pressing question', to cite the title of another *Narodopravtsy* pamphlet. 'Political free-dom is not only the first step to socialism, but a necessary circum-stance for its existence.'[2]

Narodnoe Pravo offered the first clear repudiation of an idea from which few narodniks had ever liberated themselves—the feeling that the Tsar was capable of putting things right and that only the bureaucrats about him were to be feared. Even *Narodnaya Volya*, after killing a Tsar, had addressed its appeal for justice to his successor. *Narodnoe Pravo* was the first organized radical movement, apart from the lonely Jacobin revolu-tionaries of the Nechaev tradition, to question not just specific injustices of the Tsar, but his very right to determine what justice is. *Narodnaya Volya* eventually killed a Tsar, but *Narodnoe Pravo*, under Mikhailovsky's tutelage, was threatening to kill the very idea of autocracy. What Mikhailovsky's role might have been in the struggle of *Narodnoe Pravo* to bring about political reforms in Russian society must remain a matter for speculation, for the movement was crushed with greater finality and at an earlier stage of development than *Narodnaya Volya*. In April 1894 its press was seized and most of its leaders arrested in a sudden series of movements which destroyed the party before it had succeeded in drawing up a practical programme for gaining the desired political rights.[3]

These arrests represented the final triumph of Alexander III over the narodnik radicals. His policies of social reaction had demoralized them; his police had crushed them utterly when they gave signs of regrouping for the struggle. By the time of his death on 1 November 1894, Alexander had crushed the last

[1] 'Manifesto of the Party of the People's Right', in Serge Kravchinsky, *Nihilism as it is*, London, 1895, p. 120.
[2] Quoted from Angel Bogdanovich, *Nasushny Vopros*, in Aptekman, '*Narodnoe Pravo*', loc. cit., p. 201.
[3] See *Note A^a*, p. 195.

great social movement to be launched by the narodnik intelligentsia of the seventies. By the time his successor, Nicholas II, was crowned in 1895, the radical intelligentsia had been rent asunder by an internal debate, which would determine the future direction of Russian radical thought, and indeed of all Russian history.

X

THE END OF AN AGE

WHEN Alexander III died late in 1894, he left a very different Russia from that to which he had fallen heir in 1881. He had made it clear that the economic, educational, and political development of Russia were to be directed and supervised by the centralized state; and in so doing he had effectively crushed narodnik radicalism as a social movement. The visionary aspects of *narodnichestvo* could not survive nearly fifteen years of frustration. No one greeted the arrival of Nicholas II with anything like the messianic expectancy that had greeted his predecessor.

The most striking new feature of Russian society as a whole in the mid nineties was the growth of the cities and the emergence of an urban working class. To be sure, Russia was still an overwhelmingly agrarian society. Only one-sixth of her 91,000,000 population lived in cities in 1894. Yet this urban population was twice as great as that of the late sixties, and the total increase had been especially concentrated in the larger cities. The population of Moscow and St. Petersburg was particularly swollen after the famine and typhus epidemic of 1891–2. St. Petersburg passed the million mark during that winter, and Moscow reached it a few years later.[1]

Clearly, by the mid nineties, the permanency and importance of the city in Russian life could no longer be overlooked; nor could the growth of large-scale industries which had taken place under Alexander III. By the early nineties Russia had acquired the beginnings of an urban proletariat analogous to those of Western European countries. And in the 1893–7 period the size of the working force suddenly increased by one-third to reach a figure well over two million.[2]

[1] M. W. Kovalevsky, *La Russie*, p. 313; Brockhaus-Effron, *Entsiklopedichesky Slovar*, xxvii. 82–83.

[2] M. Tugan-Baranovsky, *Russkaya Fabrika*, pp. 276, 305. The rate of industrialization really began to accelerate in the late eighties under the finance ministry of Vyshnegradsky. By 1889 the annual value of factory-produced goods in Russia had passed one billion roubles. N. Danielson, *Ocherki Nashego Poreformennago Obshchestvennago Khozyaistva*, St. Petersburg, 1893, pp. 124–5.

By any Western scale of measurement, the movement to the cities was still in its infant stage; yet in Russia it was a symptom of sudden and disrupting change. The village fairs, where the domestic craft industries had conducted a flourishing business throughout the seventies, were in sharp decline. The competition of American grain was causing increasing poverty in the countryside. By the mid nineties a huge new railroad expansion programme had already built the trans-Siberian railroad, and a vastly expanding metallurgy industry was further helping to transform the face of Russia.

The governmental economic policies of the early nineties were administered by a former railroad official, Count Witte, and involved a good measure of state capitalism—protective tariffs, increasing government ownership, and the accumulation of gold reserves. Witte had already been in control of the Russian economy for two years when Nicholas II became Tsar, and he remained the main architect of this aspect of policy until his dismissal in 1903. He was opposed within the government by Durnovo, Plehve, and most of the old-style conservatives, who looked on him as an outsider and a dangerous innovator. For the narodniks, Witte symbolized all that was reprehensible— heartless capitalism with its amoral doctrine of social development. However, for the rising Marxists Witte was an ally (albeit temporary) in the cause of Russian social progress. His new world of economic activity, in which the moral aspirations of the intelligentsia were viewed with disdain, was uniquely suited for a new world view; and it was in the early years of Witte's reign that Marxism emerged as a coherent force to challenge populism for the leadership of Russian radicalism.

The Marxist Challenge

The establishment of Marxism as a serious alternative to *narodnichestvo* among the radical intelligentsia was almost completely the work of one man, George Plekhanov. A protégé of Mikhailovsky on the *Annals*, Plekhanov had been throughout the seventies an ardent narodnik. He had, like Mikhailovsky, rejected the terrorism of *Narodnaya Volya*, defending the evolutionary narodnik concern for land redistribution in his splinter group of 1879, 'Black Redistribution'. Nevertheless, after his flight abroad in 1880, Plekhanov slowly adopted a new philosophy and began an attack on Mikhailovsky, the prophet of the old.

Plekhanov launched his attack on Mikhailovsky and the narodniks by insisting that the *obshchina* be dissolved so that Russia could reach socialism through a capitalist phase. Marx had never insisted unequivocally that the commune could not serve as the germ of socialist development in Russia. In answer to repeated requests from his Russian readers, Marx had written in a letter to Mikhailovsky in November 1877 that Russia was tending to become capitalist and thus subject to the laws of *Capital*. He spoke also of the necessity of 'changing a considerable number of her peasants into proletariat'.[1] But in the early eighties, Marx wrote that '*Capital* is neither for nor against the *obshchina*', recognizing that it might serve as a 'point of support for social regeneration'.[2] The interest of Marx and Engels in this question was, in any case, subsidiary to their interest in revolutionary developments in the West, for which they hoped Russian unrest might prove a catalyst.[3] Not until the years immediately after Marx's death in 1883 was the Marxist case against the efficacy of the *obshchina* made detailed and unequivocal by Plekhanov.

'Not only in the near future but in the present, capitalism belongs to us.'[4] With these blunt words, Plekhanov challenged the narodnik view of Russian society in his pamphlet of 1884 'Our Differences'. Plekhanov contended that the commune was vanishing and any attempt to preserve it would be vain. Plekhanov's views became a major force among his fellow *émigrés* almost immediately. In 1882 he published in Geneva the first Russian translation of *The Communist Manifesto*; and in the following year he organized in the same city the first explicitly Marxist 'circle' in the history of the Russian intelligentsia: 'The Liberation of Labour'. These two events mark the introduction into the Russian scene of Marxism as a rival force to *narodnichestvo*.[5] But

[1] *Perepiska Marksa i Engelsa s Russkimi Politicheskimi Deyatelyami*, Moscow, 1947, p. 178. Addressed to Mikhailovsky in his official capacity as editor of the *Annals*, but in answer to his own article of October 1877, 'Karl Marx before the Court of Yu. Zhukovsky'.

[2] Letter to Vera Zasulich of 8 March 1881, *Narodnaya Volya v Dokumentakh i Vospominaniyakh*, Moscow, 1935, pp. 240–1.

[3] See *Note B[b]*, p. 195.

[4] G. V. Plekhanov, *Nashi Raznoglasiya*, Leningrad, 1938, p. 272.

[5] See *Note C[c]*, p. 195.

Marxism did not grow significantly within Russia during the eighties,[1] in part because of the arguments advanced by two of Mikhailovsky's protégés on the *Annals*, Danielson and Vorontsov.

As the co-translator of *Capital* and Marx's leading Russian correspondent, Danielson was well acquainted with Marx's ideas. But in his 'Sketches of our Post-Reform Social Economy', during 1880, Danielson insisted that the pattern of social development outlined in *Capital* had no validity for Russia.[2] Vorontsov repeated this idea with less erudition but greater polemic skill during 1881 in a series of articles for the *Annals*, which were published the following year under the title: *The Fate of Capitalism in Russia (Sudba Kapitalizma v Rossii)*. 'A popular party would play a great role in practical affairs', Vorontsov argued, if 'to its belief in the vitality of popular principles was united an affirmation in the historical impossibility of the development of capitalist production in Russia.'[3] Vorontsov argued that the absence of external markets, the lack of transportation across Russia, and the hallowed communal forms of Russian life all made the likelihood of capitalism in Russia a diminishing rather than a growing possibility.

Both Vorontsov and Danielson joined Mikhailovsky on *The Wealth of Russia* in 1892, and all three began to concentrate their resources for a broadened narodnik attack on the Marxist position. Danielson, in the 1893 edition of his *Sketches of our Post-Reform Economy*, blamed the famine of 1891 on the dislocations of Russian economic life that incipient capitalism (and, by implication, its Marxist apologists) was causing.[4] Vorontsov, in his *Our Tendencies* of 1893, put aside his earlier concern with the factual question of whether or not capitalism was possible, in order to launch a broad philosophic attack on Marxism for reducing man to a 'docile tool' of history.[5]

It was on this level that Mikhailovsky entered the lists

---

[1] The earliest date at which Marxism can be said to have existed as an independent movement within Russia was 1885, when the first Russian Social Democratic circle and journal were founded and the first Russian publication of the *Critique of Political Economy* published in St. Petersburg. For details see P. Orlovsky, *K Istorii Marksizma v Rossii*, Moscow, 1919, pp. 21 ff.

[2] Published in 1880 in the journal *Slovo* and expanded into a book in 1893.

[3] Quoted in Fedor Dan, *Proiskhozhdenie Bolshevizma*, New York, 1946, p. 162.

[4] N. Danielson (Nikolai-on), *Ocherki Nashego Poreformennago Obshchestvennago Khozyaistva*, pp. 257–66, 333–46.

[5] V. P. Vorontsov (V.V.), *Nashi Napravleniya*, St. Petersburg, 1893, pp. 138–40.

against the Marxists. In the seventies Mikhailovsky had praised Marx as a fellow socialist and defender of human values. One of the most widely read books by the uncritical narodniks during the early nineties even went so far as to call Mikhailovsky 'the most hateful of our Marxists'.[1] Yet Mikhailovsky had been impressed with the criticism Uspensky advanced as early as 1888: that Marxism erred in appealing to necessity rather than free moral choice, in separating the question 'What is to be?' from the question of 'How should one live in the world?'[2] With the publication of his first 'Literature and Life' column in January 1894, Mikhailovsky began to amplify Uspensky's position and identify his own great prestige with the radical opposition to Marxism. He decried the growing tendency to speak in the name of 'pure art' or 'pure science'; attacking 'German Marxist literature' for saying that 'in a quarter of an hour one can assimilate an entire philosophy of history which is guaranteed to be scientific'.[3]

Mikhailovsky was also shocked at the advice given in 1894 by the Russian Marxist Peter Struve to 'recognize our backwardness and enter on to the path of capitalism'.[4] And in October he established the pattern of narodnik rebuttal by linking Struve and the Marxists with Orlov-Davydov and the capitalistic industrialists, who also sought to break up the social structure of Russia.[5] Mikhailovsky had not closed his eyes to the changes which were taking place. He did not, like the narodniks on the *Week*, pine for the vanished Eden of old Russia. But he felt it inhuman not to express concern for maintaining the moral type

[1] I. I. Kablits (Yuzov), *Osnovy Narodnichestva* (second ed), 1888, p. 361. Critical narodniks like Mikhailovsky were to Kablits 'intellectual-bureaucratic people-lovers' (p. 504). Mikhailovsky attacked Kablits's work in *R.B.*, 1893, no. 10 (*Lit. V*. II. 140–58), and continued to dissociate himself from Vorontsov and the purely pacific narodniks. Nevertheless, the Marxists continued to group Mikhailovsky among the uncritical narodniks, just as the latter considered him a Marxist.

[2] Letter to V. M. Sobolevsky, editor of the *Russian News*, as quoted by Mikhailovsky in his biographical introduction to G. I. Uspensky, *Poslednie Sochineniya*, St. Petersburg, 1905, i. 189–91. Uspensky's ire had been aroused by a reading of Marx's letter to the editor of the *Annals*, which had been written originally in French and was not published in Russian until October 1888 in *Yuridichesky Vestnik*. On Uspensky's opposition to Marxism and his attempt to attack it in some of his stories, see N. M. Piksanov, 'Gleb Uspensky on Karl Marx', *Novy Mir*, 1933, no. 3.   [3] *Lit. V*. II. 274.

[4] P. B. Struve, *Kriticheskie Zametki k Voprosu ob Ekonomicheskom Razvitii Rossii*, St. Petersburg, 1894, p. 288.

[5] *Lit. V*. II. 442–3.

of social relationships in the old order, while moving to the higher level which industrial development would bring.

Mikhailovsky criticized the 'Marxist onlookers' for whom living held no more excitement than going to a play which one had already read. Always knowing the ending made one feel 'very comfortable', but something was always missing from the experience. He also attacked the 'active Marxists', those who seize upon each event that seems to further social development along a Marxist pattern and foster it regardless of consequences to individuals. The logical Marxist attitude towards the famine of 1891–2, in Mikhailovsky's view, must include a considerable amount of indifference to suffering, born of the belief that such a disaster would aid in transforming the peasantry into an urban proletariat. He cited a pamphlet expressing this view by a group of Marxists in Orenburg as evidence that this was the true Marxist position.[1] In his February column, Mikhailovsky broadened his attack to the entire philosophy of dialectical materialism. All Hegelianisms he saw as similar to Calvinism in denying the individual real freedom of choice.[2]

Mikhailovsky's attack provoked a vigorous response from the Marxist camp. He received a large number of personal letters from young Marxists. Some argued with Mikhailovsky in respectful tones, urging him to make common cause with Marxism in furthering the goals which both parties were alleged to share.[3] A less conciliatory line was adopted by the young Lenin in a series of pamphlets illegally published in 1894 and later collected as *What the 'Friends of the People' are and How They Fight the Social Democrats*.

However, it was to Plekhanov—who had first applied the economic arguments of *Capital* to the Russian scene and first organized a Marxist group abroad—that the Russian Marxists turned for a full philosophical defence of Marxism. In the early autumn of 1894 a young Marxist publisher, A. N. Potresov, set off for London to obtain such a work, and returned with Plekhanov's *On the Question of the Development of the Monistic View of History*. Later known by its less cumbersome sub-title, *In Defense*

---

[1] *Lit. V.* II. 270–3.
[2] *Lit. V.* II. 275–98.
[3] This 'popular front' tone was taken by N. E. Fedoseev in two letters to Mikhailovsky in 1894: 'From the Unpublished Literary Legacy of N. E. Fedoseev', *Literaturnoe Nasledstvo* (7–8), Moscow, 1933, pp. 182–221.

of Materialism, Plekhanov's book proved a skilful attack on the
ideological foundations of *narodnichestvo* and one of the best ex-
positions of Marxist philosophy ever written. In it, many radical
thinkers professed to find a new *Weltanschauung,* a new source of
hope that populism in the age of small deeds had not provided.

Monistic, objective truth—this was the intoxicant which
Plekhanov found in Marx and offered to the young generation.
The 'subjective' personality that 'thinks feels and suffers'—the
touchstone of truth and value in Mikhailovsky's world-view—
was irrelevant to Plekhanov, who contended that 'the criterion
of truth lies not in me, but in the relations which exist outside of
me'.[1] Marx, the 'new Copernicus', has made objectivity possible
in social theory; and 'subjectivist' becomes Plekhanov's chief
term of abuse for those who build social science on 'hollow and
long-since hackneyed reflections on the theme of human nature'.[2]
Plekhanov groups the narodniks with the French 'utopian'
socialists, who 'still call all the sciences bearing on human
society "moral and political sciences" as distinct from "science
in the strict sense of the word" '.[3]

Objective social science alone can bring together the 'ought'
and the 'is', can 'build a bridge across this seemingly bottom-
less abyss'.[4] This science is for Plekhanov dialectical materialism: 'that communist teaching which began to evolve in the
beginning of the forties from utopian socialism under the strong
influence of Hegelian philosophy on the one hand and of
classical economics on the other.'[5] Thus the ideological forces
from which Plekhanov fashioned his world-view were the very
two that had been consistently derided by Mikhailovsky and
the narodniks: English economics and German philosophy.

The moral idealism of Mikhailovsky had rebelled at the
classical economists' assumption that economic forces determined social development. In the mid nineties the narodniks
were still following him in labelling the Manchester School
economists as heartless apologists for English capitalism. Uspensky had sardonically suggested writing a tragedy, *The Power of
Capital,* as a successor to his famous *The Power of the Land,* and

[1] G. V. Plekhanov, *In Defense of Materialism* (tr. Rothstein), London, 1947,
p. 220.   [2] Ibid., p. 191.
[3] Ibid., p. 178.   [4] Ibid., p. 73.
[5] As described by Plekhanov shortly after his conversion to Communism in his
Sotsializm i Politicheskaya Borba, Leningrad, 1939, pp. 24–25.

Danielson had written sadly of the 'Apologies for the Power of Money as Signs of the Times'.[1] Plekhanov blazed the trail that made it possible for radical thinkers to rid themselves of the sense of uncleanness which they had felt during the populist era in speaking of man primarily in terms of economic categories.

The moral humanism of the populists had rejected even more decisively the historical determinism of Hegel, whom Mikhailovsky had bitterly labelled a 'Berlin state philosopher' and a product of the bygone age of metaphysics. Mikhailovsky had contended that 'there is no philosophical system which treats the individual with such withering contempt and cold cruelty as the system of Hegel'.[2] Plekhanov—author of the warm official tribute of the Second International to Hegel in 1891[3]—became the first important Russian radical in the late nineteenth century to attempt a thoroughgoing vindication of the German. He defends Hegel's dialectic from Mikhailovsky—just as Engels and Marx had defended it from Dühring, Proudhon, and Bruno Bauer—by attacking the attacker. He demonstrates the palpably unscientific nature of Mikhailovsky's all but forgotten 'formula of progress', and shows that Mikhailovsky's understanding of the Hegelian dialectic was not very deep.[4] Although Plekhanov never substantiated his own claims of scientific truth for the dialectic, he succeeded in fixing the dreaded labels of 'metaphysical' and 'unscientific' on Mikhailovsky and the populists.

Mikhailovsky recognized the seriousness of this challenge to his position. 'I am so frightened with Beltov (Plekhanov) that I do not dare enter into combat with him', Mikhailovsky declared in his article of January 1895, pointing out how irreconcilable was the opposition between them.[5] Despite urging from his friends, Mikhailovsky rejected the opportunity to construct a systematic counter-doctrine; for the very point at issue with Plekhanov was whether or not social reform should be related to a body of 'scientific' dogma. To emphasize this point,

---

[1] R.B., 1895, nos. 1, 2.   [2] R.B., 1894, no. 10, p. 55.

[3] On the sixtieth anniversary of his death, printed in G. V. Plekhanov, Les Questions fondamentales du Marxisme, Paris, 1947, pp. 107–35.

[4] G. V. Plekhanov, In Defense of Materialism, pp. 84–90, 99–130. Plekhanov attacked not only Mikhailovsky, but his idol, Belinsky, whose celebrated break with Hegel was thus deprecated for the first time by a leading Russian radical.

[5] Ot. I. 30.

Mikhailovsky withdrew in his January article his earlier claim to have set forth a scientific theory of progress, admitting that his formulas are metaphorical, that his own case rests ultimately on subjective ideals.[1]

In replying to Plekhanov, Mikhailovsky rightly pointed out that his much discussed articles, 'The Hero and the Mob' (1882) and 'More on Heroes' (1891) were not endorsements of Carlyle's great-man theory of history. Mikhailovsky had expressed admiration for many of Carlyle's observations, but had refused to accept 'the positive side of his programme, which can be expressed literally in two words: find a hero'.[2] Mikhailovsky sought only to describe dispassionately the behaviour of demagogues and the general laws of mob psychology.[3] But, by discussing social phenomena as the product of general human characteristics rather than specific historical circumstances, Mikhailovsky placed himself at odds on another score with the German historicistic tradition in which Plekhanov stood.

In January and February 1896 Mikhailovsky denounced once more the Marxist tendency to explain everything by economics as a throwback to the 'third-rate' propagandists of the sixties.[4] In November 1897 he launched a final attack on the Marxist concept of history, seeking to rescue populism from the caricatured description Plekhanov had given it.[5] The supporting fire for Mikhailovsky's counter-attack was provided by a host of articles, beginning with those of Danielson and Rusanov in the March 1895 issue of *The Wealth of Russia* and climaxing in Kareev's *Historical-Philosophical and Sociological Études* of 1896. Another child of French thought who had been attacked by Plekhanov, Professor Kareev, systematically developed such Mikhailovskian themes as the centrality of the individual

---

[1] *Ot.* I. 24.

[2] II. 379. Mikhailovsky clearly explained in the first of these studies that 'the problem lies in the mechanics of the relationship between the mob and the man whom it considers great and not in a search for the standard of greatness'. II. 99.

[3] In so doing, Mikhailovsky reflected and often anticipated the views of the great French pioneers of descriptive sociology. His studies preceded and closely resembled Émile de Tarde's *Les Lois de l'imitation*, Paris, 1890; and even in the midst of his polemics with the Marxists he found time to introduce into Russia the works of Émile Durkheim, whose *De la Division du Travail Social* bore many resemblances to Mikhailovsky's writings on this subject. See P. Mokievsky, 'N. K. Mikhailovsky and Western Science', *R.B.*, 1904, no. 3, pp. 45–50.

[4] *Ot.* I. 293 ff.   [5] *Ot.* I. 169–95.

personality and the difference between the natural and the human sciences. Kareev's work prompted Plekhanov to publish in 1898 his final contribution to the debate: 'The Role of the Individual in History.'[1] This article, which received no direct answer from the narodniks, restated the difference in world-view of the two camps and, in effect, brought to a close the great debate of the nineties.

Despite its peculiarly Russian aspects, the debate between Mikhailovsky and Plekhanov mirrored in broad outline the conflict that was developing throughout European socialist thought in the late eighties and nineties. Engels in his later days was fully aware of the broad implications of the Russian struggle, when he wrote to Vera Zasulich that 'it is necessary to fight *narodnichestvo* everywhere—be it German, French, English or Russian'.[2]

In the years before the formation of the Second International in 1889—and even more decisively thereafter—a split was becoming increasingly evident in continental socialism between the French and the German, the subjective and the objective camps. Like Mikhailovsky, the French socialists (along with Lange and a few of the Germans) based their appeal on subjective ethical arguments and a sense of continuity with the French revolutionary tradition. Like Plekhanov, the German socialists (along with Jules Guesde and a few of the French) argued rather from objective, *a priori* assumptions about the true society and the meaning of the historical process, with no particular interest in the revolutionary heritage of France. Whereas the French socialists were for the most part against the growth of the state and centralized political power as such, the German Social Democrats thought in terms of taking over the newly formed and much revered institution of the German state. This rift between subjective and objective socialism, which had set Proudhon off from Marx and Lassalle, was, in essence, the same which separated Jean Jaurès from Liebknecht, and Mikhailovsky from Plekhanov. Indeed Plekhanov, Akselrod, and the other early Marxists had close personal and ideological

---

[1] Originally published in *Nauchnoe Obozrenie* under the pseudonym Kirsanov, republished London, 1950. For this and other material see G. V. Plekhanov, *Literaturnoe Nasledie (Sbornik IV) Borba s Narodnichestvom*, Moscow, 1937.

[2] Letter of 3 April 1890, in M. Potash, 'Marx and Engels on Narodnik Socialism in Russia', *Proletarskaya Revolyutsiya*, 1929, no. ii, p. 53.

links with the Germans, just as *Narodnaya Volya* and *Narodnoe Pravo* maintained close contact with the French. *Das Proletariat* of Marx, of Guesde, and of Plekhanov was concerned with the dogmas of class struggle in relation to objective social conditions. *Les Classes ouvrières* of Proudhon, of Jaurès, and of Mikhailovsky were concerned with moral truths which to them transcended the dictates of expediency or the historical context. In Russia, as elsewhere on the Continent, the struggle among socialists in the nineties was between German and French, objective and subjective, 'scientific' and 'utopian', dialectical materialist and moral idealist.[1]

The results of the debate were far from decisive in Russia, yet on the whole Plekhanov and the Marxists emerged the victors. They won few converts from among the narodniks; but they made great gains among the young and uncommitted intelligentsia. Most of the new 'thick journals' founded in the last years of the century were Marxist in orientation.[2] The trend among the intelligentsia in the nineties was away from narodnik subjectivism, which had turned to pessimism and 'small deeds', toward some new 'objective' basis for thinking through the problems of the day.[3]

As the great narodnik pioneer Shelgunov observed shortly before his death in 1891: 'The eighties thought only of themselves . . . and ended with the idea of social indifference. Present day youth are beginning with the study of those social facts, from which as a logical consequence must follow of its own accord what is to be done.'[4]

Nevertheless, to Mikhailovsky and a substantial portion of the young intelligentsia the very objectivism (which they distinguished from objectivity) of Plekhanov's position made it frighteningly inhuman. To Mikhailovsky and his followers

[1] See *Note D^d*, p. 196.

[2] Most important were *Novoe Slovo* (taken over from narodniks in March 1897 and shut at the end of the year), *Nauchnoe Obozrenie* (founded 1894, effectively taken over by Marxists in 1897 and dominated by them until its failure in 1903), *Zhizn* (founded in 1897 and dominated by Marxists from 1899 until shut in 1901), and *Nachalo* (founded by Marxists in 1899 and shut that year after five numbers).

[3] Other less socially oriented 'objective' viewpoints that were gaining converts among the intelligentsia in the early nineties were the symbolist school of pure art (which wrested a major journal—*Severny Vestnik*—from narodnik control in 1891) and the transcendental idealism of Vladimir Solovev.

[4] N. V. Shelgunov, *Ocherki Russkoy Zhizni*, St. Petersburg, 1895, pp. 1093–4.

Plekhanov stood 'on the heights of objective truth',[1] aloof from the sufferings of the day. Mikhailovsky's socialism remained steeped in the moral idealism and passionate anti-systematic subjectivism of Proudhon. When Mikhailovsky analysed social phenomena, he continued to do so through the eyes of a French sociologist, opposing to historicism a belief in the universality of man's quest for wholeness. He was and remained an opponent of Marxist socialism, which had brought together under one banner the two streams of thought he most feared: German metaphysics and English economics.

The Emergence of the Masses

Although the early Marxists had brought to an end the un-challenged dominance of the narodnik ideology, the battle had still been waged within the confines of an intelligentsia. New developments in the late nineties were heralding the end, not just of Mikhailovsky's authority, but of the Russia in which social questions could be confined to a small group of aristo-cratic radicals.

Mikhailovsky had sought to have Russian society rebuilt by repentant yet critical members of the old nobility, for 'only in that type of Russian is it possible to find ... some sort of order not prescribed from above, but developed from within'.[2] Yet, throughout the nineties a new and very different force was rising in Russia—that of the mass passions and movements of the urban proletariat. Unlike the workers of an earlier genera-tion who still thought of themselves as displaced peasants, those who swelled into St. Petersburg and the rapidly expanding cities to the south and west in the years after the great famine of 1891–2 knew that there was no turning back. With the strike of 30,000 textile workers in St. Petersburg in 1896 it became clear that the uprooted and inarticulate masses were seeking a direct voice in the remaking of Russian society.

Mikhailovsky was deeply apprehensive of this new force, in which the 'struggle for individuality' could lose its meaning. He sensed that the moral impulses of the individual would be dis-torted by the passions of the mob and its 'hero' of the moment.

---

[1] The title of Rusanov's hostile article on Plekhanov in *R.B.*, 1895, no. 3.
[2] Quoted approvingly from Dostoevsky's *Raw Youth*, p. 557 in IV. 211–12.

As early as 1891 Mikhailovsky had become pessimistic over the extent to which urbanization would bring grief to Russia:

Insofar as the division of labour impresses itself deeper and deeper into society, the striving for unity (*unison*) changes its nature and direction; in place of feeling one gets only mimicry. Feeling wanes and imitation increases to such an extent that bloody struggles and deep mutual hatred between different branches of the divided labour of society become possible. . . .[1]

Thus, Mikhailovsky began to see in the inner dynamics of these new mass movements a return to the irrationalism and 'pathological magic', that he had long considered outmoded by the forward march of history. In October 1894 he wrote of 'a great and heavy sadness' that had come over him, adding in November that 'it is difficult for me to sleep because on the whole it is difficult for me to go on living'.[2] Seeking the solace of the countryside, he left St. Petersburg to spend the summer of 1895 with the painter Yaroshenko in Kislovodsk; and when he returned in the autumn he brought with him for the first time a servant to help attend his wants. In the spring of 1896 he began to have trouble with his heart as well as his nerves, and went off for a long summer in Yalta with his friend and colleague on the *Wealth of Russia*, Ivanchin-Pisarev.

Throughout this period he spent his time increasingly on non-political matters—his memoirs, literary criticism, the work of the literary fund,[3] and visits to Moscow to see his elder son perform in the Art Theatre. Symptomatic of his sense of failure in his social mission was the statement at the beginning of his memoirs that 'other memories than literary I could not offer the reader, since all my life has passed through literature'.[4] Mikhailovsky remained, nevertheless, a deeply revered figure for

[1] II. 190.
[2] From a letter to V. Nikolenko-Gilchenko in her 'Memoirs of N. K. Mikhailovsky', *Zavety*, 1913, no. 1, pp. 32, 34.
[3] For details of the operation of this fund, its bi-weekly meetings, and the petty controversies in which it became involved, see N. K. Mikhailovsky, 'A Note on the Literary Fund', *R.B.*, 1894, no. 9, pp. 72–80.
[4] Such an obvious misrepresentation of his past may have been, as E. E. Kolosov suggests ('Toward a Characterization of the Social World-View of N. K. Mikhailovsky', *G.M.*, 1914, no. 2, pp. 217–18 and note), his 'Aesopian' way of assuring his readers that he did have a large store of other memories. There is, however, a measure of literal truth to the statement, if one keeps in mind the broad meaning he and the populists ascribed to the word 'literature'.

many active radicals such as Nicholas Rusanov and Victor Chernov, who worked under him on the *Wealth of Russia* and were drawing together in the late nineties the nucleus of the new Socialist-Revolutionary (S.-R.) Party. Despite his sympathy for the narodnik ideals of the new group, Mikhailovsky was apprehensive of its terrorist plans and mass appeals and turned down repeated offers to lend his active advice and support.

Even deeper was Mikhailovsky's opposition to the second of the movements seeking to arouse the masses politically in the late nineties: revolutionary Marxism. By the late nineties, he sensed that the moral socialism of the populists was being supplanted by a less civilized, authoritarian force, by the new communism, which Herzen had long ago characterized as 'the socialism of revenge'.[1] A friend recalled that in 1896 'he was very upset by the appearance of students censuring him for his lack of understanding of the new social movement'.[2] In the course of the next year he characterized Marxism as a 'spreading epidemic', contending that its apologists 'do not want to stand in any continuous relationship with the past and decisively cut themselves off from their heritage'.[3] Yet, for Mikhailovsky, revolutionary extremism was only the logical result of government repression. In July 1898 he wrote sadly to Rusanov:

All talented and energetic youth risk exile or banishment, and then are sucked into the muck away from books, conversations, acquaintances. . . . Each year the cream is skimmed off and thrown away leaving us only skimmed milk. . . . This explains all our mental unrest and in particular the spread of Marxism. . . . To master Marxism . . . neither mind nor knowledge is needed, but only vaunting up one's own importance under a scientific sauce, and unloading work on the worker while flattering and reassuring him. . . .

'The result', Mikhailovsky predicted, 'will be one of two in the indeterminate, but not too distant future. Either [we will] master . . . the liberal current and gain freedom from a frozen

---

[1] A. I. Herzen, *Sobranie Sochinenii*, Petrograd, 1919, vi. 117.
[2] V. Nikolenko-Gilchenko, 'Memoirs', loc. cit., pp. 137–8.
[3] *R.B.*, 1897, no. 10, i. 179. P. Yakubovich, 'Letters of N. K. Mikhailovsky', *R.B.*, 1910, no. 1, p. 237.

society, while it warms up as well, or else we will return to terror with all its unforeseeable consequences.'[1] Mikhailovsky would have had Russia take the former path; but in the world of rising mass movements, mob passions, and world wars, it was 'terror with all its unforeseeable consequences' which was eventually to prevail. Already in the late nineties Vladimir Lenin, the prophet of this new revolutionary Marxism, was rising to prominence within the Russian Social Democratic movement. With few roots in the traditions of the radical intelligentsia, Lenin had in fact been committed to a 'socialism of revenge' long before he became a Marxist. For, while Vladimir was still a schoolboy in Kazan in the late eighties, his elder brother had been executed for participation in a crude attempt to revive terrorism. When he followed his brother to St. Petersburg in the early nineties, he turned eagerly to the world of mass passions, and to the ideology of Plekhanov which promised to 'awaken in the crowd the heroic consciousness of self'.[2] He was to challenge not just Mikhailovsky and the populists, but the very world from which they came.

'You boast that the Russian non-estate intelligentsia has always been distinguished by the purity of its ideas', Lenin said of Mikhailovsky in 1894, 'but that is exactly why it has always been impotent'.[3] In his contempt for 'purity of ideas', his fascination with the concept of a revolutionary *élite*, and his attacks on the motives as well as the ideas of his opponents, Lenin was the heir to the lonely Jacobin tradition of Nechaev and Tkachev. By insisting in his attack on Mikhailovsky that 'the direct purpose of science is to provide a true slogan for the struggle',[4] Lenin cut at the very foundations of the intelligentsia's lofty concept of science and truth.

For Lenin, all truth had to be realized in society; and, since material power rules society, the realization of truth simply required the attainment of power. This preoccupation with the problem of power set Lenin off most strikingly from the moral idealism that had dominated the radical intelligentsia. The guiding principles of Lenin as a revolutionary leader followed

[1] N. S. Rusanov, 'The Politics of N. K. Mikhailovsky', *Byloe*, 1907, no. 7, p. 137.
[2] G. V. Plekhanov, *In Defense of Materialism*, p. 247.
[3] V. I. Lenin, 'What the "Friends of the People" are and how they fight the Social Democrats', *Selected Works*, London, 1939, xi. 635.
[4] Ibid., p. 606.

logically from this preoccupation and were well developed by
the turn of the century: his emphasis on seizing political power
rather than winning economic gains, and his insistence on a
disciplined core of professional revolutionaries.[1] Lenin's revolutionaries were not to be distracted from material realities by such
speculative concerns as absolute moral standards or ideal concepts of truth. For Lenin there could be no subjectivity, only
the cold appraisal of given conditions; no *pravda* apart from the
revolution he was creating; no ethic higher than that of revolutionary expediency. It is not surprising that in his key formative
writings at the turn of the century, Lenin should profess particular admiration for the very ideas which had most repelled
Mikhailovsky and the populists: the revolutionary *élitism* of
Tkachev, the ethical utilitarianism of Chernyshevsky, and the
disciplined *étatist* socialism of Lassalle and the German Social
Democrats.[2]

The victory of Lenin's brave new world was for the future
however; and, despite his own growing detachment from the
activities of the rising revolutionaries, Mikhailovsky still found
many listeners in his last years. His message to the many who
still looked to him for counsel was a restatement of the vital beliefs of the old radical intelligentsia: in an absolute truth and in
the worth of the human personality. His belief in *pravda* was
becoming almost transcendent at the end. 'All who serve truth',
he wrote in March 1893, 'serve the deity, if he exists, because if
he is, then he is of course Truth itself.'[3] He reiterated his belief
in the 'two-sided' truth in the introduction to the six-volume
edition of his works in 1896, and soon after explained to a friend:

In my sky I need a star—one alone, clear and marvellous—so
that I can go to it to cry and laugh, and live on and praise my God,
the God of truth and justice.[4]

---

[1] Lenin's political emphasis began in the late nineties in his struggle with
Struve and the 'economists' who were ignoring the prophetic side of Marxism.
His concept of a professional revolutionary vanguard was expounded in his correspondence with Potresov (V. I. Lenin, *Sochineniya*, Moscow-Leningrad, 1931,
xxviii. 19–31) and his meeting with Tsederbaum (Martov) in the late nineties.
These ideas were systematically developed in his 'Where to Begin?' in May 1901
and 'What is to be done?' in February 1902 (*Selected Works*, ii. 15–23, 24–192).

[2] See *Note E*⁶, p. 196.

[3] N. S. Rusanov, 'The Archives of N. K. Mikhailovsky', *R.B.*, 1914, no. 1,
p. 146.

[4] E. Letkova, 'From the Letters of N. K. Mikhailovsky', *R.B.*, 1914, no. 1, p. 372.

On 10 May 1898 in a speech commemorating the fiftieth anniversary of the death of Belinsky, Mikhailovsky restated his own moral idealism and its frankly subjective basis. He cited Belinsky's famous letter to Botkin:

The fate of the subject, of the individual, of personality is more important than the fate of the whole world. . . .

'This', said Mikhailovsky at the close of his speech, 'is an eternal idea. In these words Belinsky found himself—this man who did not wish to be a slave of history, society, or humanity.'[1]

Around him, as of old, a large group of radical thinkers gathered in the late nineties. Many of the greatest writers of the early twentieth century—Gorky, Andreev, and Kuprin—were beginning their careers under his general supervision on the *Wealth of Russia*. A host of young reformers, as well as influential professors like Kareev of St. Petersburg and Kovalevsky and Chuprov of Moscow, entered into correspondence with him.[2] Even more than before, his birthdays and name days had become occasions for dinners and celebrations.

His name days and birthdays served in St. Petersburg as days of pilgrimage to him. . . . His door was in motion from morning till late at night. . . . Close and distant friends, acquaintances, and people he had never met, representatives of young groups of all sorts—all appeared in this kaleidescope. And he was eternally friendly, attentive, sagacious, with his gentle, slightly provocative laughter, kindly words, and jokes . . . to know him meant to love him, to love him very much. . . .[3]

These affairs were not without their amusing side. At one of Mikhailovsky's birthday celebrations, an unannounced appearance was made by the nominal editors of the *Wealth of Russia*, two elderly and completely inactive conservatives whom Mikhailovsky referred to as 'the drowned ones'. When the time arrived for the usual endless toasts, one of the unrecognized 'drowned ones' rose and proposed: 'God save the Tsar.' Amazed shouts of protest came from the radical gathering, and only Mikhailovsky's reference to the inebriated editor as an illustration of 'the sad, abnormal circumstances in which the

[1] V. G. Belinsky, *Izbrannye Filosofskie Sochineniya*, p. 162; and *Ot.* II. 332.
[2] N. S. Rusanov, 'Archives', loc. cit., pp. 151–2.
[3] N. Karyshev, 'Memories of N. K. Mikhailovsky', *R.B.*, 1904, no. 3, pp. 12–13.

Russian progressive press finds itself' brought silence to the jeer-ing crowd.[1] Although some considered these dinners over-senti-mental occasions dominated by a self-important figure,[2] most young students found inspiration in them.

Testimony to the unique position that Mikhailovsky had come to hold in Russian radicalism was the vastness of the jubilee held in 1900 to honour the fortieth anniversary of his début as a journalist. All 3,000 copies of a testimonial book of articles specially written for the occasion by his friends and admirers were rapidly sold at the relatively high price of three roubles. Included in the book, *At the Sacred Post* (*Na Slavnom Postu*), were articles by former protégés of Mikhailovsky on the *Annals* (Lesevich, Annensky, and Yuzhakov), by socialist writers on the *Wealth of Russia* who were to become the leaders of the S.R. and N.S. parties (Victor Chernov and A. V. Peshekhonov), and by leaders of the rising constitutional liberal movement who were equally indebted to him ideologically (Alexander Chuprov and Paul Milyukov).[3]

More than 20,000 people signed letters or telegrams of con-gratulation to Mikhailovsky during the course of 1900;[4] and the testimonial dinner on his birthday, 15 November, provided a dramatic climax to the widespread homage being rendered him. The government had shut the *Wealth of Russia* for three months in 1899 and rebuked Mikhailovsky for allowing his journal to criticize Tsarist policies in Finland. As a result, Minister of the Interior Sipyagin was apprehensive about a mass meeting in honour of Mikhailovsky. All mention of the occasion in the public press was forbidden, and a large corps of police was sent to forestall possible disturbances. Despite this obstacle (perhaps even because of it) and the further deterrent of a driving snow-storm, the banquet hall of the Severny Hotel was full for the dinner, and the nearby Hall of the Union of Writers overflowing

---

[1] E. K. Pimenova, *Dni Minuvshie*, p. 177 (and 175–9). Of the two nominal editors, P. V. Bykov and S. S. Popov, the latter was particularly disliked for having sent a wreath to the funeral of Alexander III on behalf of the journal.

[2] A. Tyrkova-Williams, *Na Putyakh k Svobode*, New York, 1952, pp. 30–32.

[3] See P. Yakubovich, 'Letters of N. K. Mikhailovsky', *R.B.*, 1910, no. 1, p. 226. Short stories were contributed by Korolenko and Mamin-Sibiryak; Chekhov and Kareev were prevented from contributing because of ill health; and Rusanov's important article 'What Russian Social Life Owes to N. K. Mikhailovsky' was not published until the second edition in 1906 because of fear of the censorship.

[4] N. Karyshev, 'Memories', loc. cit., p. 12.

for the ceremonies of tribute. The theme of the speeches by his admirers was the constancy of Mikhailovsky's principles, his undaunted adherence to the noblest social ideals of the intelligentsia. Even ideological opponents like Peter Struve joined with Mikhailovsky's followers to pay him tribute.[1]

The climax of the jubilee was Mikhailovsky's own address. He always considered himself a poor public speaker; but his brief and pointed remarks produced, as they had often done before, a profound impression on his listeners. He admitted to having made

simple mistakes in many cases, but there were never any changes in direction. . . . I always wore one and the same literary frockcoat; I never changed it. Perhaps it did not fit well. Some people didn't like it; but it was always the same. It was my personal pride. . . . As for my social thought, I consider myself the continuer and follower of the school of Belinsky, Herzen, and Chernyshevsky. Personally, I did not want this veneration; I wanted to return to the provinces, but I was held back by the thought that in my person was being honoured not I myself so much as the years of the sixties.

Then Mikhailovsky brought his remarks to a moving conclusion:

The most noted representatives of this time are already silenced with the eternal dream, and their ranks are nearly exhausted. I propose that those present at my jubilee rise from their places and pay reverence in silence to the memory of the deceased who were so dear to us.[2]

The audience, in the words of one eyewitness 'rose as a man' in complete silence;[3] and, according to another present, many wept openly as Mikhailovsky left the hall after the silent tribute.[4] The incident marks a fitting close to the age which Mikhailovsky had dominated. Occurring as it did in the first year of the new century, the tribute stands as a kind of requiem for the narodnik religion of humanity, commemorating the passing not just of the men who believed, but of the nineteenth-century belief in human perfectibility itself.

In his final years Mikhailovsky remained true to his own

[1] V. Nikolenko-Gilchenko, 'Memoirs', loc. cit., pp. 45–46.
[2] Quoted by A. Faresov, 'N. K. Mikhailovsky', *Ist V.*, 1904, no. 3, p. 1043.
[3] Ibid., p. 1043.
[4] V. Nikolenko-Gilchenko, 'Memoirs', loc. cit., p. 46.

moral idealism and opposed to the extremists of both right and left. Asked to address a student meeting in February 1901 during a period of radical unrest, Mikhailovsky urged them to

> work for the creation of the great two-sided truth, fight with those things in life which hinder such work, disfigure human personality, and disturb its many-sided development.[1]

Later in the year he reiterated his opposition to terrorism, which had received new impetus from the newly formed 'Fighting Organization of Socialist Revolutionaries'.[2] Despite this attitude Mikhailovsky was suspected of some form of complicity when Sipyagin was assassinated on 2 April 1902. Plehve, Sipyagin's successor as Minister of the Interior, summoned Mikhailovsky in December to provide information on the movement. He had long known of Mikhailovsky's earlier affiliation with *Narodnaya Volya*, and felt sure that Mikhailovsky stood in a similar relationship with the new movements. Mikhailovsky maintained that he knew nothing about the new terrorism; and Plehve responded by requesting Mikhailovsky to leave St. Petersburg— for the fifth time in his journalistic career.[3]

The Mikhailovsky whom Plehve sent away from St. Petersburg was a sick man. Early in the year he had been stricken with angina pectoris and left seriously weakened. He sought to recoup his health during his forced exile by visiting for the first time in many years his relatives in Kostroma, and then by setting off on a long boat trip down the Volga. When he returned to St. Petersburg late in 1903, however, he further taxed his heart by refusing to cut down seriously on his activities. He ceased his editorial work on the *Wealth of Russia*, but continued his own writing and his work for the literary fund of the Union of Writers. On the night of 27 January 1904 he attended a meeting of the fund at the home of an old colleague on the *Annals*, the poet P. I. Weinberg. He seemed in his usual good spirits, but felt tired and returned home early. When his son, Mark, and

    [1] V. Nikolenko-Gilchenko, 'Memoirs', loc. cit., p. 50.

    [2] See his prognosis of 'troubled and dark times coming upon us' in a letter to Rusanov of 19 November 1901, in N. S. Rusanov, 'Politics', loc. cit., p. 138.

    [3] See Mikhailovsky's posthumously published account of the meeting in his *Vospominaniya*, Berlin, 1906. Plehve is reputed to have asked Mikhailovsky why he wanted freedom of the press when he could express in 'Aesopian' language as much as he wanted. See V. M. Chernov (Gardenin) *Pamyati Mikhailovskago*, Geneva, 1904, p. 49. Plehve was himself assassinated on 15 July 1904.

his nephew returned to the house later in the evening they found the body of Mikhailovsky seated at his desk, where he had died of a heart attack.

In these final months Mikhailovsky's pessimism had been deepened by the appearance of a new form of mass movement and mob passion: the modern war. News of the Boer War and of multiplying diplomatic crises had depressed him; and in his last article, published the month of his death, he had written sadly: 'Some years ago thinkers like Spencer thought that industrial activity was by its very nature peaceful, and would bring an end to war. This is a mistake.'[1] He spoke of the 'terrible struggles' he foresaw for European civilization; and, in a last letter written two days before his death on the eve of the Russo-Japanese War, he wrote prophetically: 'It seems to me that I can hear already the sound of weapons from the Far East . . . the guns of a new Sevastopol are sounding.'[2]

Mikhailovsky was spared the horror of seeing the first of the great twentieth-century wars which left the legacies of unrest from which modern totalitarianism would spring. News never reached his ears of the surprise Japanese attack on Port Arthur, which occurred on the very day of his death. This attack brought on the war, which in turn made possible the revolutions of 1905, just as the war of 1914–18 made the triumph of Bolshevism possible. It may have been symbolic that Mikhailovsky's funeral cortège of 5,000 filing by the offices of the literary fund and the *Wealth of Russia* out to the burial grounds by the Volkovsky Cathedral was interrupted and dwarfed by an unruly mob, which, fired by news of the Japanese attack, was demonstrating for war with Japan.[3]

The world of mass wars, demonstrations, and mob passions was, for Mikhailovsky, one which he could analyse sociologically, but in which he could not live. This world was more congenial for a man like Lenin, who in this same month was printing abroad his calculating 'Letter to a Comrade on our Organizational Tasks' as a brochure guide for the revolutionary vanguard he would eventually lead to power. Mikhailovsky, like

[1] X. 63.
[2] N. S. Rusanov, *V Emigratsii*, p. 267.
[3] See E. K. Pimenova, *Dni Minuvshie*, pp. 191–3; the obituary by Korolenko in *R.B.*, 1904, no. 2; and the anonymous obituaries in *Mir Bozhy*, 1904, no. 3, and *Novy Mir*, 1904, no. 8.

the radical intelligentsia of which he was the last great spokesman, was spared the necessity of coming to terms with a world
in which total war shattered faith in human perfectibility, and
revolutionary seizure of power shattered the hope for evolutionary abolition of the very exercise of autocratic power. Mikhailovsky was laid to rest near two of the great creative artists of the
narodnik period; his lifelong friend, Uspensky, and the poet
Nadson. The traditional oration at the grave was delivered not
by one of the active young revolutionaries, but—most appropriately—by Semevsky, a historian of the radical intelligentsia.

EPILOGUE

WHAT was the significance of Mikhailovsky and the populists? Historically, they left a dual legacy. On the one hand they exerted a powerful direct influence on a whole host of important movements that flourished during Russia's brief period of experiment with democratic forms between 1905 and 1917. On the other hand, they played an unmistakable if indirect role in preparing the path for the very forces they opposed—the Marxist extremists who would come to power in November 1917.

Mikhailovsky's influence on the non-Communist left was no less extensive after his death than before. During the period when political parties were first taking shape in the early twentieth century his work played an important part in winning many of the original propagators of Marxism in Russia to a new and less doctrinaire radical faith. Many so-called 'legal Marxists'—Struve, Filippov, and Kuskova—came strongly under the influence of Mikhailovsky during the early years of the new century as did others like Berdyaev who were sympathetic to Marxism in their earlier days. Mikhailovsky's influence was also profound on the party to which most of these reformed Marxists would attach themselves, the Constitutional Democratic or Kadet party. This party, which dominated the short-lived first Duma of May 1906 and remained the largest legal radical party until the Bolshevik Revolution, included in its ranks many old friends and associates of Mikhailovsky, such as Petrunkevich, Chuprov, and Milyukov. The programme of the Kadets in this first 'duma of national indignation' reflected the critical *narodnichestvo* of Mikhailovsky by calling both for a constitution and for agrarian redistribution. In the second Duma of March 1907 an even more Mikhailovskian party appeared, the *Narodnye Sotsialisty* or popular socialists. The N.S.'s split from the Socialist Revolutionary party over the issue of participating in the elections to the second Duma. Just as Mikhailovsky had castigated *Narodnaya Volya* for neglecting the political arena in 1879, so his closest followers—Annensky, Rusanov, and Peshekhonov—would rally from abroad or from other parties to lend support to the new N.S. party which became the fourth largest in the second Duma.

In a host of journals both within Russia and abroad, Mikhailovsky's influence lived on even after the dissolution of the second Duma, and indeed became briefly triumphant with the final overthrow of Tsardom and the establishment of a democracy in March 1917. Kerensky, the head of the provisional government, was, like many of his fellow S.R.'s an admirer of Mikhailovsky, while cabinet members like Peshekhonov and Milyukov had been active followers of Mikhailovsky. The S.R.'s like the other less extreme non-Marxist radicals were deeply committed to Mikhailovsky's emphasis on the individual, and to his Proudhonist idea that the final struggle for emancipation would be not between classes, but between individuals and the very idea of class.[1]

Mikhailovsky also exerted an important direct influence on Russian sociology. His popularization of Western sociology and his distinctive emphasis on the centrality to all social phenomena of the personality and its 'struggle for individuality' left an indelible mark on Russian sociology in the 1905–17 period.

Indeed, his attempt to free the science of man from all pretence of comparability to the natural sciences met with such widespread approval that Mikhailovsky's school was called by some the 'Russian school of sociology'.[2] For Berdyaev, whose first book was written on Mikhailovsky, and for the other great historians of the Russian intelligentsia—Masaryk, Milyukov, and Ivanov-Razumnik—Mikhailovsky's ideas also exerted a profound direct influence. In their noble and often lonely opposition to totalitarian socialism, all of these figures would argue, like Berdyaev, that 'Proudhon, and in Russia, Herzen and Mikhailovsky, were nearer the truth in asserting socialism for the sake of the individual, for the sake of man'.[3]

Although these anti-authoritarian socialists and sociologists were Mikhailovsky's truest heirs, it must be recognized that he

[1] See the typical article by the S.R. leader, Michael Gots (Rafailov), 'Systems of Truth and our Social Relationships', *Na Slavnom Postu*, pp. 209–14.

[2] First so designated by his former colleague Yuzhakov, and most vigorously propagated by Professor Kareev, who held, until the Bolshevik Revolution, the principal chair on the history faculty of St. Petersburg University.

[3] Nicholas Berdyaev, *The Realm of Spirit and the Realm of Caesar*, London, 1952, p. 59.

and the populists also played an important if unwitting role in preparing the way for the triumph of Bolshevism. Although most surviving populist leaders would strongly oppose the Bolsheviks in power and although Lenin consistently denounced Mikhailovsky and his generation as a 'step back' from the materialism of Chernyshevsky,[1] there was, none the less, a deep historical relationship between populism and Bolshevism.

From the early stages of his career, Lenin supplemented his own Marxist vocabulary with traditional narodnik terms of praise ('party-spirited') and abuse ('careerist', 'ideal-less'), carefully seeking to 'utilize' manipulable aspects of the ill-defined narodnik faith.[2] On the deeper level of social mythology Lenin gained much from the narodniks. For the two great undispelled and undefined myths of the populists—the idea of the narod and the vision of a coming utopia—were both used by Lenin with telling effect in consolidating his revolutionary power. By destroying the old bases of belief and attaching value connotations to the terms 'people's' and 'popular', the populists had subtly conditioned many to believe that goodness and right were not so much absolute concepts in themselves as necessary attributes of 'the people'. Thus, when Lenin assumed dictatorial power in the name of the masses, he was able to draw on the reservoir of emotional appeal that had been built up around these terms when affixing labels to the institutions and laws of the new régime.

Of even greater value to the young revolutionary movement of 1917 was the established will to believe in a coming utopia. The proclivity of the radical intelligentsia to believe in the most extreme and improbable of utopias helps explain the support rendered by so many articulate intellectuals to the Bolshevik insurgents. Even men like Berdyaev and Ivanov-Razumnik rallied around Lenin rather than Kerensky in the critical early months of the Revolution; for the latter seemed, in this moment of renewed expectation, too tied down to mediocrity

---

[1] V. I. Lenin, *Sochineniya*, xx. 100–1.

[2] See Lenin's rubric for Communist participation in popular fronts in his letter to Potresov of 26 January 1899. Lenin contended that *narodnichestvo* should not be rejected *en bloc*, that common action should be undertaken with populists where advantageous—remembering, however, 'that "utilize" is much more suitable than support and union'. *Letters of Lenin* (tr. Hill and Mudie), London, 1937, p. 73.

and practical programmes. He could not satisfy the thirst of the radical intelligentsia for a 'new revelation' in society.[1]

Had he lived, Mikhailovsky would almost certainly have opposed this uncritical messianism and stood by Kerensky's government. It is unlikely that Mikhailovsky would have countenanced at any stage the Bolsheviks' use of the idea of the narod and the vision of a coming utopia—any more than he would have given to one of his own journals the hallowed name of *Pravda*. But, historically speaking, the great myths of *narodnichestvo* left a more enduring imprint on the Russian scene than the critical method or subjective values which Mikhailovsky had held most high.

Above and beyond this ambiguous historical legacy of the populists, there is still the question of what was their real intrinsic significance. Many will be inclined to agree with Dostoevsky and the critics of the right who contended that for the tortured radical of the period 'love of the people was but an outlet of his personal sorrow about himself'.[2] Others will sympathize with the harsh judgement of Tkachev and the critics of the left, who contended that

The soil, the village, culture, the West, etc.—all these are no more than despicable and stupid words, carrying no fixed meaning . . . and saying nothing either 'to the mind' or 'to the feeling'. . . .
Thanks to the emptiness of these formulas, they can be used painlessly . . . by Mikhailovsky and Suvorin and P. Ch. and V. M. and X.Y.Z. and everyone else. . . .[3]

Now, as then, however, anyone seeking a full-dimensioned understanding must look beyond the extremist critics of left and right. For, with all their personal problems and philosophical inconsistencies, Mikhailovsky and the populists had a deep and sustaining faith. They believed in a humanitarian socialism that was rooted as much in the religious idealism and messianism of Russia as in the secular socialism of the West. They believed that all social reform was to be undertaken only for the sake of the individual personality, the supreme source of all value.

Some insight into the populists' significance in Russian history

---

[1] For amplification see my article, 'The Bolshevik Debt to Russian Populism', *Occidente*, 1956, no. 4.
[2] F. M. Dostoevsky, *The Diary of a Writer*, New York (tr. Brasol), 1954, p. 946.
[3] P. N. Tkachev, *Sochineniya*, iv. 26.

is perhaps provided by Mikhailovsky's German contemporary, Willhelm Dilthey, who contended that human thought had produced only three types of world-view. There were the objective idealists, the naturalists, and the idealists of freedom. Each had a respectable lineage of adherents in history. Each carried its own basic assumptions and particular satisfactions. Applied to Russian thought in the nineteenth century one could say that the Hegelians of the thirties and the early Slavophils were the objective idealists; while the 'men of the sixties' were the naturalists. The Marxists of the nineties combined the metaphysics of the former with the language of the latter. Standing apart in the seventies and eighties was the longing and pathos of the populists, and the teaching of Mikhailovsky, the idealist of freedom.

The influence of the populist movement extended, in its time, well into Eastern Europe, where it provided a kind of satisfaction which Marxism did not offer. As the greatest of all Serbian revolutionaries explained, 'The International has in view only governmental and economic relationships; the Russian movement seeks to reform our entire life . . . '.[1] Despite posthumous criticism from both left and right, Mikhailovsky's own ideas lived on through the impact they made on the greatest chroniclers of nineteenth-century Russian thought, Masaryk, Berdyaev, and Ivanov-Razumnik. Indeed, in our own times, when, in the words of a writer in Poland, 'A spectre is haunting Eastern Europe, the spectre of humanitarian socialism'[2] and when the most-discussed novel in the U.S.S.R. bears the title 'Not by Bread Alone',[3] who is to say that history has seen the last of the populists' faith and the strivings of the Russian intelligentsia?

[1] Svetozar Markovich as quoted in V. Viktorov-Toporov, 'Svetozar Markovich', *G.M.*, 1913, no. 3, p. 51. A famed Bulgarian revolutionary writer, Vlaykov, confessed that Mikhailovsky's writings were directly responsible for leading him away from a materialistic world-view. See Vivian Pinto, 'The Civic and Aesthetic Ideals of Bulgarian Narodnik Writers', the *American Slavic and East European Review*, June 1954, pp. 361-2.

[2] Edda Werfel, 'To the Comrades of the Sister Parties', *Przegląd Kulturalny*, 7 November 1956.

[3] V. Dudintsev, 'Not by Bread Alone', *Novy Mir*, 1956, nos. 8, 9, 10.

NOTES

NOTE A, p. 15. As early as 1856 the Slavophil Ivan Aksakov wrote: 'I have been all over Russia: the name of Belinsky is known to every youth who does any thinking. . . . One hears nothing about Slavophilism.' (Alexander Kornilov, 'Social Movements under Alexander II', *M.G.*, 1908, no. 2, p. 97.) With the death of the Kireevsky brothers in 1856, the failure of the journal *Moskvityanin* in the same year, and the passing of Khomyakov and Constantine Aksakov in 1860, the Slavophil movement can be said to have come to an end. The frequent similarities between subsequent movements and Slavophilism do not imply any direct influence as V. Ya. Yakovlev (Bogucharsky) has misled many into believing in his *Aktivnoe Narodnichestvo Semidesyatykh Godov*, Moscow, 1912, pp. 3–22.

NOTE B, p. 22. As early as 1860 Proudhon had observed with justice: 'I am read and asked about even in the extremities of Siberia.' (Raoul Labry, *Herzen et Proudhon*, Paris, 1928, p. 199.) Subsequently Proudhon's works exercised a decisive influence on the important circle of young seminarists in Saratov under A. Kh. Khristoforov in 1861–2, on the anti-aesthetic and anti-étatist polemics of Pisarev and Zaitsev in the *Russian Word* throughout 1862–3; and on many of the leaders of the short-lived *Zemlya i Volya* circle of 1862. (See Labry, pp. 236–40; Coquart, *Pisarev*, pp. 110–14, 165–7, 251–6; and 'The Karakozov Attempt', *K.A.*, 1926, no. 4, pp. 96 ff.) The death of Proudhon in January 1865 precipitated another wave of interest in him, with Yury Zhukovsky's 'Proudhon and his *System of Economic Contradictions*', *Sov.*, 1865 nos. 2, 3, 7, the most discussed of a series of articles.

NOTE C, p. 27. The *Contemporary Review* was the product of Eliseev's ideological opponents on the *Contemporary*: the utilitarian followers of Chernyshevsky. This group—which included Alexander Pypin (Chernyshevsky's cousin), Michael Antonovich (Chernyshevsky's choice to succeed Dobrolyubov as literary editor of the *Contemporary*), and Yury Zhukovsky—had come under attack by Mikhailovsky's friends Sokolov and Zaitsev for their amoral and rationalistic view of social questions. Mikhailovsky also attacked them for misrepresenting Proudhon early in 1866 (X. 505–6).

The group solidified its utilitarian faith after the closing of the *Contemporary*, when Zhukovsky and Pypin collaborated on the first Russian edition of Bentham's works, and Antonovich went abroad, in part to procure more complete editions of Bentham and Mill for translation. They collaborated on the *Contemporary Review*, on its short-lived successor, *Kosmos*, and finally on the *laissez-faire* liberal *Herald of Europe*, infra, pp. 68, 69, 73. During the late sixties they disputed with Eliseev and the moral idealist wing of the *Contemporary*. (See the 1869 brochure by Zhukovsky and Antonovich, *Material for the Characterization of Contemporary Literature*, and Eliseev's answer, 'A Reply to my Critics', *O.Z.*, 1869, no. 4.) The deep mistrust with which Mikhailovsky and Eliseev viewed doctrinaire utilitarians as apologists for 'the power of money' would seem justified in the case of Antonovich and Zhukovsky; for both of them entered into the permanent employ of the Ministry of Finance in the early eighties.

NOTE D, p. 30. Herbert Spencer, 'Manners and Fashion', *Westminster Review*, April, 1854, p. 377. Quoted (without acknowledgement) by Mikhailovsky in *Q.Q.P.*, p. 196.

Only two volumes of publisher Nicholas Tiblen's projected seven-volume translation appeared, because of Tiblen's flight abroad after the bankruptcy of the *Contemporary Review*. Spencer was amazed at the reception he received in Russia (see his *Autobiography*, London, 1926, ii. 126, 288, and esp. 308–9), and was apparently convinced by Tiblen that the latter's flight abroad was the result of charges of treason by the Russian authorities for distributing his (Spencer's) book: ibid., pp. 156–7.

NOTE E, p. 32. Comte's influence in Russia dates from the study of his works by Valerian Maikov in Paris in the early forties, and the formation in Russia of Maikov's influential 'society of thinking people' in the late fifties. Interest was widespread by the time Eugene Watson published a series of articles on 'August Comte and Positivist Philosophy', *Sov.*, 1865, nos. 8, 11, 12. In the same year, P. D. Boborykin, former editor of the *Library for Reading (Biblioteka dlya Chteniya)*, went to Paris to study under Comte (and later to join two other Russians on the editorial board of *La Philosophie Positive*); and Pisarev wrote in his 'Historical Ideas of Auguste Comte' that 'Russia will know and appreciate Comte much more thoroughly than he is known and appreciated in Western Europe', *R.S.*, 1865, no. 11, in Coquart, *Pisarev*, p. 350.

NOTE F, p. 48. One of the Russian colony in Florence described the conflict: 'Here face to face clashed two generations far removed from one another . . . for Bakunin revolution had already succeeded in revealing itself finally and definitely in the form of a grandiose ritual, and in several formulas: anarchy, negation of the state, and socialism . . . Nozhin almost never used the word "revolution". With all his powerful insight he saw that it was necessary to pass over to another more just basis of society and morality . . . but to him the means to this longed-for change were not clear.' L. I. Mechnikov, 'M. A. Bakunin in Italy in 1864', *Ist V.*, 1897, no. 3, pp. 819–20.

NOTE G, p. 48. This is the conclusion one draws from E. E. Kolosov, 'N. K. Mikhailovsky in the Karakozov Affair', *Byloe*, 1924, no. 3, pp. 62–73.

Nozhin's death was officially reported to have been caused by a blood clot, but suspicion was aroused by the fact that none of his close friends saw him after or immediately before his death. Mikhailovsky, who was called to court on 3 August 1866 to answer questions about his friend's activities, said he knew nothing of the circumstances of Nozhin's death (Kolosov, pp. 58–59). However, in his story, 'In the Interim', Mikhailovsky hints at foul play saying of Bukhartsev (Nozhin) that 'he died under such strange and unclear circumstances that all of his material and possessions were destroyed with him'. IV. 267. That Nozhin had knowledge of Karakozov's intentions and sought to forestall him seems probable from the testimony of the military governor of St. Petersburg, Prince Alexander Suvorov, that he had received a note from Nozhin several days before his death saying that he (Nozhin) had an important secret to disclose (Kolosov, p. 73). Thus the failure of government investigators to trace the cause of Nozhin's death was probably a by-product of their failure to gain any information on the activities of *Hell*.

NOTE H, p. 69. IV. 412. See also N. S. Rusanov, *V Emigratsii*, Moscow, 1929, pp. 80–81, and, for Mikhailovsky's interest in Dühring, Rusanov, 'The Politics of N. K. Mikhailovsky', *Byloe*, 1907, no. 7, p. 130. Lavrov had been one of the first to introduce Lange's work into St. Petersburg circles in the late sixties (V. Lesevich, 'A Page from my Memoirs', *Na Slavnom Postu*, p. 155), and Mikhailovsky first mentioned Lange in April 1870 (IV. 132–3).

Lange may also have exercised a direct personal influence on Professor Ziber of Kiev, who had studied under Lange in the early seventies at Zürich and was the only other figure to join Mikhailovsky in defending Marx in the latter part of the decade. Ziber developed a non-materialistic interpretation of Marx in his *Economic Theories of Ricardo and Marx*, Kiev, 1871, and was personally picked by Mikhailovsky to help defend Marx from Zhukovsky on the pages of the *Annals*. In addition to the article which Mikhailovsky persuaded him to write ('Several Observations on the Appearance of the Article by Yu. Zhukovsky on Marx's *Capital*', *O.Z.*, 1877, no. 11), Ziber later defended Marx from attacks by an apostle of government reformism ('Chicherin *contra* Marx', *Slovo*, 1879, no. 11).

NOTE I, p. 74. Lavrov and Lopatin were active in the Commune and journeyed to England to plead for help from both Marx and Gladstone. Important roles inside Paris were played by M. P. Sazhin, A. V. Korvin-Krukovskaya, wife of Blanquist leader, Charles-Victor Jaclard, as well as Dombrowski and a host of Poles. R. V. Ivanov-Razumnik, 'Lavrov and the Commune', *Sbornik Statey Posvyashchenykh Petru Lavrovu*, Petrograd-Moscow, 1920; Ivan Knizhnik-Vetrov, *A. V. Korvin-Krukovskaya (Jaclard)*, Moscow, 1931, esp. pp. 36–89.

The exaggerated official view (shared by many radicals) that Russian and Polish participation was on a very large scale (see 'The Paris Commune of 1871', *K.A.*, 1931, no. 2, pp. 4, 18–20) was probably caused by the erroneous belief that Bakunin was mustering up a revolutionary army. Actually, Bakunin had been disillusioned by the failure of his own uprising in Lyons the year before and predicted failure of the Paris uprising, while Zaitsev was busy organizing an uprising in Turin at the time. Other Russian intellectuals in Paris at the time—Sleptsov, Boborykin, and Vyrubov—actually opposed the Commune.

NOTE J, p. 75. *Uspensky v Zhizni*, p. 119. Cf. Uspensky's articles 'A Sick Conscience', *O.Z.*, 1873, nos. 2, 4.

The importance of the disillusionment of 1871 in preparing the doctrine of a special path for Russia is reflected in the two best novels on the populist movement: Dostoevsky's *A Raw Youth* (1874) and Turgenev's *Virgin Soil* (1877). In the former the leading character says: 'One seemed to hear the death knell ringing over Europe in those days . . . it was not only the bloodshed in those days that appalled me, and it was not the Tuileries, but all that was bound to follow it. They are too doomed to strife for a long time yet because they are still too German and too French.' *A Raw Youth*, London (Heinemann), 1950, pp. 462–5. One of the figures at the end of *Virgin Soil* says of the narodnik hero, Solomin: 'Our true salvation lies with the Solomins, the dull, plain but wise Solomins. Remember that I say this to you in this winter of 1870 when Germany is preparing to conquer France.' *Virgin Soil*, London (Everyman), 1948, p. 316.

NOTE K, p. 83. The title would seem to indicate that the journal stood for everything that Mikhailovsky's group held most contemptible; but the new version that began to appear in January 1875 with the Kurochkins, Demert, Skabichevsky, and others from the *Annals* as collaborators had little in common with the journal as it had existed previously. The alliance between the *Annals* and V. A. Poletika, the wealthy owner of the journal, was based on weak foundations and would end in 1876; but in 1874, the alliance seemed more a conquest for the narodniks than a weakening of their moral purity. See Kozmin, *Zhurnalistika 70kh i 80kh Godov*, p. 31; and Skabichevsky, *Vospominaniya*, pp. 315–22.

NOTE L, p. 99. Led by two Bakuninists, Sazhin and Kravchinsky, who after reading the first news of the uprisings in Hercegovina, set off from Paris to recruit fighters for the ideal of Slavic federation. Sazhin went via Locarno to confer with Bakunin; and Kravchinsky via northern Italy to see Volkhovsky, the former leader of the Odessa *Chaikovtsy*. At about the same time Bakunin's Ukrainian friend, Michael Dragomanov, returned to Kiev, and, together with a group of Russians and other Slavs, laid plans for recruiting volunteers to join the fight of the southern Slavs against the Turks. During 1875–6 a number of recruits slipped into Serbia through Bucharest, while Sazhin and Kravchinsky were directing a smaller group of Slavic *émigrés* and former members of Garibaldi's legions into Serbia through Zagreb.

This early intervention of the radicals in the Balkans (best discussed in V. Ya. Yakovlev, *Aktivnoe Narodnichestvo*, pp. 262–94) is an episode missing from B. H. Sumner *Russia and the Balkans*, Oxford, 1937, and must modify his conclusion (p. 582) that unofficial Russian support was of no importance until 1876.

NOTE M, p. 100. The vision of a loose, multi-cultural federation, which was particularly dominant among non-Great Russian revolutionaries, derived both from the participation of many radical *émigrés* in Bakunin's federal experiments in Switzerland and from an idealized picture of the U.S.A. The Kievan *Chaikovtsy* were even called *Amerikantsy*. Hopes for a decentralized federation were dashed not only by the chauvinism of the war, but by a decree of May 1876 outlawing the use of Ukrainian and several other minor Slavic languages for literary or academic purposes in the Russian Empire.

NOTE N, p. 105. The programme of the *Zemlyavoltsy* (Serebryakov, op. cit., pp. 9–15) offers a final illustration of the fusion of the traditions of north and south. They described themselves as 'Russian socialist-federalists', thus combining the social ideal of the north with the political ideal of the south. Following the former, the *Zemlyavoltsy* based their case solely on its 'moral rightness', calling for the redistribution of the land, capital, and means of production to those who engaged in productive labour, and advocating extension of the *obshchina* and artel. Following the latter (southern) tradition, they called for a decentralized federal system and the creating of local revolutionary councils (*soviets*) throughout Russia.

NOTE O, p. 105. Lavrov's bookish approach and his unsympathetic attitude toward the Balkan uprising of 1875 hastened the decline of his influence during the seventies. Kravchinsky was typical in rebuking Lavrov for his failure to support the liberation of the south Slavs, and for being 'a man of thought not passion'. (Yakovlev, *Aktivnoe Narodnichestvo*, p. 126.) A particularly popular verse among the anti-intellectual extremists of the late seventies was:

Ex-professor, ex-filosof	Ex-professor, ex-philosopher
Revolyutsii oplot	Bulwark of revolution
On zasel verkhom na raka	He sat high on a crayfish
I krichit, vpered! vpered!	Crying out, forward! forward!

Ibid., p. 115.

NOTE P, p. 110. This article on the subject of landholding was designed as a refutation of the circular of 16 July 1879, in which the Minister of the Interior, L. S. Makov, had reaffirmed the inviolability of private property as a warning to revolutionaries planning on sudden redistribution. However, Krivenko printed an article on the same subject in the first issue, and two other major contributions were by friends and followers of Mikhailovsky, N. Kurochkin and Ivanchin-Pisarev. Only Tikhomirov's article and Morozov's 'Chronicle of Persecutions' were contributed by the terrorist wing. See Ivanchin-Pisarev, 'Reminiscences of N. K. Mikhailovsky', loc. cit., esp. p. 106.

NOTE Q, p. 124. Many of the details as well as the name of the esoteric 'Hell' group within the *Ishutintsy* point to a probable link with some esoteric religious sect: vows of secrecy, celibacy, and an original intention to assassinate the Tsar on Easter. Similarly, some of the *Nechaevtsy* swore oaths on a gun and a bible, and the last of them, the *Dolgushintsy*, used as their symbol a cross with 'liberty, equality, and fraternity' engraved on it in four languages. All of these groups displayed a certain diabolistic inspiration foreign both to the schismatics, who generally opposed violence, and to the main stream of the populist tradition.

NOTE R, p. 126. 'The American Sects', *O.Z.*, 1868, nos. 4, 6, 7, 8, published anonymously and inspired by *New America*, a book on American sectarianism by the Englishman, William Hepworth Dixon, the year before. Dixon wrote in 1868 a second book on sectarianism, *Spiritual Wives*, which was translated into Russian by Zaitsev in 1869 and enjoyed great popularity in radical circles. See Coquart, *Pisarev*, pp. 408–9.

Dixon himself toured through Russia in 1869, met Zaitsev and other radicals, and published in 1870 a two-volume study, *Free Russia*, which was almost entirely devoted to a survey of dissenters, pilgrims, and Old Believers, and to a discussion of the religious and secular elements in the struggle of 'this new country—hoping to be pacific, meaning to be free' (London, 1870, i. v).

NOTE S, p. 130. Romans xiii. 8, 9, at the beginning of St.-Simon's final work *Le Nouveau Christianisme* (*Œuvres*, Paris, 1869, xxii. 99). Among other European thinkers who developed varying concepts of a new Christianity which influenced Russian radicals were Cabet (*Le Vrai Christianisme suivant Jésus Christ*) and Ludwig Feuerbach (*Das Wesen des Christentums*). The vision of a coming new form of Christianity, which the Russians derived largely from Parisian thought of the forties, was in turn profoundly influenced by Polish romantic messianism. See M. Kridl, 'Two Champions of a New Christianity: Lamennais and Mickiewicz', *Comparative Literature*, 1952, no. 3, pp. 239–67.

NOTE T, p. 142. The negotiations between official and radical circles during this period were greatly complicated by factionalism in each camp, and by an almost psychotic attitude of suspicion among the extremists. Nikoladze was distrusted abroad and may actually have been in the employ of the Holy Brotherhood. (See V. Ya. Yakovlev, *Iz Istorii*, pp. 347–9.) The extremists' fear of betrayal was only heightened by the seeming amity which had prevailed in a set of talks between relatively moderate elements in each camp: Peter Shuvalov's 'Volunteer Bodyguard' on the one hand and Lavrov, Dragomanov, and Debagory-Mokrievich on the other. (See articles on these conversations in *Byloe*, 1907: no. 4, pp. 56–61; no. 8, pp. 125–7; o. 10, pp. 123–67.)

Nikoladze eventually secured Tikhomirov's agreement to Vorontsov-Dashkov's proposals with Tikhomirov's caveat that Chernyshevsky rather than Isaev be released; but, when Nikoladze returned to St. Petersburg in 1883, Mikhailovsky had been exiled to Lyuban and Vorontsov-Dashkov's faction was no longer dominant in the Imperial Court. Nikoladze thus had to deal with Shuvalov, whose connexion had been with a different radical faction; and the only result of all the talks was Shuvalov's agreement to release the aged Chernyshevsky in 1883. (See N. Ya. Nikoladze, 'The Liberation of Chernyshevsky', *Byloe*, 1906, no. 9, esp. pp. 248–81.)

NOTE U, p. 144. The police informer, Degaev, had been responsible for Figner's arrest, subsequent mass arrests, and the virtual dissolution of the 'fighting organization' in 1883. Motivated either by repentance or anger over terms of payment, he shot Sudeikin, his employer as head of the Third Section, for which action he too was arrested and shot later in 1883. Degaev's multiple change of sides and his role in the disruption of *Narodnaya Volya* foreshadowed that of the celebrated Azef among the Socialist Revolutionaries of the early 1900's. (See N. P. Makletsovaya (Degaev's sister), 'Sudeikin and Degaev', *Byloe*, 1906, no. 8, pp. 265–72.)

NOTE V, p. 145. Mikhailovsky had already partially revised his earlier harsh judgement of Dostoevsky in his 'Pisemsky and Dostoevsky' of February 1881 and his 'Cruel Talent' of September and October 1882. Mikhailovsky recognized in Dostoevsky a genuine feeling for the people, but rejected Dostoevsky's preoccupation with suffering 'without any moral meaning'. Mikhailovsky rejected the earlier radical view of Dobrolyubov that Dostoevsky had little talent but great concern for suffering humanity, contending conversely that Dostoevsky had great talent for depicting suffering, achieved at the expense of moral concern for the condition. IV. 50–51.

NOTE W, p. 146. The leading narodnik journals during the rest of the eighties were published abroad and little read within Russia. The revolutionary narodniks clustered about *Vestnik Narodnoy Voli*, which was founded in 1883 in Geneva by Tikhomirov, Rusanov, and Lavrov, but published only five issues before collapsing in 1886. A more evolutionary—even constitutional—populism was expounded abroad on the pages of the *Common Cause*. Published in Geneva by the old Saratov Proudhonist, A. Kh. Khristoforov, and two of Mikhailovsky's early friends, Sokolov and Zaitsev, the *Common Cause* developed from a Bakuninist outlook at its inception in 1877, to a position closely akin to that of Mikhailovsky in the years before its demise in 1890.

NOTE X, p. 149. Kolya entered the theatre directly without any higher schooling, and performed increasingly important roles, including several at the Moscow Art Theatre under Stanislavsky. He became director of the Riga State Theatre on the eve of the Bolshevik Revolution during which all trace of him was lost. Mark achieved distinction as a brilliant student at St. Petersburg University and a member of major scientific expeditions to the White Sea and Spitzbergen. He became one of the principal zoologists of the Museum of Natural Sciences and wrote a number of technical articles for German and Russian publications. He died of consumption on 28 August 1904—exactly seven months after the death of his father. See S. N. Yuzhakov, 'Memorial for Mark N. Mikhailovsky', *R.B.*, 1904, no. 9; and V. A. Nikolenko-Gilchenko, 'Memoirs of N. K. Mikhailovsky', *Zavety*, 1913, no. 1, pp. 7–8.

NOTE Y, p. 151. As editorial adviser to the *Northern Herald*, Mikhailovsky had probably come in contact with Chekhov by June 1886, when his first work to gain wide critical approval, *Motley Stories (Pestrie Rasskazi)*, began appearing in the journal. In addition to bringing Chekhov into the discussion circle, Mikhailovsky was one of the first literary critics to draw attention to Chekhov's writings—in one of his infrequently appearing columns in September 1887. Together with Skabichevsky, the former literary critic of the *Annals*, Mikhailovsky was almost alone in recognizing Chekhov's extraordinary talent in the days before he became a playwright and celebrity in the nineties. (See N. Klestov, 'Chekhov and Mikhailovsky', *Sovremenny Mir*, 1915, no. 12, esp. pp. 1–4.)

Chekhov saw little of Mikhailovsky in the nineties, but never forgot the early encouragement he received from him and wrote a special letter of tribute to the organizer of the Mikhailovsky jubilee in 1900: 'I have deeply esteemed Nicholas Konstantinovich ever since I first knew him; and I am very much indebted to him.' (P. Yakubovich, 'Letters of Mikhailovsky', *R.B.*, 1910, no. 1, p. 226.)

NOTE Z, p. 157. Founded in 1876 as a bi-weekly commercial journal, the *Wealth of Russia* was taken over as an artel monthly in 1880 by some of the younger writers on the *Annals* (including Zasodimsky and Garshin), who transplanted it from Moscow to St. Petersburg where it became known as 'the literary colony of the *Annals*'. From late 1882 until taken over by Mikhailovsky in 1892, the *Wealth of Russia* was an organ of 'cultural *narodnichestvo*' and declined steadily in popularity. Mikhailovsky was co-editor with Krivenko from 1892–5, sole editor from 1895–1900, then co-editor with Korolenko till his death in 1904.

NOTE A^a, p. 159. See the anonymous 'Government Punishments for 1894', *Byloe*, 1907, no. 5. The repudiation by the *Narodopravtsy* of all methods of secret organization was pointed to by their terrorist enemies as the reason for the ease with which all were located and arrested.

The major leaders arrested in addition to Natanson were Peter Nikolaev, a nobleman and former member of the Ishutin circle who had been active abroad in *Self-Government*, and S. N. Tyutchev, a Kievan nobleman who had turned terrorist after 'going to the people' in 1875, and had been in prison from 1878 to 1887.

NOTE B^b, p. 163. Thus, in the preface to the first Russian edition of the *Communist Manifesto* in 1882, Marx and Engels declared: 'If the Russian revolution can be used as a signal to the revolutionary proletariat of the West and thus both fulfil themselves, then the existence of the communal agricultural form in Russia can serve as a fountainhead of communal development.' (*Narodnaya Volya v Dokumentakh*, p. 241.) Engels amplified this idea in 1883 after Marx's death: 'Russia is the France of a former century; to her belongs the revolutionary initiative.' His interest in Russian development seems related to his conclusion that Russia may succeed in creating a situation of unrest which 'Germany can use to make gains at the expense of Tsarism' (letter of Lopatin of September 1883 recording his talk with Engels, ibid., p. 246).

Engels appears to have been less interested in and sympathetic with the Russian movement than his more famous associate. Whereas Marx had numerous Russian correspondents and made an effort to learn the language and study Russian materials, Engels tended to write off the entire Russian movement as 'puerile' as early as 1875 in *Vorwärts*. ('Letters of Marx to Nikolai-on', with intr. by Lopatin, *M.G.*, 1908, no. 1.) According to Paul Lafargue, Engels once rebuked Marx mildly for his interest in Russia: 'I would with pleasure burn the Russian edition of land-village ownership statistics, as they have already kept you for several years from finishing *Das Kapital*.' (*Die Neue Zeit*, 29 July 1905, p. 560; cf. N. S. Rusanov, *V Emigratsii*, pp. 196–7.)

NOTE C^c, p. 163. The primary initial cause of the Marxists' break with the narodniks abroad in this 1882–4 period was a tactical insistence on political struggle as the most conducive means to socialism. See the programme Engels suggested to Lopatin, after the death of Marx and the waning of *Narodnaya Volya*, in *Narodnaya Volya v Dokumentakh*, pp. 244–6; and Plekhanov's *Sotsializm i Politicheskaya Borba* (1883) and *Programma Sotsial-Demokraticheskoy*

Gruppy 'Osvobozhdeniya Truda' (1884). Tactical priority on the political question had been also suggested by Mikhailovsky in his 'Political Letters' of 1879. Thus, Plekhanov is hardly justified in placing him among the narodniks opposed to political action, although Plekhanov may have been in ignorance of the authorship of the anonymously published 'Letters'.

NOTE D^d, p. 71. Lines did not become sharply drawn among Russians abroad until the mid nineties. August Bebel's failure to effect a *rapprochement* among the Russians in 1892 may have been a turning-point. (N. S. Rusanov, *V Emigratsii*, pp. 194–5.) Debagory-Mokrievich became Plekhanov's principal narodnik opponent outside of Russia. (G. V. Plekhanov, *Literaturnoe Nasledie*, pp. 40–41, and 42–43 notes.) For accounts of the debate as waged among political prisoners of the period, see L. S. Fedorchenko, 'In Prison and Exile', *K. i S.*, 1928, no. 8, pp. 117–18, and Yu. Steklov, 'Memoirs of a Yakutsk Exile', ibid., 1923, no. 6, pp. 74–75.

NOTE E^e, p. 176. All three of these Leninist affinities are brought out in 'What is to be done?' the first real bible of Bolshevism. The title of the work was deliberately taken from Chernyshevsky; and the citation at the beginning of the book was not one of the familiar outbursts of moral indignation from the French socialists, but a quotation from Lassalle about the need for organizing a party. Although Lenin thought Tkachev's method naïve, he thought that 'the attempt to seize power after the ground for the attempt had been prepared by the preaching of Tkachev and carried out by means of the "terrifying" terror which really did terrify was majestic'. (V. I. Lenin, *Selected Works*, ii. 182.)

BIBLIOGRAPHY

I. THE WORKS OF MIKHAILOVSKY

Sochineniya N. K. Mikhailovskago, St. Petersburg, 1896–7 (ed. *Russkoe Bogatstvo*), 6 vols., second revised edition.

Literaturnyya Vospominaniya i Sovremennaya Smuta, St. Petersburg, 1900 (ed. *Russkoe Bogatstvo*), 2 vols.

Otkliki, St. Petersburg, 1904 (ed. *Russkoe Bogatstvo*), 2 vols.

Posledniya Sochineniya, St. Petersburg, 1905 (ed. *Russkoe Bogatstvo*), 2 vols.

Polnoe Sobranie Sochinenii N. K. Mikhailovskago, St. Petersburg, 1913 (ed. M. M. Stasyulevich), Vol. X, third, complete edition.

Revolyutsionnyya Stati, Berlin, 1906 (Hugo Steinitz), 63 pp.

Vospominaniya, Berlin, 1906 (Hugo Steinitz), 48 pp.

Qu'est-ce que le progrès, Paris, 1897 (tr. Paul Louis), 200 pp.

The six volumes of the 1896–7 edition cover virtually all of his legal writings from 1869 to 1892. They are arranged topically rather than chronologically; and the dating of articles is often inaccurate. This is the most readily available of his works. It is more complete than the first collected edition of his writings (in three volumes: 1879–81) and was not materially altered in the subsequent, third edition of his works in 1907–14. The two volumes of *Literaturnyya Vospominaniya* contain his invaluable memoirs of the 1860–90 period. *Otkliki* and *Posledniya Sochineniya* contain his publicistic writings in *Russkoe Bogatstvo* during the last decade of his life.

The six volumes of the 1896–7 edition average about 1,000 numbered-column pages each, with the other volumes averaging more than half that many full-sized pages. Volume X is the only part of the complete fourth edition which must be consulted. Volumes I–VIII contain only reprinted material from the other volumes; while Volume IX was never published. Volume X is indispensable, however, containing his early publicistic articles of the sixties and his anonymous and illegal writings thereafter. Published under the editorial supervision of Mikhailovsky's elder son, this rare tenth volume also contains important introductory articles by Rusanov and Kolosov, together with a detailed list of books and articles touching on Mikhailovsky up to 1912. Since this volume is unobtainable in most of the major libraries of the West, I have given references wherever possible to other volumes in which articles in the tenth volume have appeared—particularly the readily available *Revolyutsionnyya Stati* and *Vospominaniya*, which contain some of his illegal pamphlets and posthumously published accounts of contact with revolutionaries.

In the only case in which it was possible so to do, I have given reference to a translation of Mikhailovsky's work: Paul Louis's French translation of 'What is Progress?', which is better and more easily obtainable than the German translation by I. Seitz in *Vierteljahrsschrift für wissenschaftliche Philosophie*, 1899, Heft I, Band xxiii. I have not been able to locate a copy of *Iz Romana*

'*Karera Oladushkina* (in *Sbornik 'Russkogo Bogatstva'*, St. Petersburg, 1899), which contains reprinted fragments of his unfinished novel, or of his translation of Proudhon's *De la capacité politique des classes ouvrières*, which was published as *Frantsuzkaya Demokratiya*, St. Petersburg, 1867.

The most complete bibliography of Mikhailovsky's written works is D. P. Silchevsky, 'Towards a Bibliography of the Works of N. K. Mikhailovsky', *Na Slavnom Postu*, St. Petersburg, 1900, pp. 510–16, which should be supplemented by the bibliography at the end of Volume X (through 1912) and that found in Vladislavtsev, *Russkie Pisateli*, Moscow–Leningrad, 1924, pp. 265–9 (through 1923). The best working catalogue of Mikhailovsky's works in the West is in the New York Public Library, which lists periodical as well as book entries under his name.

II. BASIC MATERIALS ON MIKHAILOVSKY AND THE POPULISTS

A select bibliography, with an asterisk placed before studies of particular value.

A. *Books and Articles on Mikhailovsky*

CHERNOV, V. M. (Gardenin), 'The Key to Understanding Mikhailovsky', *Zavety*, 1913, no. 3.

—— 'N. K. Mikhailovsky as Ethical Thinker', *Zavety*, 1914, nos. 1, 5.

—— *Pamyati N. K. Mikhailovskago*, Geneva, 1904.

*FARESOV, A. I., 'N. K. Mikhailovsky', *Ist. V.*, 1904, no. 3.

FRANGIAN, E., *N. K. Michailowsky als Soziologe und Philosoph. Eine sozialphilosophische Studie*, Berlin, 1913, 93 pp.

GIZETTI, A., 'Individuality and Sociality in the World-View of Mikhailovsky', *Zavety*, 1914, no. 1.

GOLDMAN, B. I. (Gorev), 'N. K. Mikhailovsky and Revolution', *Pechat i Revolyutsiya*, Moscow, 1924, Book 1.

—— *Nikolai Konstantinovich Mikhailovsky. Ego Zhizn, literaturnaya deyatelnost i mirosozertsanie*, Leningrad (Moladaya Gvardiya), 1931, 94 pp.

*IVANCHIN-PISAREV, A. I., 'From Memories of N. K. Mikhailovsky', *Zavety*, 1914, no. 1.

IVANOV-RAZUMNIK, R. V., 'A. I. Herzen and N. K. Mikhailovsky', *Voprosy Zhizni*, 1905, no. 8.

KAREEV, N. I., 'Memories of Mikhailovsky as a Sociologist', *R.B.*, 1904, no. 3.

*KARYSHEV, N., 'Memories of Nicholas Konstantinovich Mikhailovsky', *R.B.*, 1904, no. 3.

KLEINBORT, A., 'N. K. Mikhailovsky as Publicist', *Mir Bozhy*, 1904, no. 6.

KLESTOV, N., 'Chekhov and Mikhailovsky', *Sovremenny Mir*, 1915, no. 12.

*KOLOSOV, E. E., 'Towards a Characterization of the Social World-View of N. K. Mikhailovsky', *G.M.*, 1914, nos. 2, 3.

—— 'M. A. Bakunin and N. K. Mikhailovsky in the Old *Narodnichestvo*', *G.M.*, 1913, nos. 5, 6.

*——— 'Mikhailovsky and the Narodnik Movement from the Second Half of the Seventies', *Kievskaya Mysl*, 1914, no. 28.

*——— 'N. K. Mikhailovsky in the Karakozov Affair', *Byloe* (Paris), no. 23.

——— 'N. K. Mikhailovsky and the Russian Revolution', *Sotsialist-Revolyutsioner*, Paris, 1910, i; 1911, iii.

*——— 'N. K. Mikhailovsky in the Eighties', *Byloe* (Paris), no. 9/10.

——— *Ocherki Mirovozzreniya N. K. Mikhailovskago. Teoriya razdeleniya truda, kak osnova nauchnoy sotsiologii*, St. Petersburg, 1912 (*Obshchestvennaya Polza*), 434 pp.

*——— 'P. L. Lavrov and N. K. Mikhailovsky on the Balkan Events of 1875–6', *G.M.*, 1916, no. 5/6.

——— 'The Views of Mikhailovsky on Government', *R.B.*, 1910, nos. 2, 3.

KOROLENKO, V. G., 'Nicholas Konstantinovich Mikhailovsky', *R.B.*, 1904, no. 2.

KOVALEVSKY, M., 'Mikhailovsky as Sociologist', *Vestnik Evropy*, 1913, no. 4.

KOVARSKY, B., *N. K. Mikhailovsky i Obshchestvennoe Dvizhenie 70kh Godov*, St. Petersburg, 1909, 75 pp.

KRASNOSELSKY, A., *Mirovozzrenie Gumanista Nashego Vremeni. Osnovy Ucheniya N. K. Mikhailovskago*, St. Petersburg, 1900, 96 pp.

——— 'N. K. Mikhailovsky on Religion', *R.B.*, 1907, no. 4.

*LETKOVA, E., 'From the Letters of N. K. Mikhailovsky', *R.B.*, 1914, no. 1.

MARKERT, WERNER, *Eine politische Soziologie in Russland*, Leipzig, 1931.

MILYUKOV, P., 'N. K. Mikhailovsky', *Rech*, 1914, no. 27.

MOKIEVSKY, P., 'N. K. Mikhailovsky and Western Science', *R.B.*, 1904, no. 3.

MYAGKOV, A., 'The Banishment of N. K. Mikhailovsky from St. Petersburg', *G.M.*, 1914, no. 2.

NEVEDOMSKY, M. 'N. K. Mikhailovsky', *Mir Bozhy*, 1904, no. 4.

*NIKOLENKO-GILCHENKO, V., 'Memories of N. K. Mikhailovsky', *Zavety*, 1913, no. 1.

RANSKY, S. P., *Sotsiologiya N. K. Mikhailovskago*, St. Petersburg, 1901 (M. M. Stasyulevich), pp. 228.

ROZENBERG, V., 'Mikhailovsky in *Russkiya Vedomosti*', *R. Ved.*, 1914, no. 22.

*RUSANOV, N. S. (Kudrin), 'The Archives of N. K. Mikhailovsky', *R.B.*, 1914, no. 1.

——— 'N. K. Mikhailovsky as a Publicist-Citizen', *R.B.*, 1905, no. 1.

——— 'N. K. Mikhailovsky and the Social Life of Russia', *G.M.*, 1914, no. 2.

*——— 'The Politics of N. K. Mikhailovsky', *Byloe*, 1907, no. 7.

*——— 'What does Russian Social Life owe to N. K. Mikhailovsky?', *Na Slavnom Postu*, St. Petersburg, 1906 (2nd ed.), (Lit. Fund).

SHCHETININ, PRINCE V. A., 'N. K. Mikhailovsky and the Students of Moscow', *Ist. V.*, 1914, no. 3.

*YAKOVLEV, V. YA. (Bogucharsky, Bazilevsky), 'The Events of March 1 and Mikhailovsky', *Byloe*, 1906, no. 3.

*YAKUBOVICH, P., 'Letters of N. K. Mikhailovsky', *R.B.*, 1910, no. 1.

Numerous other articles of importance on Mikhailovsky can be found in the first edition of *Na Slavnom Postu* (*literaturny sbornik posvyashchenny N. K.*

Mikhailovskomu, St. Petersburg, 1900), which differs from the second edition only in the exclusion of Rusanov's above-mentioned article. The only articles on Mikhailovsky in reference works which have any scholarly value are S. Vengerov, 'N. K. Mikhailovsky', *Novy Entsiklopedichesky Slovar* (Brockhaus-Effron), xxvi. 744–7; and N. S. Rusanov, 'N. K. Mikhailovsky', *Encyclopaedia of the Social Sciences*, London, 1933, x. 445–6.

B. *Collections, Memoirs, and Materials on Populism*

ALTMAN, M., *Ivan Gavrilovich Pryzhov*, Moscow, 1932.

ANATOLEV, P., 'Towards a History of the Shutting of the Journal *Otechestvennye Zapiski*', *K. i S.*, 1929, no. 8/9.

ANTONOVICH, M. A., *Vospominaniya, Shestidesyatye Gody*, Moscow (Akademiya), 1933.

APOSTOL, PAUL, *L'Artèle et la Coopération en Russie*, Paris, 1899.

APTEKMAN, O. V., *Zemlya i Volya 70kh Godov*, Rostov, 1907.

*——— 'The Party of *Narodnoe Pravo*', *Byloe*, 1907, no. 7.

AVVAKUM, *The Life of the Archpriest Avvakum by Himself* (tr. Harrison and Mirlees), London, 1924.

BAKALOV, T., 'The Russian Friends of Khristo Botev', *Letopis Marksizma*, 1926, ii.

BELINSKY, V. G., *Izbrannye Filosofskie Sochineniya*, Moscow, 1941.

BELOKONSKY, I. P., 'The Zemsevo Movement', *Byloe*, 1907, no. 4.

Berdyaev, N. M., *Leontiev*, London, 1940.

——— *Subektivizm i Individualizm v Obshchestvennoy Filosofii*, St. Petersburg, 1901.

——— *Towards a New Epoch*, London, 1949.

*BERNSTEIN, E., 'Karl Marx and the Russian Revolutionaries', *M.G.*, 1908, nos. 10, 11.

*Bervi, V. V. (Flerovsky), 'Memoirs: the Idea of a New Religion', *G.M.*, 1916, no. 2.

*——— *Polozhenie Rabochago Klassa v Rossii*, St. Petersburg, 1869.

BOBORYKIN, P. A., *Le Culte du peuple dans la Russie contemporaine*, Paris, 1883.

BRAGINSKY, M. A., 'The Dobrolyubov Demonstrations of 1886', *Byloe*, 1907, no. 5.

BURTSEV, V. (V. B-VA), 'Memoirs of a Citizen of Petersburg on the Second Half of the Eighties', *M.G.*, 1908, no. 11.

CALVOCORESSI, M. D., and ABRAHAM, GERALD, *Masters of Russian Music*, New York, 1944.

CARR, E. H., *Michael Bakunin*, London, 1937.

CHAADAEV, P. YA., *Sochineniya i Pisma* (ed. Gershenzon), Moscow, 1913, i; 1914, ii.

*CHAIKOVSKY, N. V., 'Through a Half-Century', *Golos Minuvshago na Chuzhoy Storone*, 1926, no 7.

CHARUSHIN, N. A., *O Dalekom Proshlom*, Moscow, 1926, i; 1931, ii.

CHEKHOV, ANTON, *The Cherry Orchard and Other Plays* (tr. Garnett), London, 1950.

——— *The Life and Letters of Anton Tchekhov* (tr. and ed. Koteliansky and Tomlinson), London, 1928.

*CHERNYSHEVSKY, N. G., *Chto Delat* (intr. Kirpotin), Moscow–Leningrad, 1933.
—— *Sochineniya*, Moscow, 1951, x.
CHICHERIN, B. N., 'Russian Dilletantism and Communal Land-holding', *Sbornik Gosudarstvennykh Znanii*, St. Petersburg, 1878.
CHUKOVSKY, K., *Nekrasov*, Leningrad, 1926.
CONYBEARE, F. C., *Russian Dissenters*, Harvard, 1921.
COQUART, ARMAND, *Dmitri Pisarev (1840–1868) et L'Idéologie du nihilisme Russe*, Paris, 1946.
CORBET, CHARLES, *Nekrasov: L'Homme et Le Poète*, Paris, 1948.
*DAN, F., *Proiskhozhdenie Bolshevizma*, New York, 1946.
DANIELSON, N. (Nikolai-on), *Ocherki Nashego Poreformennago Obshchestvennago Khozyaistva*, St. Petersburg, 1893.
DEBAGORY-MOKRIEVICH, V. K., *Vospominaniya*, St. Petersburg, 1906.
DEUTSCH, L., *Tvorchestvo Bakuninizma*, Berlin, 1922.
DOBROVOLSKY, L., 'The Condemnation and Destruction of the Books of V. V. Bervi-Flerovsky', *Literaturnoe Nasledstvo*, Moscow, 1933, no. 7/8.
DOLLÉANS, EDOUARD, *Proudhon*, Paris, 1948.
DOSTOEVSKY, F. M., *Letters of Fyodor Michailovitch Dostoevsky* (tr. Mayne), London, 1914.
—— *The Possessed* (tr. Garnett), London, 1950.
—— *A Raw Youth* (tr. Garnett), London, 1950.
DZHABADARI, I. S., 'The Trial of the Fifty', *Byloe*, 1907, nos. 8, 9, 10.
DZIEWANOWSKI, M. K., 'Social Democrats vs. Social Patriots', *American Slavic and East European Review*, 1951, no. 2.
EISENSTOCK, I., 'French Writers in the Evaluation of the Tsarist Censorship', *Literaturnoe Nasledstvo*, Moscow, 1939, no. 33/34.
ELISEEV, G. Z., *Pisma G. Z. Eliseeva k M.E. Saltykovu-Shchedrinu*, Moscow, 1935.
—— *Vospominaniya, Shestidesyatye Gody*, Moscow (Akademiya), 1933.
FEDORCHENKO, L. S., 'In Prison and Exile', *K. i S.*, 1928, no. 8.
FEDOSEEV, N. E., 'From the Unpublished Literary Legacy of N. E. Fedoseev', *Literaturnoe Nasledstvo*, Moscow, 1933, no. 7/8.
FIGNER, VERA, *Memoirs of a Revolutionist*, London, 1929.
—— *Studencheskie Gody (1872–6)*, Moscow, 1924.
FOOTMAN, DAVID J., *Red Prelude, a life of A. I. Zhelyabov*, London, 1944.
FROLENKO, M., 'Chaikovsky and his God-Manhood', *K. i S.*, 1926, no. 5.
—— 'From the Distant Past', *M.G.*, 1908, no. 7.
GARSHIN, V. M., *Sochineniya* (intr. Byaly), Moscow–Leningrad, 1951.
—— 'An Unpublished Letter of V. M. Garshin', *K.A.*, 1934, no. 3.
GESHINA, E. V., 'The Shelgunov Demonstration', *M.G.*, 1908, no. 11.
GUDKOV, I., 'New Materials on Uspensky', *K.A.*, 1941, no. 3.
HANS, NICHOLAS, *History of Russian Educational Policy (1701–1917)*, London, 1931.
HECHT, DAVID, *Russian Radicals Look to America 1825–1894*, Harvard, 1947.
HECKER, JULIUS, *Russian Sociology*, New York, 1915.
HEPNER, BENOÎT-P., *Bakounine et le Panslavisme Révolutionnaire*, Paris, 1950.

HERZEN, ALEXANDER, *The Memoirs: My Past and Thoughts* (tr. Garnett), London, 1924–7, six vols.
—— *Polnoe Sobranie Sochinenii i Pisem* (ed. Lemke), Petrograd, 1919–23, 21 vols.
ISKOV, A. S. (Dolinin), *V Tvorcheskoy Laboratorii Dostoevskogo Istoriya Sozdaniya Romana 'Podrostok'*, Moscow, 1947.
ITENBERG, B., 'The Activities of the South Russian Union of Workers', *Voprosy Istorii*, 1951, no. 1.
IVANCHIN-PISAREV, A. I., *Khozhdenie v Narod*, Moscow, 1929.
KABLITS, I. I. (Yuzov), *Osnovy Narodnichestva* (2nd ed.), St. Petersburg, 1888.
KACHAROVSKY, K. R., *Narodnoe Pravo*, Moscow, 1906.
—— *Russkaya Obshchina*, Moscow, 1906.
KAREEV, N. I., *Osnovnye Voprosy Filosofii Istorii*, St. Petersburg, 1883, ii.
—— *Starye i Novye Etyudy ob Ekonomicheskom Materializme*, St. Petersburg, 1896.
KELSIEV, VASILY, *Perezhitoe i Peredumannoe*, St. Petersburg, 1868.
KHUDYAKOV, I. A., 'Memoirs', *Ist. V.*, 1906, no. 11.
KISTYAKOVSKY, V. A., *Stranitsy Proshlago. K Istorii Konstitutsionnago Dvizheniya v Rossii* [Moscow?], 1912.
KOROLENKO, V. G., *Polnoe Sobranie Sochinenii*, St. Petersburg, 1914, ii.
*—— *Vospominaniya o Pisatelyakh*, Moscow, 1934.
KOVALEVSKY, MAKSIM, *Sotsiologiya*, St. Petersburg, 1910, i.
KOVALIK, S. F., 'Movements of the Seventies', *Byloe*, 1906, no. 10.
KOZMIN, B. P., *Nechaev i Nechaevtsy*, Moscow–Leningrad, 1931.
—— *Revolyutsionnoe Podpole v Epokhu 'Belogo Terrora'*, Moscow, 1929.
—— 'S. G. Nechaev and his Enemies in 1868–9', *Revolyutsionnoe Dvizhenie 1860kh Godov*, Moscow, 1932.
*—— *Tkachev i Revolyutsionnoe Dvizhenie 1860kh Godov*, Moscow, 1922.
—— 'Two Words on the Word "Nihilism" ', *Izvestiya Akademiya Nauk S.S.S.R.* (otd. lit. i yaz.), 1951, x, no 4.
—— *Zhurnalistika Shestidesyatykh Godov XIX Veka*, Moscow, 1948.
—— *Zhurnalistika Semidesyatykh i Vosemidesyatykh Godov XIX Veka*, Moscow, 1948. (These are stenographs of lectures given in the journalistic section of the higher party school in Moscow.)
KRAVCHINSKY, S. (Stepnyak), *Nihilism as it is*, London, 1895.
—— *Underground Russia* (pref. Lavrov), New York, 1883.
KRIDL, M., 'Two Champions of a New Christianity: Lamennais and Mickiewicz', *Comparative Literature*, 1952, no. 3.
KROPOTKIN, PRINCE P. A., *The Great French Revolution, 1789–93*, London, 1909.
—— *Memoirs of a Revolutionist*, New York, 1899.
—— *Mutual Aid: a factor in evolution*, London, 1902.
LABRY, R., *Herzen et Proudhon*, Paris, 1928.
LAVROV, PETER (MIRTOV), 'The Birth of Christ', *G.M.*, 1916, no. 7/8.
*—— *Formula Progressa N. K. Mikhailovskago*, St. Petersburg, 1906.
*—— *Istoricheskie Pisma* (3rd ed.), St. Petersburg, 1906.
*—— *Narodniki-Propagandisty 1873–78 godov*, St. Petersburg, 1907.
LEMKE, M. K., *Epokha Tsenzurnykh Reform (1859–65)*, St. Petersburg, 1904.

—— *Ocherki po Istorii Russkoy Tsenzury i Zhurnalistiki XIX Stoletiya*, St. Petersburg, 1904.

—— *N. M. Yadrintsev*, St. Petersburg, 1905.

LENIN, V. I. (pseud. of Ulyanov), *Letters of Lenin* (tr. Hill and Mudie), London, 1937.

—— *Selected Works*, London, 1936–9, 12 vols.

—— *Sochineniya* (3rd ed.), Moscow, 1930–3, 30 vols.

LIWOFF, GRÉGOIRE, *Michel Katkoff et son Epoque*, Paris, 1897.

LUKASHEVICH, A. O., 'To the People', *Byloe*, 1907, no. 3.

MARTOV, YU. O. (pseud. of Tsederbaum), with Potresov and Maslov, *Obshchestvennoe Dvizhenie v Rossii v Nachale XXogo Veka*, St. Petersburg, 1909, i.

MECHNIKOV, L. I., 'M. A. Bakunin in Italy in 1864', *Ist. V.*, 1897, no. 3.

MIKHAILOV, A. D., *Pisma Narodovoltsa*, Moscow, 1933.

MOROZOV, NICHOLAS, 'In the Name of Brotherhood', *G.M.*, 1916, no. 8.

NEKRASOV, N. A., *Izbrannye Sochineniya*, Leningrad, 1947.

—— *Literaturnoe Nasledstvo*, Moscow, 1946, no. 49/50.

NEKRASOVA, E., 'Journals for the People', *Russkaya Mysl*, 1891, no. 3.

NORMANO, J. F., *The Spirit of Russian Economics*, New York, 1945.

*ORLOVSKY, P. (pseud of V. Vorovsky), *K Istorii Marksizma v Rossii*, Moscow, 1919. Bolshevik bias, but well documented, and preferable for this period to Martov and Dan, *Geschichte der russischen Sozialdemokratie*, Berlin, 1926.

*OVSYANIKO-KULIKOVSKY, D. N., *Istoriya Russkoy Literatury*, Moscow, 1911–12, iii–v (photo repr. Ann Arbor, 1948).

—— *Istoriya Russkoy Intelligentsii*, St. Petersburg, 1909–11, 2 vols. The history of literature collects valuable articles from many writers; but his own history of the intelligentsia tends too much to view literary characters as real historical figures.

—— *Sobranie Sochinenii*, St. Petersburg, 1909, v.

PANTELEEV, L., *Iz Vospominanii Proshlogo*, Moscow (Akademiya), 1934.

PESHEKHONOV, A. V., 'On Alternate Themes, Our Program', *R.B.*, 1906, nos. 6, 8.

PIKSANOV, N. K., 'Gleb Uspensky on Karl Marx', *Novy Mir*, 1933, no. 3.

*PIMENOVA, E. K., *Dni Minuvshie. Vospominaniya*, Leningrad, 1929.

PISAREV, D. I., *Izbrannye Sochineniya* (ed. Kirpotin), Moscow, 1934, i.

—— *Sochineniya* (3rd Pavlenkov ed.), St. Petersburg, 1901, iii.

*PLEKHANOV, G. V. (Beltov, Kirsanov, Valentinov), *In Defence of Materialism* (tr. Rothstein), London, 1947.

—— *Literaturnoe Nasledie: Sbornik IV, Borba s Narodnichestvom*, Moscow, 1937.

—— *Nashi Raznoglasiya*, Leningrad, 1938.

—— *Les Questions Fondamentales du Marxisme*, Paris, 1947.

—— *The Role of the Individual in History*, London, 1950.

—— *Sochineniya*, Moscow–Petrograd, 1923, i.

—— *Sotsializm i Politicheskaya Borba*, Leningrad, 1938.

*POLYANSKY, V. (ed.), *Russkaya Zhurnalistika. I. Shestidesyatye Gody*, Moscow (Akademiya), 1930.

*POPOV, I. I., *Minuvshee i Perezhitoe. Vospominaniya za 50 let*, Leningrad, 1924.

POTASH, M., 'Marx and Engels on *Narodnik* Socialism in Russia', *Proletarskaya Revolyutsiya*, Moscow–Leningrad, 1929, no. 11.

PRIBYLEVA-KORBA, A. P., *Narodnaya Volya, Vospominaniya o 1870kh i 1880kh Godov*, Moscow, 1926.

REINHARDT, N. V., 'Memoirs', *Bayan*, 1908, no. 1.

*REUEL, A. L., *'Kapital' Karla Marksa v Rossii 1870kh Godov*, Moscow, 1939.

RIASANOVSKY, N. V., *Russia and the West in the Teaching of the Slavophiles*, Harvard, 1952.

ROZENBERG, VLADIMIR, *Iz Istorii Ruskoy Pechati*, Prague, 1924.

RUSANOV, N. S. (Kudrin), 'The Influence of West European Socialism on Russia', *M.G.*, nos. 5, 6, 9–12.

—— 'Lavrov, Man and Thinker', *R.B.*, 1910, no. 2.

—— 'Literary Memoirs', *Byloe*, 1906.

—— *Sotsialisty Zapada i Rossii*, St. Petersburg, 1908.

*—— *V Emigratsii*, Moscow, 1929.

RYAZANOV, N., *Two Truths: Narodnichestvo and Marxism*, St. Petersburg, 1906.

SALTYKOV, M. E. (Shchedrin), *Izbrannye Sochineniya*, Moscow–Leningrad, 1946.

—— *Literaturnoe Nasledstvo*, Moscow, 1934, no. 13/14.

—— *Pisma, 1845–89*, Leningrad, 1924.

SAMARIN, YU. (with F. Dmitrev), *Revolyutsionny Konservatizm*, Berlin, 1875.

SAMORUKOV, N., 'The Social-Political Activity of G. A. Lopatin', *Voprosy Istorii*, 1951, no. 3.

*SEREBRYAKOV, E. A., *Obshchestvo Zemlya i Volya*, London, 1912.

SHCHAPOV, A. P., *Sochineniya*, St. Petersburg, 1906, i.

SHCHEGOLEV, P. E., 'From the History of the "Constitutional Murmurings"', 1879–81', *Byloe*, 1906, no. 12.

—— 'The Event of March 1 and Solovev', *Byloe*, 1906, no. 3.

SHELGUNOV, N. V., *Ocherki Russkoy Zhizni*, St. Petersburg, 1895.

*—— *Sochineniya* (3rd ed., Intr. Mikhailovsky), St. Petersburg, 1905, 3 vols.

—— *Vospominaniya*, Moscow–Petrograd, 1923.

SHEVCHENKO, TARAS, 'The Heretic', *Byloe*, 1906, no. 6.

SHIRYAEV, S. G., 'Letters to Lavrov', *Golos Minuvshago na Chuzhoy Storone*, 1927, no. 5.

SHISHKO, LEONID, *Sotsialnye Dvizheniya v 60kh i pervoy polovine 70kh Godov*, Moscow, 1921.

SIMONENKO, GREGORY, *Gosudarstvo, Obshchestvo i Pravo s Tochki Zreniya Zakonov Narodnogo Khozyaistva Opyt Politiko-Ekonomicheskago Analiza Gosudarstvennoy i Obshchestvennoy Deyatelnosti*, Moscow, 1870–2, 2 vols.

*SINEGUB, S., *Zapiski Chaikovtsa*, Moscow–Leningrad, 1929.

*SKABICHEVSKY, A. M., *Literaturnye Vospominaniya* (ed. Kozmin), Moscow–Leningrad, 1928.

SLOBOZHANIN, M., 'S. N. Krivenko', *M.G.*, 1908, nos. 5, 6.

SOKOLOV, N. V., *Die Abtrünnigen*, Zurich, 1872.

SOLOVEV, VLADIMIR, *Lectures on God-manhood* (intr. and tr. P. Zouboff), New York, 1944.

STRUVE, P. B., *Kriticheskie Zametki k Voprosu ob Ekonomicheskom Razvitii Rossii*, St. Petersburg, 1894.
—— *Na Raznyya Temy, 1893–1901*, St. Petersburg, 1902.
TIKHOMIROV, L. A., 'From the Archives of Leo Tikhomirov', *K.A.*, 1924, no. 6.
*—— *Russia Political and Social*, London, 1888, 2 vols.
—— *Vospominaniya*, Moscow, 1927.
TIMOFEEVA, V. V., 'Memoirs', *M.G.*, 1908, no. 4.
TKACHEV, P. N., *Izbrannye Sochineniya*, Moscow, 1932–3, 5 vols.
TOLSTOY, LEO, *Anna Karenina*, The World's Classics, Oxford.
—— *My Confession*, The World's Classics, Oxford.
TSITOVICH, P. P., *Chto Delali v Chto Delat*, Odessa, 1879.
—— *Novye Priemy Zashchity Obshchinnago Zemlevladeniya*, Odessa, 1878.
—— *Otvet na Pisma k Uchenym Lyudyam*, Odessa, 1879.
TUGAN-BARANOVSKY, M., *Russkaya Fabrika v Proshlom i Nastoyashchem, Tom I. Istoricheskoe Razvitie Russkoy Fabriki v XIX Veke* (7th ed.), Moscow, 1938.
TURGENEV, I. S., *Virgin Soil*, London (Everyman), 1948.
TYRKOVA-WILLIAMS, A., *Na Putyakh k Svobode*, New York, 1952.
USPENSKY, G. I., *Gleb Uspensky Materialy i Issledovaniya*, Moscow–Leningrad, 1938.
*—— *Gleb Uspensky v Zhizni*, Moscow (Akademiya), 1935.
VESELOVSKY, B., 'Ideological Currents of Contemporary *Narodnichestvo*', *Obrazy*, 1907, no. 1.
VIKTOROV-TOPOROV, VLADIMIR, 'Svetozar Markovich', *G.M.*, 1913, no. 3.
VORONTSOV, V. P. (V. V.), 'Memoirs', *G.M.*, 1916, no. 5/6.
—— *Nashi Napravleniya*, St. Petersburg, 1893.
—— *Sudba Kapitalizma v Rossii*, St. Petersburg, 1882.
*YAKOVLEV, V. YA. (Bogucharsky, Bazilevsky), *Aktivnoe Narodnichestvo Semidesyatykh Godov*, Moscow, 1912.
*—— *Iz Istorii Politicheskoy Borby v 70kh i 80kh Gg. xix Veka*, Moscow, 1912.
YASINSKY, I. I., *Roman Moey Zhizni*, Moscow, 1926.
YUZHAKOV, S. N., 'Memorial to Mark N. Mikhailovsky', *R.B.*, 1904, no. 9.
ZIBER, N. I., *Sobranie Sochinenii*, St. Petersburg, 1900, 2 vols.
ZLATOVRATSKY, N. N., *Izbrannye Proizvedeniya*, Moscow, 1947.

C. Published Documents on the Period

BURTSEV, VLADIMIR, *Za Sto Let*, London, 1897, part 2. The best extant calendar of the revolutionary period up until the mid-nineties.
DEUTSCH, L. (intr.), *Delo Pervogo Marta 1881*, St. Petersburg, 1906.
KALLASH, V. (intr.), *Protsess 193kh*, Moscow, 1906.
LEMKE, M. K., *Politicheskie Protsessy v Rossi 1860kh Gg. po Arkhivnym Dokumentam*, Moscow-Petrograd, 1923.
Literatura Sotsialno-Revolyutsionnoy Partii 'Narodnoy Voli' [Paris], 1905. Official S.R. publication of all the literature and correspondence of *Narodnaya Volya*.
Narodnaya Volya v Dokumentakh i Vospominaniyakh, Moscow, 1935. Contains best calendar of organization's movements.

SHILOV, A. A. (pref.), 'The Karakozov Attempt', *K.A.*, 1926, no. 4.
YAKOVLEV, V. YA. (Bazilevsky, Bogucharsky), *Gosudarstvennyya Prestupleniya v Rossii v XIX Veke*: i, Stuttgart, 1903, covers 1825–76; ii, iii [Paris, 1905], covers 1877.
—— *Materialy dlya istorii revolyutsionnago dvizheniya v Rossii v 60kh Gg*, Paris, 1905.
—— *Revolyutsionnaya Zhurnalistika Semidesyatykh Godov*, Paris, 1905. The only one of a projected multi-volume series to appear, containing complete reprints of *Nachalo* and the second *Zemlya i Volya*.

D. *Journals of the Period*

This is a list of those legal and illegal periodical publications of the period which played a significant role in the development of Russian thought during the narodnik age. Many of these journals are unavailable in the West; and many more, available only in part. But this list is made as comprehensive as possible, as there is no other short reference work available on the subject. The journals listed are those of importance up until the turn of the century, together with the figures who were instrumental in shaping their social outlook (who are not necessarily the editors or publishers). Principal sources for this information are E. E. Kluge, *Die russische revolutionäre Presse*, Zürich, 1948, and A. V. Mezer, *Slovarny Ukazatel po Knigovedeniyu*, Moscow–Leningrad, 1931, i. Other sources have been used, however, particularly in drawing up the characterizations of the journals. Crosses (†) indicate that the journal was forcibly shut by the government.

1. *Legal journals to which Mikhailovsky contributed*

Delo, St. Petersburg, radical democratic under Shelgunov till 1882, conservative from 1884 (1866–88).
Knizhny Vestnik, St. Petersburg, radical, bibliographical, Zaitsev, Nozhin, V. Kurochkin, 1860–6.
Nedelya, St. Petersburg, weekly, romantic narodnik under Gaideburov from 1869.
†*Otechestvennye Zapiski*, St. Petersburg, radical narodnik under Nekrasov, Saltykov, Eliseev, 1868–77; Mikhailovsky, Saltykov, Eliseev, 1877–84.
Rassvet, St. Petersburg, women's rights, V. Krempin, 1859–62.
Russkaya Mysl, Moscow, zemstvo liberal, from 1880 under V. Lavrov; from 1885 under V. Goltsev.
Russkiya Vedomosti, St. Petersburg, daily from 1868, favourable to zemstvo liberals, and under V. Sobolevsky (from 1882) to radical narodniks.
Russkoe Bogatstvo, St. Petersburg, from 1880 romantic narodnik, from 1892 radical narodnik under Mikhailovsky (actual editorship from 1895–1900, co-editorship with Korolenko 1900–4).
Severny Vestnik, St. Petersburg, moderate liberal, largely literary, under A. M. Evreinova from 1885; from 1891 conservative, symbolist school of art.

2. *Illegal journals to which Mikhailovsky contributed*

†*Letuchy Listok*, St. Petersburg (press of *Nachalo*), 1878, 1 no.

†*Listok Narodnoy Voli*, St. Petersburg (press of *Narodnaya Volya*), 1884, 3 nos., revolutionary narodnik, Tikhomirov, &c.

†*Narodnaya Volya*, St. Petersburg–Moscow–Rostov, 1879–84, 10 nos., Tikhomirov, &c.

Samoupravlenie, Geneva, 1887–9, 4 nos., Belevsky, Debagory-Mokrievich, Dragomanov, &c., narodnik constitutionalist.

3. *Other important journals*

Epokha, Moscow, romantic narodnik, Zlatovratsky, Vorontsov, 1888.

Mir Bozhy, St. Petersburg, moderate liberal from 1892 under A. Davydova; becoming revisionist Marxist at turn of century under influence of A. Bogdanovich.

Nauchnoe Obozrenie, St. Petersburg, revisionist Marxist from 1894, under M. Filippov (from 1899).

Novoe Slovo, St. Petersburg, radical narodnik 1894–7 under Sleptsov and Skabichevsky; economist Marxist from 1897 under Struve and Tugan-Baranovsky.

Russkaya Rech, St. Petersburg, conservative, A. Navrotsky, E. Markov, 1879–82.

Russky Vestnik, Moscow, autocratic chauvinist, under M. Katkov till 1887.

Sbornik Gosudarstvennykh Znanii, St. Petersburg, official conservative, V. Bezobrazov, B. Chicherin, 1874–80.

Ustoy, St. Petersburg, romantic narodnik under S. Vengerov, 1881–2.

Vestnik Evropy, St. Petersburg, *laissez-faire* liberal under M. Stasyulevich.

Yuridichesky Vestnik, Moscow, official publication of Moscow Juridical Society, favourable to zemstvo liberalism, 1867–92.

Zarya, St. Petersburg, autocratic conservative, N. Danilevsky, 1869–72.

Zhensky Vestnik, St. Petersburg, women's rights, P. Lavrov, G. Uspensky, &c., 1866–8.

Znanie, St. Petersburg, liberal positivist, Yuzhakov, P. Lavrov, 1870–77.

4. *Publications other than monthly journals (appearing daily, weekly, or thrice weekly)*

Bereg, St. Petersburg, official conservative under P. Tsitovich, 1880.

Birzhevyya Vedomosti, St. Petersburg, evolutionary narodnik under V. Poletika, Skabichevsky, 1875–7, then moderate liberal under Poletika, 1877–9.

†*Golos*, St. Petersburg, moderate liberal under A. Kraevsky until 1884.

Grazhdanin, St. Petersburg, chauvinistic conservative under V. P. Meshchersky from 1872.

Iskra, St. Petersburg radical narodnik, chiefly satirical, under N. Kurochkin until 1873.

†*Molva*, Moscow, radical Slavophil, under I. Aksakov, 1867–8.

†*Molva*, St. Petersburg, moderate liberal, under V. Poletika, 1879–81.

Moskovskiya Vedomosti, Moscow, autocratic chauvinist, under Katkov till 1887.

Novoe Vremya, St. Petersburg, moderate liberal till 1876; thereafter autocratic chauvinist under A. Suvorin.

Pravitelstvenny Vestnik, St. Petersburg, official organ of Ministry of the Interior from 1869.

†*Russkoe Obozrenie*, St. Petersburg, liberal constitutional, under G. Gradovsky, 1876–8.

Rus, Moscow, conservative chauvinist under I. Aksakov, 1880–6.

Syn Otechestva, St. Petersburg, conservative till 1886; then moderate evolutionary narodnik under Sheller-Mikhailov till 1896, and Krivenko till 1900.

5. *Chief provincial journals sympathetic to narodnichestvo*

Aziatsky Vestnik, St. Petersburg, evolutionary narodnik, V. Kurochkin, one issue, 1872.

Kievlyanin, Kiev, narodnik, but anti-federalist, pro-Russification, V. Shulgin; thrice weekly till 1879, thereafter daily.

†*Kievsky Telegraf*, Kiev, zemstvo liberal, Ukrainophil, M. Dragomanov, approx. monthly till 1876.

†*Novorossiysky Telegraf*, Odessa, evolutionary narodnik, under A. Serebrennikov, thrice weekly, 1869–73.

†*Obzor*, Tiflis, evolutionary narodnik, N. Nikoladze, daily, 1878–83.

†*Odessky Listok Obyavlenii*, Odessa, evolutionary narodnik, A. Serebrennikov, V. Navrotsky, irregular, 1872–80.

Vostochnoe Obozrenie, St. Petersburg–Irkutsk, radical narodnik, under N. Yadrintsev, 1882–90; thereafter, I. Popov.

6. *Principal illegal journals*

Bomba, Geneva, Jacobin revolutionary, G. Tursky, 2 nos., 1889.

Cherny Peredel, Minsk, narodnik, G. Plekhanov, 5 nos., 1880–1.

Gromada (Ukr.), Geneva, constitutional federalist, M. Dragomanov, 5 vols. and 2 nos., 1878–82.

Letuchie Listki, London, evolutionary narodnik, N. Chaikovsky, S. Kravchinsky, 46 nos., 1893–9.

Listok Zemlya i Volya, St. Petersburg, revolutionary terrorist, N. Morozov, 6 nos., 1879.

Nabat, Geneva, Jacobin revolutionary, P. Tkachev, G. Tursky, 4 nos., 1875–7.

Nachalo, St. Petersburg, revolutionary narodnik, P. Karonin, 4 nos., 1878.

Narodnaya Rasprava, Geneva, 1869–70, Jacobin revolutionary, S. Nechaev, 2 nos.

Narodnoe Delo, Geneva, anarchist revolutionary, M. Bakunin, N. Zhukovsky, 17 nos., 1868–70.

Obshchee Delo, Geneva, evolutionary narodnik, Zaitsev, Sokolov, Khristoforov, 112 nos., 1877–90.

Obshchina, London, Jacobin revolutionary, S. Nechaev, 2 nos., 1870.

Obshchina, Geneva, anarchist revolutionary, N. Zhukovsky, P. Akselrod, 9 nos., 1878.

Podpolnoe Slovo, Geneva, radical democrat, N. Nikoladze, M. Elpidin, 2 nos., 1866.

Rabochaya Gazeta, Kiev-Ekaterinoslav, orthodox Marxist, B. Eidelman, 3 nos., 1897–8.

Rabochaya Mysl, St. Petersburg–Berlin, orthodox, then economist Marxist, K. Takhtarev, N. Dokhovy-Olkhin, 16 nos., from 1897.

Rabochy, St. Petersburg, orthodox Marxist, D. Blagoev, 2 nos., 1885.
Rabotnik, Geneva, anarchist revolutionary, N. Zhukovsky, 15 nos., 1875–6.
Rabotnik, Geneva, orthodox Marxist, G. Plekhanov, P. Akselrod, 6 nos. 1896–9.
Sotsial-Demokrat, Geneva, orthodox Marxist, G. Plekhanov, P. Akselrod, 4 books, 1890–2.
Sotsialist, Geneva, revolutionary narodnik, 1 no., 1889.
Sovremennost, Geneva, radical democrat, N. Nikoladze, L. Mechnikov, 7 nos., 1868.
Svoboda, Geneva, Jacobin revolutionary, G. Tursky, 15 nos., 1888–9.
Svobodnaya Rossiya, Zürich–Geneva, narodnik constitutional, V. Burtsev, V. Debagory-Mokrievich, 3 nos., 1889.

E. *Western Writings of Importance*

BLANC, JEAN JOSEPH LOUIS, *Histoire de la révolution française*, Paris, 1866, 2 vols. (abbr.).
COMTE, AUGUSTE, *Cours de philosophie positive* (ed. Littré), Paris, 1864, 6 vols.
CUSTINE, MARQUIS DE, *Russia*, London, 1854.
DARWIN, CHARLES, *On the Origin of Species by Means of Natural Selection, or the Preservation of Favoured Races in the Struggle for Life*, London, 1859.
DIXON, WILLIAM HEPWORTH, *Free Russia*, London, 1870, 2 vols.
—— *New America*, London, 1867.
HAXTHAUSEN, BARON AUGUST VON, *The Russian Empire*, London, 1856, 2 vols.
LANGE, FRIEDRICH ALBERT, *History of Materialism* (2nd Eng. ed.), London, 1877–81, 3 vols.
MARX, KARL, *Capital*, London (Wm. Blaisher), 1920.
—— *Letters to Dr. Kugelmann*, London, 1934.
—— *Perepiska K. Marksa i F. Engelsa s Russkimi Politicheskimi Deyatelyami*, Leningrad, 1947.
—— *The Poverty of Philosophy*, London, 1936.
—— *Sochineniya Marksa i Engelsa* (ed. Adoratsky), Moscow, 1932, &c.
MILL, JOHN STUART, *On Liberty*, London, 1859.
PROUDHON, PIERRE JOSEPH, *Les confessions d'un révolutionnaire, pour servir à l'histoire de la révolution de fevrier*, Paris, 1850.
—— *De la capacité politique des classes ouvrières* (vol. iii of *Œuvres*, ed. Bougle and Moysset), Paris, 1924.
—— *De la justice dans la révolution et dans l'Église*, Paris, 1858, 3 vols.
—— *The General Idea of the Revolution in the Nineteenth Century* (tr. Robinson), London, 1923.
—— *Le Système des contradictions économiques, ou Philosophie de la misère*, Paris, 1846, 2 vols.
QUATREFAGES, JEAN LOUIS ARMAND DE, *L'Unité de l'Espèce Humaine*, Paris, 1860–1.
ST.-SIMON, COMTE HENRI DE, *Le Nouveau Christianisme* (*Œuvres de St.-Simon et d'Enfantin*, vol. xxii), Paris, 1869.
SPENCER, HERBERT, 'Manners and Fashion', *The Westminster Review*, 1854, April.

SPENCER, HERBERT, 'Progress, its Law and Cause', *The Westminster Review*, 1857, April.
—— *An Autobiography* (2nd ed.), London, 1926, 2 vols.
—— *Social Statics: or, the conditions essential to human happiness exemplified and the first of them developed*, London, 1851.
STRAUSS, DAVID FRIEDRICH, *Der alte und der neue Glaube* (4th ed.), Bonn, 1873.
VICO, GIOVANNI BATTISTA, *Œuvres Choisies de Vico* (tr. Michelet), Paris, 1835, 2 vols.

III. BASIC REFERENCE MATERIALS

A. Relevant Histories and Interpretations

BERDYAEV, N. M., *The Origins of Russian Communism*, London, 1937.
IVANOV-RAZUMNIK, R. V., *Istoriya Russkoy Obshchestvennoy Mysli*, St. Petersburg, 1909–11, 2 vols. Sympathetic to narodniks.
KORNILOV, ALEXANDER, *Modern Russian History* (tr. Kaun), London, 1916, 2 vols. Important for financial and agrarian policy, but lacking valuable documentation of original in *M.G.*, 1908, no. 2, &c.
KUCHARZEWSKI, JAN, *The Origins of Modern Russia*, New York, 1948. Attacks the chauvinism of the Russian movement from extreme pro-Polish position.
LOSSKY, N. O., *History of Russian Philosophy*, New York, 1951. Unbalanced, little on the radicals.
MASARYK, THOMAS GARRIGUE, *The Spirit of Russia*, London, 1919, 2 vols. Still the best short history of Russian thought, liberal, neo-Kantian position.
MAYNARD, SIR JOHN, *Russia in Flux*, London, 1946.
MAVOR, JAMES, *Economic History of Russia*, New York, 1925, ii.
MILYUKOV, PAUL, *Histoire de Russie*, Paris, 1933, iii (with Seignobos, Eisenmann, &c.). Valuable on internal political developments.
—— *Russia and its Crisis*, London, 1905.
MYAKOTIN, V. A., *Iz Istorii Russkago Obshchestva*, St. Petersburg, 1906.
POKROVSKY, M. N., *Brief History of Russia*, London, 1933, 2 vols. Crude Marxist.
ROBINSON, G. T., *Rural Russia under the Old Regime*, New York, 1949.
SETON-WATSON, HUGH, *The Decline of Imperial Russia*, London, 1952.
SUMNER, B. H., *Russia and the Balkans*, Oxford, 1937.
VENTURI, FRANCO, *Il Populismo Russo*, Turin, 1952, 2 vols. A wealth of material on movements through 1881, particularly on revolutionary extremists.
WALLACE, MACKENZIE, *Russia*, London, 1912. Reliable and readable, with much from his personal travels in late nineteenth century.
ZENKOVSKY, V. V., *Istoriya Russkoy Filosofii*, Paris, 1948, 2 vols. Orthodox position, little on the radicals.

B. Encyclopedias

Bolshaya Sovetskaya Entsiklopediya (ed. Shmidt), Moscow, 1926–47, 65 vols. The standard Soviet reference source, replete with labels rather than information on the narodniks, particularly on the period of the nineties. Nevertheless, containing much valuable material on many of the figures of the seventies.

Deyateli Revolyutsionnogo Dvizheniya v Rossii. Bio-bibliographichesky Slovar. Ot predshestvennikov Dekabristov do padeniya Tsarizma (ed. Vilensky-Sibiryakov), Moscow, 1932–3, ii, iii, v. Much the best and most reliable source for information and bibliography on the various revolutionaries. Incomplete, however, for the late seventies and eighties.

Entsiklopedichesky Slovar, St. Petersburg (Brockhaus-Effron), 1890–1905, 41 vols. A wealth of information and valuable articles on all aspects of Russian life and development, by such contributors as Vladimir Solovev (philosophy), Nicholas Kareev (history), and S. A. Vengerov (literature). Rigidly limited, however, in material about the revolutionaries, because of restrictions of the censorship.

Entsiklopedichesky Slovar Russkogo bibliographicheskogo Instituta Granat (12th ed.; ed. Zheleznova, &c.), Moscow, 1937–8, 55 vols. Much valuable biographical information on the revolutionaries and the movements of the late nineteenth century. More available in the myriad earlier editions, but less easily found than the other encyclopedias.

C. *Special Reference Materials*

KOVALEVSKY, M. W. DE, *La Russie à la fin du 19ᵉ siècle*, Paris, 1900. Economic and commercial data.

MASANOV, N. F., *Slovar Psevdonimov*, Moscow, 1941–9, 3 vols. Identification of pseudonyms.

MEZER, A. V., *Slovarny Ukazatel po Knigovedeniyu*, Moscow–Leningrad, 1931–3, 2 vols. Information on periodicals.

POPOV, V., *Sistematichesky Ukazatel Statey, 1830–84,* St. Petersburg, 1885. Invaluable index to periodical articles (including *Delo, O.Z.,* &c.).

RUBAKIN, N. A., *Sredi Knig*, Moscow, 1911–5, 3 vols. Rich store of bibliographical material arranged by subjects.

VENGEROV, S. A., *Kritiko-Biographichesky Slovar*, St. Petersburg, 1889–1904, i–vi. Biographical material; good only for early letters of alphabet.

VLADISLAVTSEV, I. V., *Russkie Pisateli*, Moscow–Leningrad, 1924. Best single bibliographical source for narodnik period.

INDEX OF NAMES

PRINTED IN
GREAT BRITAIN
AT THE
UNIVERSITY PRESS
OXFORD
BY
CHARLES BATEY
PRINTER
TO THE
UNIVERSITY